To Dick and Brenda —

Blessed memories,
Happy readings, and
best wishes,

V. "Kass" Kassir

5/18/20

POINTED
REFLECTIONS

POINTED
REFLECTIONS

VARTKES M. KASSOUNI, D. Min.

POINTED REFLECTIONS
Copyright © 2020 by Vartkes M. Kassouni, D.Min.

FIRST EDITION
Printed in the United States of America

Typesetting: PATTY SANCHEZ
Layout and pagination: LOUISA JANBAZIAN
Graphics: LORI RUFF-SCHMALENBERGER
Cover Design: VAHAK JANBAZIAN (Caspianseal.com)
Printing: PRINTSOLUTIONS.INFO - Englewood, NJ

ISBN: 978-0-578-59704-1

This book is dedicated to my wife, Samira, in appreciation for her untiring support, and in recognition of her retirement from teaching in 2019, after 50 years.

Quoting from a recognition she received on this occasion, "THE LEGEND HAS RETIRED"

CONTENTS

CONTENTS

CONTENTS

CONTENTS

CONTENTS

CONTENTS

CHAPTER IV. UNITED ARMENIAN CONGREGATIONAL CHURCH, LOS ANGELES, CA, 1978-1983

CONTENTS

CONTENTS

CONTENTS

CONTENTS

INTRODUCTION

It all began in the fall of 1953 when I started my theological studies at the Biblical Seminary, New York City. At the age of 22 years, I began as the pastor's assistant for English language ministries, in a small church in West New York, N.J., across the Hudson River, called the Armenian Presbyterian Church. It ended in 2007, at Morningside Presbyterian Church, Fullerton, CA 54 years later. Included in that amazing span of ministry, were ten other churches.

In each church I wrote a weekly or a monthly article for our newsletter. I have saved many of them with the intention of publishing them some day. Since retiring, I have devoted myself to writing, and this is my second book. The first one titled *"Points of Life"* was published in the spring of 2017.

These articles contain my thinking, my theological and intellectual persuasions, flowing from my heart and soul. The articles are contemporary to the year written, hence they are dated. The reader will note my growth (or need of it) in awareness of and sensitivity to issues, such as the need for being gender inclusive. I am faced with the dilemma of either changing each pronoun regarding God and humanity to be gender inclusive in each article dating back to 1955, and in doing so remove the context of time in which they were written, or by keeping them in their original language incur the irritation and frustration of our readers. Also, in a number of the articles, I refer to the husband as "the breadwinner," and to the mother as "the home maker." I know times have changed and many homes, including ours, have had two bread-winners, both the husband and the wife. Responsibility and the honor go to them both, and raising the family is a calling shared by both of them. Quotations from the Bible are from the New Revised Standard Version (NRSV) and the King James Version (KJV) unless otherwise noted.

As I write, the words from an old southern hymn drifts in and out of my brain, "Blessed memories, how they linger how they ever flood my soul..." Each article reconnects me with people with whom I associated. Literally thousands of people, young and old whose lives I touched — the elderly I comforted, the young I challenged and molded in the grace of our Lord Jesus Christ. Yes, and there were those that I disturbed and bothered as well. To them I apologize and seek forgiveness.

I say to them all, "Thank you for all you have given me; for the trust you placed in me as a pastor, and the joys we shared together as fellow human beings. For tears of sorrow we have shed together in times of suffering and pain, for peals of laughter in times of celebration, and above all for love made real in times of caring, I say thank you!"

Sometimes it was smooth sailing; sometimes it was turbulent and rough. Sometimes it was the thrill of the open road, and sometimes the stomach wrenching feel of the roller coaster. When everything is said and done, I say, it was surely worth it all!

Vartkes M. Kassouni
Orange, CA

CHAPTER I

ARMENIAN PRESBYTERIAN CHURCH
WEST NEW YORK, NJ, 1953-1956

The Herald

MONTHLY BULLETIN of the
ARMENIAN PRESBYTERIAN CHURCH
West New York, New Jersey
and the
ARMENIAN PRESBYTERIAN MISSION
Paterson, New Jersey

April 1955

EASTER 1955

I had just been reading the newspaper, "Hydrogen Bomb Tested Successfully in Nevada!" "China Defies the U.S and Pledges Invasion of Formosa — Diplomats Are Alarmed!" "Communist Party Makes Big Gains in Japan!" "New Danger of War between Israel and Egypt!" "Juvenile Delinquency on the Rise!" What a world I was living in! I felt that if I took one step, I'd be tumbling over a cliff! Fear gripped my heart. Then I began to think of the Christian Church in this world. Surely, I had thought the church must do something about all this, but I was sadly disappointed, I had just received a letter from the "old country." Things weren't going too well with the church there. Few missionaries to carry the Gospel to the world. The church there seemed to be afraid to move forward — "Not enough money," they said.

Here in America things weren't much different. People weren't much interested in the Bible anymore. Prayer meetings were empty. Spirituality lacked. The impact of the Church on society was almost nil. It too seemed to be crouched in a corner of this world hardly keeping itself alive. Frankly, I was ready to give up. Is this what Christianity was supposed to be? I was disillusioned; maybe I had been dreaming too much. I had heard of the exploits of Christians of past ages. I had read of Wesley who said. "The world is my parish," revolutionize the whole course of the British Empire. I had read of Luther who influenced a whole continent for Christ. Oh, how many victorious events I had read about... but they must have been exaggerated because the church seemed powerless today. I would talk to people about God, and they would laugh in my face and say, "I'd like to meet a man who has ever seen Him!" "No educated man can believe there is a personal God," they would tell me.

Yes, in the face of such odds, I was discouraged. If there was a God, His reality had departed from me. Christ, as far as reality was concerned, might just as well have been still in the grave. It must have been an empty endeavor on my

5

part to live as a Christian. The Christian Church must not have the answer to the problems of this sadly mixed up world after all!

As I was thinking these gloomy thoughts, suddenly there was a soft knock on my door. I opened it, thinking some friend of mine was visiting me, when I suddenly fell on my face in utter joy and amazement, for standing before me was none other than the Lord Jesus Christ Himself! He reached down to pick me up and as He laid His gentle hand upon me, I saw His nail scarred hand. His voice sounded assuring clear as He said, "Reach hither finger, and behold my hands, and be not faithless, but believing." Oh, what joy! It was true after all, Christ was living. He wasn't dead! Again he spoke, "Because thou hast seen me, thou hast believed: blessed are they that have not seen, and yet have believed." Then, I realized that my own unbelieving heart had made myself so discouraged!

Christ showed me how He was still working in this world. He showed me many faithful churches, preachers, missionaries, and laymen working faithfully bringing in the harvest. He also showed me scores of men and women who believed in Him. In the salvation they experienced in Him, they were finding true happiness and peace in the midst of a troubled world. Then, He promised me again that one day soon He would come to rule the world forever and ever.

Are you also sick of sin?
Heavy of heart and dim within?
I think I hear a whispered "Yes."
A muffled groan of deep distress!
Alas, we need not fear or doubt.
But sing with joy and work with might.

Christ is not dead, but lo He lives.
This day He rose and with Him brings
a new beginning, a new life.
For this is Easter, '55!

CHAPTER II

ARMENIAN EVANGELICAL CHURCH
NEW YORK CITY, 1959-1964

WHY WORSHIP?

Because our NATURE demands that we do, man is by nature made to worship. Primitive peoples worship trees, the sun, the moon, spirits, and a host of other beings. Who told them to worship? No one, they are following the simple dictates of their natures. Civilized man worships his modern gods. No one is exempt. The man who claims to be so modern that he does not need God still needs his pleasures, his intellect, his money, and worships these with a fervency that puts the religious man to shame!

Because our FAITH demands that we do. We, who claim to love God and believe in Christ, His Son, need to stay in communion with Him. Love always unites. This is so clearly evident in human relationships. What would one think of a man who claims to love his wife and yet never likes to talk to her or spend time with her at home? Worship unites us to God in a bond of fellowship. To adore God as our Father, means that we experience his fatherly care and strength.

"God is in His holy temple; let all the earth keep silence before Him."
Habakkuk 2:20

VARTKES M. KASSOUNI

No. 2 • January 21, 1960

A FAITH FOR OUR TIMES

It is the dead calm of midnight. The scene is a prison. The stillness of the hour is broken only by occasional bursts of song intermingled with the loud snores of men sleeping. Suddenly, without warning, the place is shaken to its foundations by a shattering earthquake and pandemonium reigns. One man, the jailer, afraid that all have fled, is ready to commit suicide. Another, the prisoner who was singing, remains completely calm and does not even attempt to escape. Quite a study in contrasts! What made the difference? Faith in Christ! (Read Acts 16:19-34, where the event is recorded).

What makes the difference in our times? What is to remove the deep insecurity gnawing at the vitals of humanity with fears and phobias? What is to give us an unmovable rock of strength, conviction and peace, in a sea of changing times, changing values, changing behaviors and morals? Faith in Christ. Not a mere religious sentimentality, but a living union with the eternal God! Faith is as timeless as God is timeless. Faith is a strong as God is strong. Faith is as real as Jesus' gentle touch on a fevered brow. Here is a changeless faith for a changing world.

No. 3 • May 1, 1960

A DISTURBING QUESTION

"Simon Peter, do you love me?" Jesus asked this three times in rapid succession. He was asking this of a man who had made great boasts about how he would defend the cause of Christ with his life, and would never desert Him, but when the crisis of the cross arose, he betrayed Christ and hid himself in fear and remorse! Now, after His resurrection, Jesus has sought Peter out and is testing the genuineness of his commitment to Him and His cause. What an embarrassing moment for Peter! "Yes Lord, I love You," he answers glibly trying to close the subject, but Jesus is not satisfied, and he repeats the question again and again.

Peter's weakness was nothing unique. We have all acted like him many, many times too! How easily and glibly we too join in our confession of Jesus Christ as our Lord. Promises, promises, promises! But the crises of hard times, temptations, call to Christian service and bearing of our crosses sends us into hiding too! Jesus is seeking us out not to embarrass but rather to remove our fear and put his power in us. Evading Him means continued fear, but facing Him means victory.

No. 4 • May 29, 1960

THE PRODIGAL'S BROTHER

Who is there in our church who has not heard of the story of the Prodigal Son, as told by Jesus? But how many of us remember this man's brother? He was the one who decided to stay home. One would first think that he stayed home because of his love for his father, but a closer look gives us a far different story. He stayed because he was a shrewd character. He knew that someday all his father's riches would be his because he chose to stay. His hypocrisy is revealed when the prodigal decides to come back. He now realizes that he is no longer the only heir, and reveals his inner self. Instead of being overjoyed with the return of his brother, he is angered and filled with jealousy!

Most church people are not like the prodigal, but like his brother. We find hardly any morally degenerate people, —the "down-and-outers," among us. Does this mean that all is well? On the contrary! The respectability of the church often becomes an excellent covering for our egos, and like the prodigal's brother, we hide our selfish motives under the thin veneer of "service to the church!" We too must repent, as did the Prodigal.

No. 5 • October 23, 1960

PULPITS, PEWS, AND POLITICS (1960)

Which will it be, Kennedy or Nixon? We wish we could say, but that is just not possible for us. What can the Church say, or does she have the right to say anything? While every instrument of communication is being used to sway the minds and consciences of the people, must the Church remain silent?

The Church must speak if she would minister to total man. Man in the market place as well as man at prayer. Christ looked over Jerusalem and wept because of its impending destruction. Politicians speak of concern for the needs of the country and humanity at large, but Christ's self-sacrifice on the cross for humanity is still the unsurpassed demonstration of real and utterly genuine concern!

The task of the Church is far deeper that mere social reform. It remains for her to resolve the deep need and anguish of humanity at the foot of the cross. The task of the church is not to remove slum buildings, but so to change the lives of people that they will not turn their homes into slums! Instead of forever talking about peace, she demonstrates it in the lives of Christ-centered disciples. A proud humanity presents lofty and high-sounding programs that somehow always fail. The church presents a crucified and risen Lord, whose Gospel has done more for mankind that we can ever imagine.

No. 6 • January 15, 1961

HOLY, HOLY, HOLY

Isaiah the prophet is one of the most striking figures in the Old Testament, and his writings, distinctly powerful and penetrating. The sixth chapter of his book is autobiographical, containing an account of his spiritual experience with God. It is divided into four parts: 1. His meeting with God in the Temple, and being overcome by the fact of God's extreme holiness. 2. Isaiah's own feeling of uncleanness and depravity in contrast to this holy God. 3. His cleansing and spiritual purification. 4. His readiness for service in response to the question asked by God "Whom shall I send, and who will go for us?"

Here is the pattern of experience which is set down for us to follow as well. Often, we urge people in churches to give, to serve, to teach, and to do many other important tasks in the service of God. The reason we get so little response is that we skip the first three steps, and jump to the fourth. No man will dedicate his life to God or his church, unless he has first of all been overwhelmed by the holiness of God and seen his own depravity, and then has sought cleansing and a new life. If a church fails to present the living and holy God to her people, the activities she indulges in will be mere "child's play" in contrast to her high and great calling!

No. 7 • March 19, 1961

THE COMMUNION OF SAINTS

Here is a rather ambiguous statement in the Apostles' Creed that is full of deep meaning, however in need of definition. Actually, our modern usage of the terms "communion" and "saint" is what causes the difficulty. The word "communion" means "fellowship, or coming together for mutual benefit," and does not always mean the celebration of the Lord's Supper. And the word "saint" does not mean a holy mystic or one who has achieved perfection. In the New Testament, this word is applied to ALL believers in Christ. The root meaning of the word is "separated and set aside for a specific purpose." St. Paul calls all the members of the church of Christ "saints," because their confession of Christ as Savior and Lord has separated them from the world and set them apart from it.

Man is a social being. He has to get together with others of his kind; otherwise he will never develop properly in his personality. Even so must Christians, otherwise their spiritual personality will languish and eventually die. Sunday television church-going is a mighty poor substitute for the fellowship of the community of believers constituting the dynamic life of the church. Which do we belong to—the television church with a bed for a pew, on the living church of God?

No. 8 • October 22, 1961

GREAT EXPECTATIONS

"Are you He who is to come, or shall we look for another?" This message was sent to Jesus by a man in jail. No, he was not a criminal, but quite to the contrary, a man of unsurpassed religious dedication—John the Baptist. The very man who stated boldly, "Behold the Lamb of God which taketh away the sin of the world," is now having doubts! Jesus was not living up to his expectations! He had fully and confidently expected Jesus to establish the Kingdom of God upon the earth in a form that would grind all human kingdoms before it and fill all the earth. His faith in this fact was so deep that he had openly defied Herod, the ruler of the land, and was now in prison as a result.

Have we also joined the vast multitude of those who are spiritually disenchanted and have lost faith in Christ and the Church, because He has refused to do what we demanded that He do? Let us beware, for if John the Baptist could be wrong how much more could we! Jesus replied to John saying, "The blind receive their sight, and the lame walk, lepers are cleaned and the deaf hear, and the dead are raised up, and the poor have good news preached to them." You see only those who confess that they are blind, lame, leprous, deaf, dead, and poor, are blessed by Jesus. All others go away empty and offended.

No. 9 • September 2, 1967

A QUESTION WORTH REPEATING

"What am I?" This question in its various forms has been asked repeatedly in all ages by thinking people. The Psalmist asks it in the 8th Psalm: "What is man…?" We are asking it again with renewed intensity in these changing times, especially so as we begin to probe the depths of our glorious universe.

Life becomes exciting and wonderful only for people who, having asked this question, receive insights and answers, which place them in a place of dignity and worth in the universe. All others are doomed to a humdrum existence of tasteless living. They become robots of either their own habits, the corporate whims of society or even more gruesome, slaves of the state.

The God-centered life is the key to the discovery of the dignity of man and his place in the timeless scheme of the universe. Man imprisons man and makes him a slave of his inventions, but God puts him in a place of command and freedom of action. The Psalmist discovered this when he said: "Thou (God) hast crowned him (man) with glory and honor. Thou madest him to have dominion over the works of thy hands." God has never intended that we be restricted in the exercise of our mental resources.

However, God does intend for us to have a measure of humility, which will make us glorify God and not man when we do cross new horizons and discover new vistas of scientific truth. There is something beautiful about man remaining humble in the midst of glorious achievement, but on the contrary, there is something monstrous and terrifying about the pride of man heaping glory and power on himself when he does achieve great things. The former paves the way for a life of peace and mutual prosperity for all, but the latter paves the way for tyranny and human bondage. Which way are we headed?

No. 10 • October 21, 1962

COME, TAKE, LEARN

"Come unto me… Take my yoke upon you … Learn of me."
— (Jesus, in Matthew 11:28, 29)

Christianity is constantly referred to as a religion of movement and practical action. There is a dynamic spirit within it which flows and streams outwards. "Out of you shall flow streams of living water," said Jesus. Acting as the conscience of society, it has often in present times as well as the past, formed the spearhead of reform movements and has been the agent of social reforms.

But before there can be movement outwards, towards inter human action, there must be movement inwards—towards Christ. Before saying "go into all the world," Jesus said, "come unto me!" Coming to Christ involves a basic commitment of body and soul, a total surrender in humble adoration and a dedication of time, talent and wealth. What will Christ do with us? Not only will He "give rest to our souls," but will fire us with His passion for humanity. He will give us His yoke, He will teach us, He will equip us for action. Without His leadership, our actions resemble the feeble and chaotic efforts of soldiers in retreat, and not of those being led by the King of Kings.

No. 11 • March 24, 1963

INSTANT RELIGION

Last week we mentioned how some people buy their religion on the "time-payment-plan," like insurance. Others do the contrary and experience their religion in a quick, once-for-all manner, like swallowing a pill.

The day of instant products is upon us! We are surrounded with instant foods, instant culture, instant education, instant travel, and even instant religion. It comes in two varieties, formal and informal. If you have grown up in a liturgical church, you are aware of the "instant" forms of your religion. You go into a ceremony and come out filled with Christian grace… through baptism, communion and a number of other acts. If you have grown up in a non-liturgical church, you know the "instant" forms of religion there. A simple prayer, a quick assent, a "yes" to the question, "Do you accept Jesus Christ as your Savior?" and it is done! Two seemingly opposite forms of Christianity thus meet on a common ground of spiritual mass production.

Religion capsules may sound like a good idea, but if you depend on them for a steady diet, the results will be devastating!

VARTKES M. KASSOUNI

No. 12 • April 14, 1963

CONDEMNED TO LIVE
(EASTER)

Condemned to die!
The sting of death has pierced my soul;
I too am mortal, I too shall fall.
Condemned to die!
My lot with mankind now is cast:
To breathe, to live, then die at last.
Condemned to die!
Is there no hope, no light, no way?
Must death be God, and man its prey?
Condemned to die!
Before the judge, He heard us cry:
"We want Him dead, yes, CRUCIFY!"
Condemned to die?
Condemned to lie in stately rest?
A shrine for pilgrims' holy quest?
No! Condemned to live!
On Easter morn behold Him rise;
Behold in Him how death now dies!

No. 13 • April 28, 1963

THE SEARCH FOR TRUTH

"And ye shall know the truth, and the truth shall make you free."
(John 9:32)

Here is one of the most quoted sayings of Jesus. It is used by politician, philosopher, educator, preacher, scientist and representatives of just about all other professions engaged in inter-human relationships. It is used to give expression to man's unlimited capacity for acquiring new knowledge and confidence in his ability to discover "truth" in its many varieties.

It is most unfortunate that we fail to quote the previous verse, which reveals to us that Jesus was making a conditional statement: "If ye continue in my word... ye shall know the truth." Ah, this makes a big difference! Jesus was not talking about "truth" as ideas arrived at by sheer mental and physical exertion, but at truth in the moral sphere.

To follow in Christ's "word" means: To accept His analysis of human nature as being corrupt and in need of re-creation! Accept Him as the source of moral revitalization, and say with Paul, "Not I but Christ." The saying therefore becomes an expression of humility and not of pride.

VARTKES M. KASSOUNI

No. 14 • September 8, 1963

THE PASSION TO LIVE

"For me to live is Christ."—St. Paul. (Philippians 1:21)

The passion to live is strong enough, but the passion to live for something is much stronger. It is said that Lenin summed up his whole purpose in life with one word, "Revolution!" Paul sums this up with one word too, "Christ."

Breathing, working, playing, singing, seeing… all these signs of life become nothing but signs of mere existence, or human vegetation, unless a unifying principle like a golden thread ties it all together and gives it meaning, purpose, drive and vision.

Have you ever asked yourself, "What is the one overall and all-encompassing thing which controls me and my work?" If you claim to be a Christian, can you say that that one thing is Christ? Does His will govern your life, your home? Do His principles direct your personal and business practices? Do you see yourself as part of a universal and eternal people of God (the Church), called out into the world with divine mission? Is your all pledged and dedicated to Him? He demands no less of one who bears His name!

No. 15 • September 22, 1963

THE WAY UP IS DOWN

"Everyone that exalteth himself shall be abased; and he that humbleth himself shall be exalted."—Jesus

One day a controversy broke out in a local church and, as it often happens, people quickly chose sides and girded themselves for battle. Tempers flared, emotions boiled, and words began to fly! Finally, a general congregational meeting was called to see if matters could be ironed out. But again, people seized on the opportunity to take the floor and lambast the other side.

The leader of one faction who could see that things were not going too well for him became most disturbed and taking the floor for one more time, began an impassioned speech. He stated most emphatically that the thing under discussion would be most harmful to the church and to its members—that if it were passed, it would be a black day for all. Finally, he ended his comments with these words: "We demand our rights!" All this time an old man was quietly sitting in one corner listening to all the talk but throughout it all had not said a word. Hearing this final "demand" of the speaker, he stood up with deliberate dignity and said he had one comment to make. "My friend, you demand your rights. Well, if God gave us what we all deserve we would then get our rights—Hell!"

No. 16 • December 8, 1963

IN MEMORIAM

"Let the word go forth from this time and place, to friend and foe alike, that the torch has been passed to a new generation of American—born in this century, tempered by war, disciplined by a hard and bitter peace, proud of our ancient heritage… Let every nation know… that we shall pay any price, bear any burden, meet any hardship, support any friend, oppose any foe to assure the survival and the success of liberty. This much we pledge—and more"—our late President, John F. Kennedy.

The despicable act of our President's assassination on November 22nd has left us all shocked beyond words. Fast breaking events that now follow this terrible event make us watch and listen in horrifying amazement, not knowing what the next moment has in store for us. Let us never forget, however, that the God of Heaven and earth is with us yet. In the words of that Negro spiritual… "He's got the whole wide world in His hands; He's got the whole world in His hands."

No. 17 • December 22, 1963

WHERE IS HE?

"Where is He who has been born King of the Jews? For we have seen His start in the East, and have come to worship Him." (Matthew 2:22)

Shepherds came searching, found Him in a lowly manger, and went out to proclaim the good news.

Magi saw the star and came westward asking the question. They found Him, worshipped Him, and then disappeared to be heard from no more. Legend tells us there was a fourth one who kept looking for Him and found Him at the Cross.

King Herod asked this question, seeking to murder Him. Fearful that his throne was in danger, he had all male children two years and under put to the sword! What will not man do to preserve his security!

Scholars asked this question, searched out the scriptures, located the city where He was born and then did nothing about it.

Where is He today? Under the Christmas tree? In the pageants? Wrapped in tinsel? In elaborate church rituals? In the slums? In the plush suburbs? In heaven? On earth? He has a way of still being born "in barns" of modern life! "Seek and ye shall find"—

No. 18 • January 5, 1964

LAY LEADERSHIP

On the occasion of the Installation of Church Officers, it is appropriate that we consider the important role that laymen play in the life and ministry of the Church.

A leader is one who takes the initiative. If there is a job to be done, he does not look to someone else, but jumps in and does it!

A leader is one who can always see beyond the immediate circumstances and works with an ideal or long-range plan in mind.

A leader is one who can work with others and can inspire a sense of loyalty in them.

A leader is one who can generate enthusiasm in the midst of apparent failure.

A leader is one who has the ability to call attention to the work at hand rather than to himself. He does not seek false praise by displaying false humility.

A church leader is one who lives daily in the knowledge that he is really a servant of his fellow men.

No. 19 • February 6, 1964

SLAVERY AND FREEDOM

"If the Son makes you free, you will be free indeed."—Jesus, (John 8:36)

Continents are in turmoil because people seeking freedom are on the march. From the depths of our souls, we are all reaching out frantically to rid ourselves of the rule of oppressors. Nothing comes first before freedom, not even food or life itself!

Who or what is our taskmaster? Some foreign country, some national, economic or political force beyond ourselves? This is the typical approach to the subject today: "The African's curse has been the colonialist;" or "Communism is the curse of free nations;" or "Capitalism is the source of all human misery." It is always "the other man, the other ideology, the other county."

Jesus tells us to look within ourselves. There is no slavery worse than slavery to our own habits, thinking way of life, prejudices—what the Bible calls "sin!" After the colonist has departed, the native still has to master himself. The enemy within can rule with greater ferocity than the enemy without. Having located your oppressor within, come to Christ, He can make you free indeed.

No. 20 • March 1, 1964

CHRIST AND THE DRUG ADDICT
(BASED ON THE TESTIMONY OF DAVID WILKERSON)

Share with me my joy, for I have seen a great thing:

Yesterday I heard and saw the Lord!

Yes, saw and heard Him, and others with me saw Him too…

With faltering speech, but radiant face the young man stood,

"I was an addict," said he. "When all others had given me up, Christ found me! From the depths of hell He saved me!"

"Today I love Him, I adore Him my Lord!"

In rapt attention, we listened as we heard the story unfold.

It began with a young preacher fired with a mission;

The ultimate challenge is to help young people in bondage to drugs.

"I passed out witnessing the revolting sight," said he.

"I could no longer preach unless God would prove that addicts too could be freed from their evil and shame, by the power of the redeeming Christ."

He started with five, and today they are fifty multiplied over. The work has spread to Boston, Houston, L.A. and more.

Human wrecks reclaimed, remade, made whole—

Christ at work where most men dread to tread.

In unbelief "Where is God?" men say…

Yesterday we saw Him in the cathedral of a former addict's soul.

No. 21 • March 22, 1964

THE KING ON A DONKEY

One wonders what people would think of Jesus if He were living in our society today. We often fail to realize that He was a man who deliberately did the unusual, was a non-conformist, and lived with complete disregard to things we call basic and most necessary. He did not live this way in order to attract attention to Himself, but on the contrary, to demonstrate the futility of man's accepted way of life and system of values. His so-called "triumphant entry into Jerusalem" is a dramatic emphasis of this fact. The picture of that man on a donkey is more like that of a Don Quixote rather than a Caesar.

We try to elevate Jesus today and put Him on the pedestal He refused while on earth. His representatives on earth today assume titles and trappings that stagger the imagination and dazzle the eye! If they were given the chance, they would refuse the donkey and ride that charger. The parade they would organize would make headlines all over the world. But alas in doing so, we would be doing away not only with the donkey, but the Christ who sat upon it!

No. 22 • April 19, 1964

A TIME TO WEEP

**"A time to weep, and a time to laugh;
a time to mourn and a time to dance."** (Ecclesiastes 3:4)

For us Armenians, April 24, is a time to weep. For on that day, we remember the hundreds of thousands of our people who were massacred close to 50 years ago—in enlightened 20th Century!

Memory is a powerful force that can either be harnessed for positive and wholesome purposes, or it can be a destructive and utterly negative influence. **How are we Armenians going to use our grief?** We can sulk and be filled with obsessive hatred for our tormentors—a worthless and completely useless thing! We can clamor for "world recognition of the dastardly act." Subconsciously, those who cry for such "recognition," are seeking satisfaction of unrealized yearning for personal and national glory!

Grief can be redemptive and in our case, it must be so. Grief in hate destroys the hater like a cancer. Grief in love saves him. Weep in love and you give life to future generations, weep in hate and you kill—yourself as well as unborn generations of Armenians!

No. 23 • May 3, 1964

BEYOND DESPAIR, WHAT?

"So I turned about and gave my heart up to despair." With this conclusion, the writer of Ecclesiastes summed up the result of his search for the key to life's meaning.

Three different approaches to the problem yielded negative results: the **philosophical** approach (1:12-18), the **sensual** approach (2:1-2), and the **cultural** approach (2:3-23).

Is this the "end of the line?" "Yes," answers the man standing on the ledge of a tall building ready to commit suicide. "Yes," answer many thinkers who see humanity tottering on the brink of universal self-annihilation. "No!" answers the Christian. Mere idealism? May be, but a lot better than introverted despair and gloom!

Our author continues, for this is not his end either: "Apart from Him (God) who can eat or who can have enjoyment? For to the man who pleases Him, (God) gives wisdom, knowledge and joy." (Ecclesiastes 2:25). Stop your search just short of the word "God" and despair does become the conclusion of the matter. The strange thing is that we often do so in the interest of intellectual maturity and freedom! It is a declaration of dependence to say "my God," but it is also the only way out of despair.

No. 24 • June 7, 1964

WHO IS, WHO WAS, AND IS TO COME

"I am the Alpha and the Omega, says the Lord God, who is and who was and is to come, the Almighty." (Revelation 1:8)

We begin today a final series of studies taken from the last book of the Bible—The Revelation of John. A series of studies creates an impact which is accumulative, while an overall sweep of the book's contents is also acquired.

Contrary to the popular belief of many, this book was not written primarily as predictive prophecy concerning future events, but to strengthen and comfort God's people who were being systematically persecuted by the Roman Empire. One must always remember that these were the times of the monster Nero! The focal point of the book therefore is not **a thing**, being Jesus' second coming, but **a person**—The King of Kings, Christ the Lord! The eternality and indestructability of the Christ and His message to the churches form the introduction to the drama now unfolding.

The message of this book is for our times. Precisely because we are involved in the mainstream of humanity's agonies today, we too must recapture the truths which will provide the inner resources "to endure till death."

CHAPTER III

FIRST ARMENIAN PRESBYTERIAN CHURCH
FRESNO, CA, 1964-1977

No. 1 • September 13, 1964

CHOOSE TODAY

Great moments in the history of mankind continue to stir our hearts today. Who dares to read of Vartan's speech to his men on the battlefield of Avarair (in 451 AD) and remain unmoved? Who can remain unstirred after hearing Churchill rally his country during the fiery days of the Blitz?

3,000 years ago the challenge "Choose today whom you will serve!" was flung at the whole nation by its veteran general Joshua. After crossing the burning deserts, they had arrived at the land "flowing with milk and honey." In the midst of a general trend to forget God, this man called the nation to a decision.

"America, America!" This modern land of seemingly infinite abundance presents our challenge. Today infinite abundance presents our challenge. Today the alternatives are clearly set before us—either enjoy our plenty in self-centered prosperity, or else dedicate it and ourselves to the glory of God and the service of our fellow-men. Choose today, and may that decision become one of the greatest moments of your life.

(Read—Joshua 24:14-22)

No. 2 • October 25, 1964

PULPIT, PEWS AND POLITICS

The pulpit is used by the church to communicate truth, both human and divine, to the hearts and minds of its people. Should the pulpit be used to communicate political truth? "Hold it pastor, you are treading on dangerous ground!"

Sure, we are treading on dangerous ground, but choosing to do otherwise would be choosing to make our Gospel totally irrelevant or unrelated to life. Politics deal with the personal and social needs of people, and the pulpit has always been immensely concerned with the subject, from Biblical times to the present.

To be honest about it, however, we must confess that the church is caught on the horns of a dilemma. The problem is that it wants to get thoroughly involved in society and yet must stop short at the point where society becomes the State. This is so because we conform to the belief that Church and State must remain separate.

"Whom shall I vote for, Johnson or Goldwater?" Do not expect the answer from the pulpit next Sunday. But do expect the church to help mold your attitudes, beliefs, values, and principles throughout the whole year so that when election time rolls around, you will be able to make up your own mind without being carried away by political agitation. This is the right and proper way. The ultimate voice of the church must therefore not be the pulpit but the pew, that is to say the lay membership without whom the church would be nothing but a hierarchy of self-delusion!

(For meditation—Amos 7:7-15)

No. 3 • November 15, 1964

WHAT PRICE GLORY?

POWER, AUTHORITY, GLORY. These are mighty and grand words which modern man understands and respects! Is it not true that most political, social and institutional concerns seek the successful attainment of all three?

The first, POWER, would provide us with the brute force necessary to get anything moving. Without it, nothing can work. Blueprints can never leave the drawing board and dreams die unfulfilled.

Having secured power and effectively utilized it to accomplish our purposes, we find out that it can produce many beneficial side-effects—such as lording it over all who need that power too but are too weak to produce it themselves! So, AUTHORITY is born and quickly degenerates into dictatorship.

Why do men seek so much power and authority? Is it not that they may rise high up and be "number one on the totem pole?" Ah, sweet glory! How wonderful to have people look and say, "There goes so and so, he runs this town!"

The tragedy of it all is that after having successfully achieved all three goals, one ends up unconsciously falling into the hands of the Devil! This is what he tried to do with Jesus, but he was successfully rejected. "Blessed are the meek," said Jesus, "For they shall inherit the earth."

(Read—Luke 4:1-13)

No. 4 • November 22, 1964

FAITH OR PRESUMPTION?

Christianity in our times is expressed in extremes. On the one hand, you have cold rationalism which says, "I will believe only that which my mind can prove to be true." As a result, there is actually the lack of faith and unbelief because the supernatural cannot be grasped and analyzed by our brains. On the other hand, you have an overabundance of faith. There are people who find it very easy to believe things and act upon those beliefs without any hesitation. In the mountains of West Virginia, there are snake-handlers in the cause of faith, for example!

Jesus' third temptation, strangely enough, was of this second type. The fact that He had faith was not questioned, but He was challenged to prove it by some spectacular means—such as throwing Himself down from a tower and believing that angels would protect Him. Would this not be a dazzling display of his deity? Would not the crowds throng after Him if he did that?

Faith is the product of humility; presumption is the product of pride. Faith produces a steadiness, a firmness, a direction in the routine of life. Presumption is born in insecurity and seeks new displays for self-assurance. Faith produces the church, but presumption produces nothing more than religious vaudeville!

(Read—Luke 4:1-13)

No. 5 • February 21, 1965

WHY DOES GOD ALLOW IT?

The wicked prosper and the righteous suffer! It seems as if this has been repeated over and over in the experiences of many people and nations. In the Bible, this is the question asked by many men of God such as Job, Jeremiah and Habakkuk. The Psalms are full of this question also.

Our own people have found themselves in the fire of suffering from the beginning of their history; we have never had a time of peace and prosperity comparable to such periods that just about any nation on the face of this earth has had. Whether it be 451 A.D. and the battle of Avarair or 1915 and the massacre of a million and a half of our people, the story has been the same! One can really understand why many an Armenian today is really in his heart a skeptic saying, "If there is a God, why has He remained silent in all this suffering?"

The irony of it is that by giving up belief in God, suffering is not removed and the problem still exists. How much more terrible is it to add darkness of the heart and soul to the pain of the body? I have personally cringed at the bitterness and utter gloom that I have seen in people who have "cursed God" and have given themselves up to complete despair!

There is only one way to rob your tormentor of his sense of triumph— by remaining unbroken in spirit. This spirit is in the final analysis what makes man to be man. And there is a paradoxical thing, which has been observed to be true—the more you torment a man, the more of a man he becomes if he keeps believing in himself and his God! We have lost millions of people in innumerable massacres, but we have come through each one looking ten feet tall!

(Jeremiah 12:1-6)

39

No. 6 • June 13, 1965

MY FATHER, MY SON

The story of the Prodigal Son holds much for us today as we seek guidance in rearing our children right. We see therein three stages of growth through which all our children pass. It would be well for us to consider them:

    1. <u>DEPENDENCE-ATTACHMENT.</u> When children are young, they obey without questioning. They are completely dependent and have no feeling of self-sufficiency.

    2. <u>INDEPENDENCE-REBELLION.</u> Self-discovery invariably means self-sufficiency. And this means "cutting off the apron strings." The prodigal left home. "I don't need you any more dad," may well have been his feelings.

    3. <u>INTER-DEPENDENCE-MATURITY.</u> Many young people stop at the second stage, and in doing so remain immature. The play-boy son is really still a child stunted in his growth. The road back to father and home is the road to responsible realization that we are members of one another, and no one (including the father) is complete without the other.

(Read Luke 15:11-32)

No. 7 • July 11, 1965

THE UNIVERSE AND I

It is increasingly being realized that man's penetration of the universe is introducing drastic changes into our thinking concerning the meaning of "man" and of "God." The space-age is here with full force and the exciting adventure of probing and conquering space has begun!

"How far will God let them go?" This is a question we have heard being asked by a number of religious people. I believe this question to be an unfortunate one because it reveals a lack of understanding about man, as God created him to be. God did not create man to be a prisoner, but a steward. And the territory he can cover is boundless! All this on one condition—that he respects laws built into nature and laws built into man to govern both, nature and himself.

Let us not be false interpreters of our Bible when we make it sound as if science is anti-God. On the contrary, it is the fruit of God-given ability, which God put into us when he created us. Let us allow science to affirm our faith rather than belittle it! Let us not be like the Christian young man who refused to look into a microscope because he said, "If God wanted me to see all those things, he would have given me eyes strong enough to see them."

Let the beauty and the wonder of nature that science reveals to us make us also to proclaim like the Psalmist of old, "O Lord our Lord, how excellent is Thy name in all the earth!"

No. 8 • October 24, 1964

OUR CHURCH MUST MOVE

This is the conclusion of an expert who is top in his field. He has made a careful study of our situation and now reports to us that the only solution to the many problems that face us is found in the decision to move! We therefore pass on this information to you so that you may study it carefully and come to church prepared to cast your vote—to move or not to move. Please discuss this matter thoroughly in your family, call in the neighbors and tell it to them also; do not hesitate to gossip about it to people from other churches and even write to your distant relatives anywhere in the world. This matter is serious and the life of the church depends on it. Come to think of it, your life depends on it too.

No, I am not talking of a building but I'm talking of the church— you and me. Before you relax in a sign of relief and say "He's joking," let me assure you that I am in dead earnest. Some churches move buildings and think **that** solves their problems. We are **not** moving our location, but we are trying to get the people "on the move." We have not even begun to fulfil our mission as a church of Christ. Let us stir ourselves up and do away with self-satisfied activity that does nothing more than tickle egos.

Oh, by the way—that expert on churches I mentioned above is Jesus Christ who said, "Go into all the world and preach the gospel." Go man go!

No. 9 • October 31, 1965

IS YOUR NAME JACOB?

Jacob is one of the best known characters of the Old Testament. He is known by his given name Israel to be the father of the Hebrew nation. But we are not interested in mere history—that is something that seems so remote now. We are rather interested in analyzing his character because we are so much like him ourselves. Here is a man who from his early age did all he could to get ahead in life—he was a "go getter!" Even family relationships held nothing really sacred for him, and he robbed his own brother and lied to his father. He kept this kind of a life up and in the process amassed a fortune, two wives and twelve children.

Much of this story is known except one often forgotten fact—that God did not let him get away with it! One day Jacob had to face himself squarely, and what he saw there was not very pretty. We read that all night he "wrestled with God." He sought God's blessing and God would not give it to him. This was his moment of truth. When it was all finally settled, Jacob came away with a permanent limp—with a body broken but a spirit reborn.

When and if you too are someday cornered by circumstances, and peace evades you, it may well be that God is finally getting through to you as he did with Jacob. "The Lord disciplines him whom he loves."

(Read Genesis 32:22-30)

No. 10 • November 7, 1965

WHEN FOUNDATIONS SHAKE

Have you ever been caught in an earthquake? Those who have tell us it is probably one of the most terrifying experiences of life. When one analyzes the reason for this, one can easily understand why. We associate stability and permanence with the ground we walk on. It is solid, hard and all of life depends upon it. When it shakes and cracks, everything shakes and cracks with it, including our minds!

It takes the shaking of foundations to reveal our inner fears. When this happens, forces arise from the depths of our hidden selves to tear us apart. This was the case with the jailer who was assigned the duty of keeping prisoners, among whom were Paul and Silas. The same earthquake produces radically opposite results among these people. Is it not amazing that the jailer who was in command of things became so shaken that he almost committed suicide, but Paul and Silas who were bruised and wounded from their previous ordeals remained calm and composed throughout the whole thing? What made the difference?

The answer is in our story. When the jailer saw the difference he asked "What must I do?" Paul said, "Believe on the Lord Jesus Christ." Faith in Christ is nothing more than trusting Him to be in us what He claims to be—the ground of our existence. This is what is meant by his name Lord. And this ground is unshakeable.

(Read Acts 16:25-34)

No. 11 • November 21, 1965

ONE THING I KNOW

"How did he do it...?" "What do you say about him?" "What did he do?" "How could he?"

Questions were thrown at him faster than he could possibly handle. Here was a man who claimed to have received his eyesight by one called Jesus, but this of course, could not be true because according to the careful judgment of the Pharisees, Jesus was a sinner and an imposter. Their conclusions about Him were based on tradition, theology and logic! And yet they were faced with a dilemma, how to explain this marvelous event of a man receiving his sight! Even after getting the theological third degree, the man would not change his story. "Many things I do not know," he said "But one thing I do know, I once was blind, and now I see!" What a glorious answer.

To believe him, his questioners would have to humble themselves and accept their own spiritual blindness. They could not accept that, so they did the next best thing—they threw the poor man out of town.

And is it not so with us today? When truth challenges us, we more often than not allow prejudice to overrule. We too at first refuse to believe, next we ridicule, then we ignore and finally, we persecute.

(Read John 9:24-41)

No. 12 • December 5, 1965

FAITH FOR A NEW AGE

Our title is the slogan being used by the American Bible Society in focusing attention on our vital and continuing need of God's written Word. December 12th, being Universal Bible Sunday, we make it the theme for our meditation also.

Our age is one in which newness is idolized. New homes, new appliances, new furniture, new world! Can the Bible continue to speak to such an age?—"If anyone is in Christ he is a new creation, the old has passed away, behold the new has come." Here is God's answer. To be alive in this new age without a vibrant and ever-new faith in Christ means nothing more than disaster.

Our age is one of sadness and pain. While our rockets climb into precision-planned orbits heralding new glories, thousands continue to die on old-fashioned battle fields. Hatreds continue to tear us apart. Personal tragedies continue to tear our hearts out! Does the Bible say anything about this? "Come unto me all who labor and are heavy laden." "The Lord is my Shepherd." "The Lord is the strength of my life, whom shall I fear?" "Perfect love casts out fear." Here are a few of the many answers God gives us in His word.

Faith out of touch with the new age is impotent. The new age without faith is a horror. A Bible-centered faith is in touch with both God and the new age. Such faith is magnificent.

No. 13 • January 9, 1966

THE PRODIGAL'S BROTHER

What young man is there who has not been cautioned both by parents, teachers and minister to be careful and not fall into the kind of life that trapped the prodigal son.

This man had a brother who never left home. He was very scrupulous and industrious. He worked hard, never wasted money. He never got involved in wild parties and obeyed his father diligently. In short, here is a man who would most probably be considered a model young man today.

The prodigal returned to his father and home one day. In the midst of all the tears of joy and the celebrating, we see one totally unexpected thing—his brother filled with anger and jealousy refusing to even come in! This sudden change in his personality was caused by his contention that his father had not appreciated him enough and was playing favorites,
And so our model young man is revealed to be motivated not by selfless devotion but shrewd scheming. He knew prestige, riches, and the whole heritage of his father would be his if he stayed home! It is quite ironic that the prodigal repented and was received back into the warmth of his father's love, but we read of no change of heart in his brother.

(Read Luke 15:11-32)

No. 14 • January 16, 1966

JESUS AND OUR PERSONALITY
(JESUS 1)

Jesus is a man with a claim on your life! You remember the wartime posters—"Uncle Sam wants YOU!" Well, such a slogan sounds rather humorous, but there is nothing humorous about Jesus' continuing claim.

"Uncle Sam" has the power to force his demands upon us and when a draft call comes we know he uses that power most effectively. Jesus does not work this way. He uses methods that are drastic in their passivity. So much so that one could easily, as is often the case, mistake them for weakness and impotence.

Jesus had divine powers, but never used them to force anyone to believe in Him.

Jesus had a magnetic personality, but he never used it to overwhelm and captivate his audience.

Jesus had superior reasoning and intellectual powers, but he never squashed his opposition in a debate and then gloated over his obvious victory.

Jesus never takes advantage of our inferiorities. However, we do when we use them as the point of contact, whereby we overwhelm and dominate. But consider the difference—Jesus makes disciples with His method, but we make slaves with ours.

(Read Luke 7:36-50)

No. 15 • January 23, 1966

JESUS AND HIS WAY
(JESUS 2)

In the early years of the Christian church Jesus' disciples were called "Followers of The Way." We read this in the Book of Acts in several places. Acts 9:2 mentions, for example, the days when Paul was a persecutor of Christians. We read that he went "to Damascus, so that if he found any belonging to the Way, he might bring them bound to Jerusalem."

"The Way" refers to a certain way of life, a certain system of values, which these people had adopted as their own. This is what distinguished them from other people and disciples of other religions. How striking and meaningful this is! When someone became a disciple of Jesus, he immediately took upon himself Jesus' way of life.

What does "Way" consist of? (I can just hear someone say, "Here come the dos and the donts!") Putting it simply and yet most strikingly, it can be found in one word "service." I deliberately did not say "love" because that is a much abused and sentimentalized word. Jesus said, "The Son of man came not to be served but to serve."

Here is the great distinguishing characteristic of Christianity, which separates it from all other religions, and even "religion" itself, as it is commonly understood. "The Way" means action, while "religion" means dogma and creed. Do you call yourself "Christian?" Fine, then START SERVING YOUR FELLOW-MEN IN THE NAME OF CHRIST.

(Read Mark 10:35-45)

No. 16 • February 13, 1966

JESUS AND GOD'S REALITY
(JESUS 3)

"Lord, show us the Father, and we shall be satisfied," asked the apostle Philip of Jesus. His question gives expression to a universal quest—to experience the reality of God. From the jungles to the most sophisticated society of modern civilization when rituals are observed, one sees this search for God to form the core of religion.

Where is God? Some say He must be approached through a host of intermediaries; others say it is impossible to know if He exists; other say there is no God; and today a by-product of "enlightened" intellectualism boldly proclaims. "God is dead!" with a "look ma, no hands!" sense of proud self-accomplishment.

Jesus taught basic truths about God: 1) Man really is not looking for God, but running away from Him. The "god" man looks for and never finds is the personification of his own wish-fulfilment which is a figment of his own imagination. 2) The God of reality is looking for us, seeking to reach and to save us. This God-toward-man approach to the question is unique to Christianity. 3) Jesus himself is the clue to the identity and reality of God. God is made accessible to man in him, and in Jesus, man experiences God in human dimension. So, for anyone seeking God, Jesus says, "I am in the Father and the Father in me."

(Read John 14:1-11)

No. 17 • February 27, 1966

JESUS AND OUR CONFLICTS
(JESUS 4)

Today we submit the fourth in our series of Jesus' "A Faith That Works," which is based on Jesus' life and teachings. Those previously covered are: "Jesus and Our Personality," "Jesus and His Way" and "Jesus and God's Reality."

Chapter 5, 6 and 7 of Matthew are commonly called "The Sermon on the Mount." Actually, they are a series of discourses which are unsurpassed in preserving for us the genius of Jesus' teaching. They are a rather full treatment of human conflicts, and we could easily have a full series just on these. For example, they include problems of hatred leading to murder, sexual immorality leading to adultery, marriage tensions leading to divorce, violence leading to war, hypocrisy leading to spiritual bankruptcy, drive for security leading to idolatry, lack of trust leading to anxiety, judging of others leading to self-condemnation and lack of genuineness leading to spiritual sterility.

How easy it is to see by even a very superficial treatment of Jesus' teachings that He is vitally interested in our well-being. Man says, "Give me health and let me enjoy life the way I please." Jesus says, "Your statement is contradictory. The reason you are unhealthy is that you are living as you please already." Turn your life over to your Lord. Trust him and then you will begin to live as you've never lived before!

(Read Mathew 5, 6, 7)

No. 18 • March 13, 1966

JESUS AND OUR PAINS
(JESUS 5)

At the very outset of his ministry, Jesus made a claim. Standing in the synagogue in his hometown, Nazareth, he read a quotation from the prophecy of Isaiah and then said, "Today this Scripture has been fulfilled in your hearing."

In this claim, Jesus revealed that the nature of his ministry would primarily be that of removing the pain and sorrow of mankind—the pain of poverty by bringing "good news to the poor," the pain of captivity by proclaiming "release to the captives," the pain of blindness by giving "recovering of sight to the blind," the pain of slavery by setting "at liberty those who are oppressed."

Claims must be backed up with action. It was a big one that Jesus made. It almost sounds like the bombastic and preposterous claims that politicians make, with no intention of ever keeping their word. But the difference is that Jesus did back up his claim with visible action. Not only did people then experience the reality of this, but people today testify of His power as well.

God, in and through the work of his Son, is dedicated to the task of helping us conquer our sorrows and pains. He has not promised us escape from suffering, but strength to bear and overcome it. Let us allow him to make this claim become a reality in our hearing today also.

(Read Luke 4:16-30)

No. 19 • March 20, 1966

JESUS AND OUR FUTURE
(JESUS 6)

This is the last in our series titled "A Faith That Works." Today we present Jesus' teaching concerning the climax of history and the establishment of His kingdom.

"When will this be?" The disciples asked this question to Jesus with the inquisitiveness of a child watching a thriller movie! Today some people claim that they "read the signs of His coming" and dogmatically state in reply to the question "He is coming soon!" Others who pretend to be more suave and sophisticated coolly say, that's all medieval stuff, and in reply to the question "When?" they say "Never!"

Jesus called it "This gospel of the Kingdom." And it forms the basis of His teachings. In theology it is called "the eschatological hope" (that big word means: concerning the end of time). No, belief in this truth is not medieval but Biblical and Christ-centered. We cannot divorce this from all else that Jesus taught, because it is the key truth on which all else hangs.

We believe in the ultimate triumph of Christ over evil and the establishment of his complete rule (Kingdom) over time and eternity. This is our hope and this is the believer's future—"Heirs of God and fellow heirs with Christ."

(Read Matthew 24:1-14)

P. S.—Oh yes, in reply to "when?" Jesus said, "No one knows, not even the Son!"

No. 20 • April 17, 1966

POST-EASTER ENCOUNTERS: DOUBTING THOMAS

Easter is over! Post-Easter blues set in very quickly, as evidenced by "back-to-business-as-usual" attitude of almost everybody in the church. The glorious claims made a week ago for the church triumphant have been filed and placed in careful storage.

"Our church was full on Easter!" This claim has dubious value for I am sure Satan waits just a few days and comes to church the week after, and then he has no lack of evidence to show to the world that Christians really do not believe all the things they talked about and sang about the week before! Even that new hat somehow has lost its luster too.

Jesus had a series of encounters with His disciples following His resurrection. And in each one his purpose was to rally them and get them on the move. Thomas was the doubter… he had to be shown by a direct experience that Christ was risen. "Unless I see, I will not believe," he said. Jesus met his challenge and reclaimed the faltering disciple. Thus Easter became the gateway to a glorious life

(Read John 20:24-31)

No. 21 • April 24, 1966

POST-EASTER ENCOUNTERS: PETER THE BRAVE

Among Jesus' post-Easter encounters with his disciples, the outstanding one is the conversation he had with Peter. In it a fundamental choice is presented to Peter—one which will determine once for all what his commitment to his Lord will mean.

Peter had to be first in everything. He had an answer for everything; he was always seeking to lead the other disciples; he was ready to defend his Lord with the sword. But when Jesus was crucified, he was the first one to say, "Let's go back to our fishing." It seems life with his Lord meant a series of sensational experiences. They are to be enjoyed but soon forgotten when the intensity of their emotion dies off.

Jesus finally faces him squarely and says in effect, "Peter, put up or shut up!" Actually the real words used are, "Peter do you love me?" "If so, tend my sheep." The measure of his love is to be determined by the measure of his love for work! Not emotion but involvement...

Our name is Peter too. We who would be first to defend our loyalty to God and his church are faced with a challenge. Service and not talk is the measure of that loyalty. Sheep tending is a menial task, but when performed in the service of Christ, it becomes a demonstration of divine power.

(Read John 21:15-19)

No. 22 • May 1, 1966

WHAT GOES ON HERE?

What is your idea of what goes on during that one hour every Sunday morning between 11 and 12 o'clock? We commonly call it the hour for worship, but that is a theological word, which your pastor suspects does not mean the same to most lay people.

Recently, during a session of our Communicants' Class, the question was asked, "What goes on during a worship service?" The written reply came from one young person in our church. "We sing, we pray, we hear the Bible read and preached and we give an offering. There is also a lot of squirming, blowing of noses, staring out the window and sleeping!"

What do <u>you</u> say? Do you come to hear the choir "perform," the "preacher lecture," or do you just "go." Many people just don't "go" at all!

Church attendance is a <u>declaration:</u> <u>First</u> of a need, for we in effect are saying "I need spiritual nourishment, strength and guidance." <u>Second</u> of a faith, for we are saying "I believe in God. I believe that God has spoken and continues to speak to me in Christ. I believe in listening to Him." Church attendance is also a <u>presentation.</u> We present ourselves not to the pastor, or to each other, but to God. In song, prayer, offering and sermon, we give ourselves to Him every time we worship Him, for He is worthy to receive total honor and glory. Remember, you have a date with God every Sunday.

No. 23 • May 22, 1966

I, EVEN I ONLY

Have you ever felt like crawling into a hole and forgetting, forsaking everything and everybody around you? If the feeling has never come to you, congratulations, you are super-human!

"The whole world is gone crazy!" "America is being taken over by communists!" "Crooked politicians are running the country!" "The churches are filled with unbelievers!" "I am the only one left who still has his senses, faith and patriotism!" The first four statements we hear often, the last we tell to ourselves secretly for we know nobody would really understand what we mean.

Elijah was a man of God who strangely enough felt this way too. One day he told God, "I, even I only am left, and they seek my life." One day he was leading the nation in a holy revolution, the next day he was hiding in a cave! God's reply was "Go, return... Yet I will leave 7,000 in Israel, all the knees that have not bowed to Baal."

Don't say "I," but "God." "I" is the negation of "God." "I" seeks recognition, security and power and when it fails to receive this despondency, sets in. "God" is the affirmation of faith, and when you say it, you no longer depend on yourself, nor crave security. When you say "God," then you have already overcome your fears and have discovered the secret of victorious living.

(Read 1 Kings 19:9-18)

No. 24 • May 29, 1966

PENTECOST 1966
(HOLY SPIRIT 1)

May 29 is Pentecost Sunday. This day the role of the Holy Spirit in giving birth to, expanding and sustaining the Christian Church is called to our attention.

Jesus called the Holy Spirit "The Counselor." In classical Greek usage this name was given to the person (usually a slave) who took the children by the hand and led or escorted them to school. Thus, the Holy Spirit is the divine Guide, one who walks alongside us in the journey of life.

The holy Spirit is "to teach us all things." The Christian must be led of the Holy Spirit in learning spiritual truth. Study of the Bible without a dependence on the Holy Spirit is bound to lead us into error instead of truth.

The Holy Spirit is "The Spirit of Truth." Truth is the foundation stone of the magnificent edifices of life that man would build. We seek it diligently; we base all human behavior upon it; we formulate systems of law on it. But how do we find truth? By yielding to the working of the Holy Spirit! God is the author of truth, and the Holy Spirit is His channel.

The Holy Spirit "Will bear witness to me" (that is Jesus Christ). A genuine experience of the infilling of the Holy Spirit produces a Christ-like person. As Paul said, "Not I but Christ."

(John 14:25-31; 15:25-27; 16:7-12)

58

No. 25 • June 5, 1966

NOT HUMANLY POSSIBLE
(HOLY SPIRIT 2)

Last week's message on "Pentecost 1966" has been expanded into a two-part series on the doctrine of the Holy Spirit.

John 16:8 contains in summary form the significant and basic work of the Holy Spirit:

1) He unmasks sin. The true nature of sin is revealed to be unbelief… "Because they do not believe in me." Belief is not intellectual assent to a dogma or creed, but a commitment of ones' self to a way of life—in this case to Christ and His way.

2) He vindicates righteousness. This vindication of the validity and rightness of Christ's ministry is tied up with Jesus' return to the Father: "Because I go to the Father." The Father's acceptance of Him is the sign of His approval. Isaiah says, "He shall see the fruit of the travail of his soul and shall be satisfied."

3) He guarantees judgment. The final overthrow and the defeat of evil and Satan has been made a matter of certainty, "because the ruler of this world is judged." The battles rage on but the outcome is guaranteed.

The Spirit-directed and oriented person is one who is sensitive to sin, committed to the right and calm in the midst of strife.

(Read again John 16:1-15)

VARTKES M. KASSOUNI

No. 26 • June 12, 1966

HONOR YOUR FATHER

"Honor your father and your mother, that it may be well with you and that you may live long on the earth." Here is a well-known commandment which needs renewed emphasis in our days.

"But they do not understand me!" With this much-used and abused exclamation many a son or daughter turns against parents. Father and child drift apart, conversation hardly transpires between them. Father comes home and sticks to his paper; son comes home, gobbles up his food and runs right out without any word. And so another day finds its conclusion. This is the tragic situation in many homes. The only thing they have in common is the roof over their heads!

The Bible has something definite to say about this problem: "Children honor your father and mother"—this is the children's responsibility. And to the parents it says, "Fathers, do not provoke your children to anger"—This is the father's responsibility. Unfortunately, the reason why many a son hates his father is that the father has really mistreated his son and denied him his dignity.

The father who is blessed with true honor is one who has carefully cultivated his role as head of the home, and who has never taken his family for granted.

(Read Ephesians 6:1-9)

No. 27 • June 26, 1966

WHAT IS FAITH?

The word Faith is probably a word that is used more than any other in conversations regarding religion. One often hears the expression, "I cannot explain it; I take it by faith."

Is "Faith" a substitute for things we cannot explain rationally? With most of us this is the case. That which knowledge lacks, faith provides! This may be a neat and simple system of assuring ourselves our beliefs are fine after all, but we overlook one simple point... All one has to do is secure more knowledge and then "Faith" begins to recede. Discovering the scientific causes of things makes "Faith" less and less necessary! In pre-scientific eras of man this kind of faith was all people could have, but today scientific man feels he no longer needs it because he understands so much more about the laws of nature.

"Faith" is not a system whereby we provide answers for gaps in our knowledge. Faith is TRUST primarily—this trust has nothing to do with knowledge for it is a declaration of personal need. This need is felt by the scientist just as much as the illiterate. It provides an ASSURANCE which acts as an under girding, holding us up. Both this trust and this assurance are centered in the reality and fact of God! Not just "faith" but "Faith in God"—this is the difference.

(Read Hebrews 11:1-12)

No. 28 • July 3, 1966

CHRISTIAN FREEDOM

How ironic that in a day when mankind universally is clamoring for liberty, the Christian Church does not enjoy the reputation of doing much about it within its own ranks. On the contrary, its role often seems to be that of a denier of freedom, as horrible as that may sound! What has happened to the ringing cry of the apostle "For Freedom Christ has set us free"?

Lack of freedom is often deliberately worked into the structure of the church or inadvertently creeps into it with the passing of years. Some churches deny freedom because of their <u>organizational structure</u>. There is a rigid hierarchy that makes the rules and enforces them rigidly. In such churches you can do nothing more than "pay and obey." Other churches practice intolerance because of rigidity in <u>dogma and doctrine</u>. The creed of the church is not, in such cases the expression of the faith of the people but the enforced rule of "correct" belief, without which the gates of paradise remain forever shut! Other churches practice intolerance by enforcing <u>tradition</u>, whether it is ancient or modern, it makes no difference. The beliefs and practices of the ancients are sanctified and idolized regardless of whether they mean anything anymore. Or the will of a local "pope" in a local church becomes the law, and woe be to anyone who would stand in his way. Or the <u>social practices</u> of a bygone era continue to make their inflexible demands on a new generation. The rallying cry of the exponents of such intolerance always is "Now, when we were young, we never…"

The hypocrisy of our position is easily made evident when we seek to win converts to Christ and the church by saying "Only through the Christian gospel will you find true freedom." People who take us seriously are appalled at what they find within the supposed ranks of God's happy family or earth—the church.

Do we then advocate anarchy? Of course not! Christian freedom demands of us responsible action based on the love of God and the love of our fellow men as opposed to self-centeredness or "flesh," as the apostle would put it. And that same freedom considers it mandatory that no one else but the individual is to decide before his God what right conduct would demand of him. As St. Paul puts it, "For you were called to freedom brethren; only do not use your freedom as an opportunity for the flesh, but through love be servants of one another. For the whole law is fulfilled in one word, 'You shall love your neighbor as yourself.' But if you bite and devour one another, take heed that you are not consumed by one another." Behold the foundation on which Christian freedom is built.

(Read Galatians 5:1-15)

No. 29 • July 17, 1966

CONTAGIOUS CHRISTIANITY

"Your faith in God has gone everywhere, so that we need not say anything." Fancy that! 'The laymen have been so effective that the preacher is out of a job… Yes, this is what St. Paul is writing to the Thessalonians. After his initial ministry in their midst, they "caught fire" and through them the Gospel spread through their town, country and whole state.

This is the secret of the rapid expansion of the early church in New Testament times. Today we must re-learn this secret or else perish. Faith must be contagious or it is no faith at all. We must seek results in the lives of those around us to whom we minister in Christ's name. Faith like a seed has inherent power for germination and growth. And seed is meant to be sown not stored away in a shelf somewhere.

"Religion is a personal matter, so I keep it to myself." It sounds good, but it is sheer unadulterated nonsense! Anyone who makes this claim is confessing that his faith is sterile. It is a natural ingredient of faith that it be contagious, for of itself it generates, joy, love, work and power. Try to contain this in yourself and you'll explode! It's "GO" all the way or else it's no good.

(Read 1 Thessalonians Chapter 1)

No. 30 • July 24, 1966

ORDER IN FREEDOM

Two weeks ago, taking our cue from Galatians chapter 5, we emphasized the freedom of the Christian way of life. Today, using the same chapter for our study, we wish to emphasize the place of responsibility and order in Christian life and action.

Historically, overemphasis of *order* has produced a strict regimentation in Christendom. The quest for freedom, within churches which have abused order has produced many reformation movements, one of which is our own Armenian Protestantism.

But in these very same reformation churches, we observe a phenomenon which is equally abhorrent—the misuse of freedom and the lack of Christian responsibility. In other words, order within freedom has been not only neglected but in many circles is being rejected outright. This type of freedom is non-biblical and nowhere does our God advocate religious anarchy! We have over 200 denominations and they are still growing in number… Where two or three people disagree with the emphasis of their pastor or the government of their church, they think they have the divine right to separate and form a new church. This is a horrible thing and is condemned outright in Scripture.

The only way we can have peace and an effective ministry is to be willing to yield ourselves to those whom God has placed amongst us as our leaders. In our type of church this means a representative form of government—beginning at the local church level and going all the way to the national. There is a distinct order in the church which is biblically validated.

How applicable to the government of the church is the Scripture verse which says, "If you bite and devour one another, take heed that you are not consumed by one another."

(Read Galatians 5:13-26)

No. 31 • July 31, 1966

SUPPLEMENTS TO FAITH

God has done all he can for you! He has already given us everything necessary to live a good life. He has given us over and over again promises assuring us of power in our quest to escape the moral disintegration of our age. Yes, and most wonderful of all, he has shared His very essential nature with us in Christ.

Is all this not enough to insure a life of spiritual productivity for us? No, it is not, for to it must be added one most vital ingredient—your active and utmost effort to translate faith into action. To do this you must supplement faith with goodness, goodness with knowledge, knowledge with self-control and self-control with endurance. To endurance must be added constant devotion to God, which must include brotherly kindness and climax in love.

It is in applying yourselves to these things that you evidence growth and productivity. Furthermore, it means that your confession of Jesus Christ as your Lord means something real and vital, and not mere lip-service. And by your own actions you are confirming the fact that God has chosen you and made you His own, affording you admission to the eternal Kingdom of our Lord and Savior Jesus Christ. But if you are foolish and blind enough to ignore these things, then you are inviting disaster and death on yourselves!

(The above is a paraphrase of 2 Peter 1:3-11)

No. 32 • August 28, 1966

BEYOND SELF-PRESERVATION

Jesus was talking about self-preservation when He said, "Do not be anxious about your life, what you shall eat or what you shall drink, nor about your body, what you shall put on." At first glance this seems a fantastic statement. Only "drifters" do not care about such things. And furthermore, is not self-preservation the very principle on which the continuity of life is based?

Jesus' statement is followed by a key question which must be taken into careful consideration if His teaching is to be understood: "Is not life more than food?" Here is the crux of the matter: Self-preservation is not life necessarily as the full potential of our humanity. And Jesus is urging us to look up and see how much more thrilling living can be, if we are not bound to this treadmill existence in search of food, drink, and clothing!

In our day and age there are many who are putting Christians to shame by showing a deeper dedication to some cause other than their own comfort. The revolutionary goes on a starvation diet gladly, depriving himself of everything but his ideal. But we Christians, we seem to be seeking churches that do the opposite—keep us smug, content and well-fed (at least at banquet times).

Emphasis has shifted from <u>mission</u> to <u>comfort</u> but in the process we seem to be enjoying life less. Ironically Jesus' other words are being realized "Those who find their life will lose it, and those who lose their life will find it." (Matthew 10:39)

(Read Matthew 6:25-34)

No. 33 • September 11, 1966

THE RACE BEFORE US

The author of Hebrews depicts the Christian life as being a race. All the elements of an exciting sport event are in it: spectators eagerly anticipating the outcome and athletes who have been trained for the occasion now ready for the big event and literally "raring to go!" Their preparation includes long disciplined training which is often painful and hard. All their powers are concentrated on one thing—to win.

The Christian has a superb trainer: Jesus is called "the author and perfector of our faith." Just as an athlete must yield himself completely to the direction of his trainer, so must we yield ourselves to our Master. He knows the track! He has endured the rigors and the great demands of the race Himself, and He has won. And a winner can train winners!

So often we wish we could get out of the field and into the spectator stands—actually many have done so. They are always watching someone else do something or other. And how true this is in church. The Christian who is truly in the race is a committed and disciplined person who is not afraid of self-sacrifice and hard work. He has learned that only those who race are crowned—a spectator can never be a winner.

(Read Hebrews 12:1-15)

No. 34 • September 18, 1966

WITH ALL YOUR MIND

The words in our reading are taken from Jesus' great commandment which states, "You shall love the Lord your God with all your heart, and with all your soul and with all your mind." We have chosen purposely to stress the use of the mind in our relationship with God for two reasons: 1) That Jesus demands of us an intellectual (the mind) approach to our faith as well as emotional (heart and soul). This is often neglected by us, and even discouraged by many, due to fears that the mind is not to be trusted. 2) With our young people back in school, with many in colleges and universities, they should be reminded that their intellectual devotion to God must keep pace with their devotion to secular education.

A purely emotional approach to our faith results in superstition, and a purely intellectual approach results in sophistication. Jesus kept the two joined together, and so should we.

The mind must be geared to study our faith in an inductive disciplined and scientific manner—just as carefully as physics or any other course is studied. If we are afraid to do so because we are afraid the results may betray us, then we have already begun to sink into superstition. Whom are we protecting, God or ourselves? God has done a pretty good job of surviving the attacks levelled against Him through the ages, but a shoddy approach to the Christian faith has ruined the effectiveness of many a Christian.

(Read Matthew 22:34-46)

No. 35 • September 25, 1966

HARD AND UNPOPULAR

"After this, many of his disciples drew back and no longer went about with Him… Jesus said to the twelve, "Will you also go away?"

Here is a picture of Jesus we seldom emphasize—the unpopular Jesus. Thousands followed Him one day and the next only a handful was left. Why?

As long as He worked His miracles, He was popular—healing the sick, feeding the hungry. But the day he shifted His emphasis from the physical to the spiritual His popularity waned. "I am the bread you must eat" He had said, refusing to feed them miraculously. And the people taking offense at this said, "This is a hard saying."

Hard sayings demand hard thinking followed by hard action, and very few people expect to have it hard when they follow Jesus. They want just the opposite—to have it easy. After all, when all else fails to give us what we want, we try God, do we not? But Jesus was never in a race for popularity. His mission is to build followers, and the hard course He has prepared for us is designed to do just that. The few that stick it through find it to be wonderfully true. "Peter answered Him, 'Lord to whom we shall go? You have the words of eternal life.'"

(Read John 6:60-71)

No. 36 • October 2, 1966

THE BREATH OF GOD

"God breathed into his nostrils the breath of life, and man became a living soul" (Genesis 2:7) "All Scripture is inspired by God." (2 Timothy 3:16)

A close study of these two verses will easily make it evident that both have two factors in common. First, in each case God is at work with creative power. Second, that God's breath is the agent in each with His life-giving force. Man was a clump of clay until God breathed into his nostrils. The Bible ("all Scripture") is a living book, made so by the breath of God. For "to inspire" in its original meaning meant "to infuse life by breathing." And don't we in the Armenian language call the Bible "The Breath of God," or "*Asdouadzashountch*?"

The first act of God brought forth man in his original birth and creation as a human being; the second act brought forth man in his rebirth and re-creation as a child of God. The record of the first is encased in the body of man and the record of the second is encased in the body of the Bible. Within its amazing pages are preserved for us, the sacred events of history, climaxing in the person of Christ, which are the carriers of God's salvation.

Consequently, the study of the Bible is the primary means whereby we bring ourselves today under the impact of God's Holy life-giving Spirit!

> "Breathe on me, Breath of God,
> Till I am Wholly Thine,
> Until this earthly part of me
> Glows with Thy fire divine"

(Read 2 Timothy 3:10-4:5)

No. 37 • October 23, 1966

THE DIVINE UNITY OF NATIONS

On the occasion of United Nations Day it is fitting that we discuss the significance of such a world organization within the perspective of the Christian faith. For Scripture used in forming the basis of our comments, we use Acts 17:26 "For He (God) made from one every nation of men to live on all the face of the earth, having determined allotted periods and the boundaries of their habitation."

We reject outright the argument that the United Nations is to be opposed because, supposedly, it is seeking to unite nations in an anti-God venture much as the builders of the tower of Babel did in ages past! A cool and sensible analysis would support the observation that the United Nations is seeking as best it can to act as an agent of reconciliation among nations, seeking to make human brotherhood a reality for all. We should be thankful that it has helped, at best, to bring an uneasy peace to many areas of the world where fires were fiercely burning.

"And he made from one every nation." The apostle asserts the essential unity of the human race in this verse. By its very nature, the universal church of Christ demonstrates this to be a reality and the church continues to give its moral support to any movement on earth that seeks to unite rather than to tear apart man from his brother man. One last word: If you cannot support the United Nations what is your alternative?

(Read Acts 17:22-31)

No. 38 • November 6, 1966

JESUS AND PAIN

"My God it hurts!" Our cries of pain are common and real. Although we avoid pain like the plague, suffering is still the experience of humanity. No sooner do we think we have eliminated one cause of pain then several others spring up to take its place!

The test of our faith takes place at the point of pain. And a genuine faith in turn becomes the key to a positive response to it. The Bible's extreme practicality is easily made evident when we note that it speaks to this point more essentially than any other.

The focal point of the Bible is the person of Jesus Christ. It follows then that His attitude to pain and suffering be deeply significant to us. And this it is. The significance lies in the fact that He experienced in His own nature the full impact of the pain of suffering humanity. He experienced it, absorbed it, suffered its full consequences and finally overcame it.

Our union with Christ by faith then should mean something most vital to us—the nearness of the God who suffers with us, that we may with Him overcome our pain. The writer of Hebrews says, "Since therefore the children share in flesh and blood, He Himself partook of the same nature... He had to be made like his brethren in every aspect so that he might become a merciful and faithful high priest in the service of God... for He Himself has suffered."

(Read Hebrews 2:1-18)

No. 39 • November 27, 1966

HOLY EXPECTANCY
(ADVENT 1)

The season of Advent begins with the fourth Sunday before Christmas. It is also called the "Season of Expectancy." Let us think this over for a minute or two...

Children expect lots of goodies. Parents with paralyzing dread look forward to late-night shopping, myriads of Christmas cards, frantic preparations for the relatives who will be "dropping in." And at the conclusion of it all, an empty pocket book, frazzled nerves and a miserable looking Christmas-tree that is tossed out on the sidewalk waiting for the trash man. Quite a symbolic climax to the American way of celebrating a holy event!

When Jesus said, "Blessed are those who hunger and thirst for righteousness," He was talking about something far different. He was talking of intellectual expectancy: the desire to learn more of the great truths that form the basis for Christian values. He was also talking of emotional expectancy: the desire to feel in one's bones, as it were, the great awe and reverential mystery in the contemplation of the event of God being revealed in the man Christ Jesus. He was talking of volitional expectancy: the great desire to be moved by God's spirit into action. The exhilarating action of working with Christ to relieve the pain and suffering of a sin-blighted world! Our prayer may well be for this season: "Spirit of the living God fall fresh on me! Melt me, mold me, fill me and use me. Spirit of the living God fall fresh on me!"

(Matthew 5:1-16, emphasis on verse 6)

VARTKES M. KASSOUNI

No. 40 • December 4, 1966

THE WAY OUT
(ADVENT 2)

"How did I get into this mess?" Have you ever asked yourself this question as you pondered your predicament? Looking back at the course of events we remember that getting in was easy... just follow your natural inclinations. But how to get out? That is the sixty-four dollar question.

Destruction, deportation and exile—this was Israel's lot, and in Babylon they had plenty of time to ask themselves, "What happened? What went wrong? What did we do to deserve this?" And the way out? A desert stretching for hundreds of miles separating them from their homeland. How vast that wilderness must have seemed to this defeated and demoralized nation! Despair and doom was the common sense approach to the predicament.

Futility, despair and doom! Words reflecting most familiar feelings in our times too. Whether reflecting personal tragedy, national trends or the moral decline of the times—it makes no difference.

And then the gloom is shattered when a voice, clear as the sound of a trumpet, cries out: "Comfort, comfort my people... Every valley shall be lifted up, and every mountain and hill be made low... and the glory of the Lord shall be revealed, and all flesh shall see it together." Yes, how true that "Man's extremity is God's opportunity." Are you willing to let Him finally take over the control of your life?

(Isaiah 40:1-11)

No. 41 • December 18, 1966

A NEW SONG

What would a worship service be without sacred song? What a marvelous creature man is that he has music in his heart and can break forth in praise of his creator God? All of nature reflects this fact also. The Psalmist talks of mountains and valleys, trees and forest, the sun the moon and the whole universe, and all of God's creation joining in a mighty chorus of adoration!

Human beings cannot feel alive without singing... By the sound of music, nations are stirred to patriotism; football teams depend on the thrill of their supporters' rallying songs to urge them on to victory; young people keep their ears glued to their transistor radios by the hour as they thrill to the beat and rhythm of music; children instinctively begin to sway and dance in response to music. In effect, music means life!

A singing church, a congregation that thrills to the sound of great music and instinctively joins in the mighty chorus in praise of the Almighty God—this is a live church! There is nothing more demoralizing than a congregation that merely stares at or at best mumbles through the hymns, and hires "professionals" to do the singing for them. Is this not too often the way we look upon our ministers, organists and choirs? But they are there not to do the singing for us but to <u>lead</u> us as we join in with one voice and heart. God has given us a "new song"—the song of salvation and life abundant—so let us sing it heartily!

(Read Psalm 40:1-5)

No. 42 • December 25, 1966

WHO IS HE?

Everybody loves a baby! It is so easy to get sentimental over a bright-eyed, dimple-cheeked, button- nosed little bundle of smiles and soft skin. Babies are to be kissed, hugged and loved. And so also with the baby Jesus, we put Him in a cradle and sing "O little Town of Bethlehem" as we rock Him to sleep!

Would you continue to love that baby if you knew He would grow up and at every point be a challenge and a threat to you, your security, your values and your beliefs? Would you coddle a revolutionary?

Let's get down to business about this Jesus whose birth we once again celebrate. He has a certain claim on your and my life. If we respond, we will never be the same person again. He makes a total claim. No dollar-in-the-plate, "I enjoyed that sermon" kind of response adequately fulfills our obligations in response to that claim. He wants YOU: "Follow me" is His standing claim. Where to? He never says ahead of time. He never guarantees ease, comfort and an easy road. On the contrary, He assures us that the kind of treatment He received in life we will too. Now that's pretty scary language coming from one who was crucified!

Herod knew his throne was at stake and sought to kill the baby Jesus. We don't kill Him but just administer a mystery drug to our mental image of the child so that He never grows up to challenge us!

(Read John 1:1-18)

No. 43 • January 22, 1967

ADORATION IN WORSHIP

The key element in worship is ADORATION. The Psalmist calls out saying, "O magnify the Lord with me, and let us exalt His name together."

Before we "get anything" out of our church services, we must "give something" first. The magnification and exaltation of God in our minds and hearts, through congregational singing and private prayer, is the key to this. A person in church who has the "spectator mentality" may have his intellectual or emotional fancy somewhat tickled but will fail completely to receive what God intends for him to have.

Through adoration of God, a person to person relationship in worship is fostered. God is not "out there somewhere" but here in our midst waiting to hear us addressing Him. And what will we tell Him? "Please God… give me… give me… give me." This is not prayer but panic! Prayer begins with adoration and praise, expressing in intimate terms our sense of overwhelming joy, love, and gratitude, for what He is and does. It is thus that an open acknowledgment is made of the fact that God holds a supreme place in our lives—He is our Sovereign Creator Sustainer God!

Worship that begins with such adoration is sure to end and on a high note of spiritual renewal.

(Read Psalm 103)

VARTKES M. KASSOUNI

No. 44 • January 29, 1967

CONFESSION IN WORSHIP

The adoration of God cannot take place without a corresponding awareness of our own sinfulness. Light produces shadow, and the brighter the light, the stronger and more clearly defined become the shadows. In worship when we bring our selves under the bright glare of God's glory and holiness we invariably sense within ourselves the fact that we stand condemned in our sins. So, confession becomes the spontaneous response of the worshipper.

Confession must be accompanied with repentance or else it becomes nothing more than just verbalizing and meaningless repetition. Reading a prayer of confession printed in a worship bulletin may be an empty exercise and a public show unless it is accompanied with a true change of heart and mind. Consequently, whether a prayer of confession be printed for us or not, we must in the privacy of our own hearts approach God with true repentance in every worship experience.

Confession is followed by assurance, when God's word speaks forgiveness and renewal: "If we confess our sins He (God) is faithful and just to forgive our sins, and to cleanse us from all unrighteousness." Such assurance is the ground for our infinite joy and "peace that passes understanding." Such a right relationship with our God is the key to a right relationship with ourselves and our fellow-men.

(Read Psalm 130)

No. 45 • February 19, 1967

GOD'S RESPONSE IN WORSHIP

In the past four weeks we have in the series, "The Meaning of Worship," defined the part we human beings play in corporate worship. We have stressed that through adoration praise, confession and commitment, we bring ourselves to God and together with fellow believers we acknowledge God to be our sovereign and creator Lord. Today we stress the second key factor that is most basic in worship—God's response. In other words, not only do we come to God, but he comes to us. Where a sense of encounter with God is lacking, true worship has not taken place.

God comes to us through the Word and Sacrament. The Bible plays a key role in the first and Holy Communion in the second. In both cases, the instrument that God uses is the minister, who at this point plays a prophetic role. Through the sermon, he exposes and interprets God's written word (the Bible), ever conscious of the fact that he remains under the control and discipline of the Holy Spirit. Through the sacrament of Holy Communion, God encounters us through the living Word (Jesus Christ). For is not Holy Communion the sacrament designated by Christ Himself to be the means whereby we remain in dynamic communication with Him ("This is my body... this do in remembrance of me"). Again, the minister plays the role of God's agent or representative in the dramatization of this fact.

(Read 2 Peter, Chapter 1)

No. 46 • February 26, 1967

COMMITMENT IN WORSHIP

Commitment in worship is the act of self-surrender to God and the dedication of oneself to the realization in life of God's will and mission.

The call to commitment comes at least twice in every worship service. First, with the call for an offering, by which means we give of ourselves in actuality. For is not our attitude concerning money the revealer of our true self? "Where your treasure is there will your heart be also. " According to this saying of Jesus, it is obviously true that very few of us have our heart (or commitment) in the church because so little of our treasure is given to it! It is most appropriate then that we should give money a central place in our worship of God.

The second opportunity for commitment given in every worship service is at the conclusion of the sermon. Every message that the minister delivers is meant to bring us to the point where we are faced with the decision: "Shall I accept God's word of judgment and grace which I have just heard? Am I willing to have God reorder my life to bring it more in line with His direction?" In the moment of quiet meditation following the service, we make that decision. And we follow up our decision with the practical application of it in our daily life.

(Read Romans 11:33-12-13

No. 47 • March 5, 1967

THE THIRST FOR REALITY

Years ago Jesus said, "Blessed are the thirsty." How true this is! I love to see a truly thirsty person—one who has a passion to seek and search for ultimate meaning in the totality of life in and around him.

Notice the restless search of the artist, seeking in self-expression to communicate reality. How fathomless this seems, for what is reality? Once reality was sought in reproduction of the outward or visible aspects of life, but today emphasis is on the inward invisible and even sub-conscious. This is true not only in art but in the disciplines who study human personality, such as psychology.

This is why people who outwardly seem to have achieved reality —the commonly accepted symbols of success, happiness, prestige, wealth, etc.—are often torn apart in their invisible selves by feelings of frustration, insecurity and outright meaninglessness. Reality eludes them like mercury eludes one's grasp!

"Ho everyone who thirsts, come to the waters." This deep need, this craving, this quest is recognized in Scripture. And the call is sent out to all to seek ultimate meaning in life from the source of life itself.—"Come to me, that your souls may live."

(Read Isaiah 55:1-9)

No. 48 • March 12, 1967

SORROW AND JOY

"Joy, Joy, Joy, tears of joy." With these words Blaise Pascal, one of the greatest French writers of the 17th Century, expresses feelings of rapture that swept over him in a deeply personal encounter he had with God. The experience is recorded in his book called *Pensees*, which is a classic in devotional literature.

Centuries before Pascal, the prophet Isaiah said, "You shall go out in joy, and be led forth in peace, the mountains and the hills before you shall break forth into singing..." Here are two men vastly separated by time and space and yet both witnessing to an identical experience.

Such joy is always preceded by deep self-evaluation and the sorrow of repentance. Isaiah says, "Seek the Lord while He may be found... call upon Him while He is near," Pascal says, "I have cut myself off from him (God); I have fled from Him, denied Him, crucified Him."

Lent begins with sorrow and ends with joy! Repentance climaxes with redemption! Death is swallowed up by Resurrection!

(Read Isaiah 55:6-13)

No. 49 • March 19, 1967

A PUBLIC CONFRONTATION

Public demonstrations are one of the identifying marks of our age. We have sit-ins, lie-ins, marches, rallies and public meetings assembled at a moment's notice for just about any cause imaginable!

"The church should stay out of it!" is the common reaction registered when the question of the church's involvement is brought up. We agree that issues debated are often so complex that it is not an easy matter to decide who is right and who is wrong. But here is a question; "If the church had remained neutral in every age, would we be where we are today?" Where would we be if Moses had not publicly confronted Pharaoh. What if Jesus had not publicly ridden into Jerusalem, the focal point of a triumphant demonstration. What if Christ had not allowed Himself to be brought publicly to trial by imperial Rome and crucified? Where would we Armenians be if men like Vartan, the leader of the nation close to fifteen hundred years ago, had not confronted publicly the Persian King and the false religion of fire-worship?

Neutrality is the "safe" position to take. But in all these cases if those involved had remained neutral, then their safety would have meant death to the cause they represented. On the contrary, their death insured the life of the church! After all, did not Jesus say, "A seed must die if it is to bear fruit?"

(Read John 12:12-26)

85

No. 50 • April 9, 1967

CONFLICT AND PEACE

It takes no effort to believe that mankind is at war today. But it does take considerably more effort and insight to suggest adequate and workable solutions. Everybody wants peace in Vietnam, for example, and eloquently stresses the reasons <u>why</u> we must have peace, but answers to the question <u>how</u> continue to remain unspoken or unheard!

Conflict, which is the basic cause of war, is the clash of two or more opposing forces. World wars, or international wars, reflect conflicts that rage in the personality of human beings. You and I have such clashing forces within ourselves —psychology recognizes and treats this as a fact. The Christian faith goes one step beyond—not only does it say we have such conflicts, but identifies the root cause as being our rebellion against and our desire for independence from God.

Peace comes to our personality when all aspects of it work in harmony and unity with each other instead of against each other. Hence, the prime purpose of psychotherapy is to help us resolve these conflicts. But how about our primary conflict with God? You solve that either by forcing yourself to believe there is no God (an undertaking of unguaranteed results!), or else being reconciled with God by faith. This is what Christ offers us with assured results…"Therefore, since we are justified by faith, we have peace with God." (Paul)

(Read Romans 5:1-11)

No. 51 • April 23, 1967

LEST WE FORGET

(52nd Anniversary of Armenian Genocide Day) "...of whom the world was not worthy."

The following is a true account taken from Viscount Bryce's documentation of the massacre of the Armenians in 1915: *(The Treatment of Armenians in the Ottoman Empire, London,1916)*

"In a mountain village there was a girl who made herself famous. Here, as everywhere, the men were taken out at night and pitifully killed. Then the women and children were sent away in a crowd, but a large number of young girls and brides were kept behind. This girl who had been a pupil in the school at X., was sent before the Governor, the Judge and the Council together, and they said her: "Your father is dead, you brothers are dead and all your other relatives are gone, but we have kept you because we do not wish to make you suffer. Now just be a good Turkish girl, and you shall be married to a Turkish officer and be comfortable and happy." It is said that she looked quietly into their faces and replied" "My father is not dead, my brothers are not dead; it is true you have killed them, but they live in Heaven. I shall live with them. I can never do this if I am unfaithful to my conscience. As for marrying, I have been taught that a woman must never marry a man unless she loves him. This is a part of our religion. How can I love a man who comes from a nation that has so recently killed my friends? I should neither be a good Christian girl nor a good Turkish girl if I did so. Do with me what you wish." They sent her away with the few other brave ones, into the hopeless land."

(Read Hebrews 11:32-12:2)

No. 52 • April 30, 1967

RECEIVE ONE ANOTHER

"Receive one another, as also Christ received us"...

How often we hear that we must receive Christ into our lives. But very seldom do we hear it stressed that we must receive each other into our lives. The irony of the matter is often clearly demonstrated when in the churches, we who claim to have received Christ into our lives act rather aloof around others and keep ourselves insulated and isolated from the rest! A kind of spiritual superiority complex develops which robs us of our effectiveness as witnesses to the very same Christ we have received.

How did Christ receive us? By making all kinds of people, including prostitutes, despised tax-collectors as well as highly respected members of the community, feel that they had his total concern for their needs. He gave of Himself to us so freely that we sensed His love "while we were yet sinners," to the extent that He died for us.

Maybe if we showed more of this kid of a spirit, more people would be willing to receive our Christ. Only thus the church becomes what Christ intends it to be—a community of people committed to each other in the bond of Christ-centered love. Anything short of this will result in complete futility. You see, the Christ we preach can be seen only in our lives and absolutely nowhere else.

(Read Roman 15:1-7)

No. 53 • May 14, 1967

LOVE'S SPLENDOR
(A MOTHER'S DAY MEDITATION)

"Love is a many splendored thing..." So go the lyrics of a very popular song. Where else but to 1 Corinthians 13 or the famous "Love Chapter" could one turn to for a description of its splendors? In just five verses, 15 of its inherent qualities are listed:

1. Love is slow to lose patience
2. Love is constructive
3. Love is not possessive
4. Love is not anxious to impress
5. Love does not cherish inflated ideas of itself
6. Love has good manners
7. Love does not pursue selfish advantage
8. Love is not touchy
9. Love does not keep an account of evil
10. Love does not gloat over the wickedness of others
11. Love rejoices when truth prevails
12. Love knows no limits to its endurance
13. Love knows no limits to its trust
14. Love knows no fading of its hope
15. Love outlasts anything else

Such love does not come easy! The easy variety is merely a desire to possess a person or thing that appeals to us. The divine variety of love is the giving of oneself to the beloved, which means acceptance of hard work and responsibility.

(Read 1 Corinthians 13 verses 4-8 especially)

No. 54 • May 21, 1967

OUR MISSIONARY OUTREACH

Two stories would illustrate the place of missionary outreach in the life and program of any church:

One day a tourist stopped at a vast oil-producing industrial complex and requested to be given a tour of the place. He was taken to the wells from where the oil was pumped, then on to all the other operations where the oil was refined and processed. When the tour was completed, he had one question. "I have seen with great interest all these operations, but I have not seen the shipping department. Where is that?" The answer was, "We do not have a shipping department. It takes all the oil we can produce to keep our machinery running!"

In Texas a church discovered oil in its back yard. Overnight they had so much money that they had no idea what they could do with it. So a congregational meeting was called to decide the matter. As soon as the meeting was called to order, a member said, "I move that we divide the money equally among all members." And then another brother jumped up saying, "I move an amendment to the motion that this church receives no new members!"

A church without a missionary outreach is a self-defeating and self-centered church. The realities of the thrilling Christian faith can be experienced only as we give ourselves in the service of Jesus Christ. Our missionary outreach is our shipping department!

No. 55 • June 4, 1967

A VISIBLE FAITH

He who has a plan of action must work it! It is so in every vocation and every phase of daily living. The evidence of the plan's rightness can be seen only then. Many a battle is won on the planning board but lost on the field.

One day a group of men wished to take a sick friend to Jesus. Ordinarily it would be a simple thing to pick up their friend and bodily carry him, but they were stopped by a barrier they did not figure on. The house where Jesus was visiting was completely packed with people, and they could not get through. At this point, <u>determination</u>, <u>courage</u>, and <u>love</u> took over. They tore a hole in the roof of the house and lowered their friend to the very feet of Jesus!

If our faith is to be any good, it must be resourceful and courageous. Faith has little to do with doctrinal formulas but much to do with daring living. When most people are either too lazy to do anything or fearful of failure, those having the kind of faith which Jesus admired, take over and push the plan through.

Life today demands of us no less. All it takes is belief in ourselves and in the God in whom is our trust.

(Read Mark 2:1-12)

No. 56 • June 18, 1967

FATHER IN THE HOME

Dad's on the spot this week! It's his turn to be pampered and praised, honored and feted. We men feel somehow cheated however, because we never get even half the fuss made over us that our wives get on Mother's Day!

On Father's Day not only must we be honored but also helped to cope with the many responsibilities that fatherhood implies. The breakdown of the modern American home is a matter of deep concern. Judge Kenneth Andreen, presiding judge of the Superior Court of Fresno, says, "All studies of the growth and development of children and of the functioning of adults in society show a close relationship between the individual's ability to function in society and the quality of the relationships within his family. Statistical studies of delinquency, crime, suicide and mental illness show that all these indices of personal failure that create problems for society are closely associated with broken homes."

If dad does not act responsibly in the home, then things are bound to deteriorate. Dad, your sole responsibility is not to make money and let mom raise the kids!! There is an Old Eastern saying, "The fish begins to rot from the head." It is so in the home too, and dad, you are that head. How wonderful if the head of the home is the source of love, respect, faith, and companionship. Blessed is the home that has such a father. Its fragrance and aroma will permeate all and rise even to the highest heaven!

(Read Colossians 3:12-25)

No. 57 • July 2, 1967

THE POWER OF NEW WINE

Jesus was an expert in using illustrations from daily life to make an impact in His teaching. A dramatic one is the illustration regarding the chemical action which new wine has on its containers. Skins of animals were used to contain wine in those days, and with use they got old and deteriorated. Often when new wine was poured in old skins, they burst, no longer having the necessary strength. Drawing His conclusion from this illustration, He likened His teaching to that of new wine for which people needed transformed and new lives. Otherwise, the truths and power of His teaching would destroy them!

Conversion, or new birth experience, introduces this newness into our personality. Paul called it a "new creation" or "the new man. " Not only do we get a new personality, but a new perspective on life, a new system of values, a new outlook and motivation. Things that would satisfy us before now become remnants of a life that no longer satisfy. Every day brings us face to face with the frontiers of the new age in which we live. Alas, however, when confronted with new and unexpected experiences, too many Christians resort to "the old wineskins," turning to tradition for direction! Churches are notorious in this, often not allowing any new experimentation because "we never did it this way." Let us listen to what Christ has for us at this point. He clashed with traditions. His person and His Word are our sole necessary equipment to move ahead with confidence. All else, apart from Him, act not as freeing agents but fetters which bind and enslave the soul.

No. 58 • July 9, 1967

THE MEASURE OF OUR WORTH

It is a game people play: In social gatherings or private conversations the question is asked, "How much is so and so worth?" We mean worth in terms of money, of course…

Jesus often talked of a man's worth too. He gauged it not by the amount of money the person had, however, but the amount of productivity found in a person's life. So much so that He condemned financial hoarding as a sign of spiritual degeneration which was destined for ultimate and total destruction. Is it not rather disturbing that what we consider a virtue Jesus condemns as totally worthless? But real worth, according to Him, was to be seen in the use to which we put our possession and our life. "The measure you give will be the measure you get, and still more will be given to you," He said. Notice that the growth of our worth is dependent on the extent of our actual giving away of ourselves. Anticipating the response which often says, "But I have so little, how can I give it away?" Jesus said, "And from him who has not, even what he has will be taken away." It is not the amount but the spirit we have which makes the difference. Invest whatever we have in the lives of others, allowing God's love to flow through us outwards, and God will respond with an overabundance we never dreamed we could have.

(Read Mark 4:21-29)

No. 59 • July 16, 1967

OUTCAST NO MORE

Society has a way of conveniently setting aside and removing from public life and influence those people considered no longer of any worth to us. In Jesus' day the mentally deranged would be chased out of town into the cemeteries and desolate territories.

In Mark chapter 5, there is a fascinating account of such a man and his encounter with Jesus. His association with the Master is symbolic of the life-giving relationship we all can have with Him too. He was a man forsaken by all because they no longer could do anything to restrain him. Their best remedy was to tie him with chains like an animal. He was a tortured and self-torturing individual.

Jesus met him and communicated with him, not as with an animal but as a human being. Jesus asked for his name, what a beautiful thing that simple gesture is—"He asked for my name!" This is highly significant, and so much more so in our day of mass media for mass communication for mass results—names are neither asked for nor learned, and human worth ignored increasingly.

And the man was healed! O glorious Spirit of God that calls me by name and touches me personally, and heals me triumphantly. O people living in the catacombs of modern alienation, listen, the Master calls us by NAME!

(Read Mark 5:1-15)

No. 60 • July 23, 1967

DISTURBED DISCIPLES

Most people want their religion to be an anesthetic which will make them insensitive to the pain and problems of life. And the kind of world we are living in is increasing our problems at a multiplying pace! Some people go to their alcohol, some to their drugs, others to their religion to find that false sense of security from their woes and the ever present crisis with which life faces them. Faith makes them so heavenly minded that they don't want to be reminded of the hard realities of earth. How significant is that most Negro spirituals, for example, sang of the ecstasies of heaven, only because they were seeking a subconscious escape from the hell of their earthly existence.

One day, Jesus with His disciples was looking for a lonely place, some leisure and peace. The hungry crowd came bursting upon them. The disciples' reaction was typical: "Send them away... we are tired... we have nothing to give them." But Jesus had "compassion on them because they were like sheep without a shepherd." People always held top priority in His agenda—all kinds of people, including those rich and poor, outcast as well as respectable, high class and low class—they were all precious and worthy of divine attention.

The disciples thought a cozy and intimate relationship with Jesus would be a heavenly experience. But Jesus taught them that God was in the crowd, and that missing the opportunity to feed them would be missing the opportunity to experience God—His presence, and His Word!

(Read Mark 6:30-44)

No. 61 • July 30, 1967

BEYOND CONFESSIONS

In response to the question by Jesus "Who do you say that I am"? Peter made a great confession. He recognized the divine mission and nature of Jesus, and he was openly commended for it. So much so that he was declared to be the person who was to be the rock on which Christ would build His Church! But notice something else—in the next sentence Peter is being denounced with the cutting words, "Get behind me, Satan! For you are not on the side of God, but of men." Peter was great when it came to formulating confessions, but he was very weak when it came to making commitments. For he did not wish Jesus to encounter the cross, and from later events we know Peter certainly did not!

Christians in America have a strong fascination for correct confessions. This is a carryover from ancient church history when heresies confused and often wrecked the churches. Over 200 denominations in this country are an eloquent witness to this fact! There is something almost satanic about it however, for subconsciously the person who accepts a confession convinces himself that he is all right. He is on the "right side," and he can relax. And in doing so he falls into the same trap Peter did—desire for preferential divine treatment and a detour around the crosses of life! It takes action beyond confession to demonstrate the correctness of your commitment.

(Read Mark 8:27-33)

No. 62 • September 3, 1967

PROFIT AND LOSS

Economics forms the heart of America today. Money talks, it talks big and it does all the talking.

We are a hard working nation. We have in relatively a very short period of history forged out of nothingness a land which is the greatest, most powerful, most envied and most copied nation in the world. It has taken work, work, work and lots of money. The parlance of profit and loss is our basic vocabulary and it is push, work and push all the way!

While the haves bask in the sunshine of their luxury, the have-nots are redoubling their efforts to inherit some of the vast wealth of this nation, seeing in economic power the secret of absolute and complete happiness. Even violence is being looked upon increasingly as a legitimate tool to satisfy demands. And so the pace quickens, efforts are redoubled and all attention is focused on the achiever of economic paradise.

But a question asked centuries ago keeps haunting us. "What profit is there if a man gains the whole world but loses his soul?" If in the process of securing our economic bliss we turn into heartless and soulless machines, automatically responding to the stimuli of our environment, what good is it? What difference is there between a multimillion dollar Univac machine that solves all kinds of intricate problems and the emerging ideal American who lives in a gold-plated home? The Bible says of the Romans, "Claiming to be wise they became fools." God said to the fat-cat businessman in his dream one night. "You fool." It may very well be that the very image we are trying to create for ourselves will someday be admired as the ultimate in human folly!

(Read Luke 12:16-21; Mark 8:35-37)

No. 63 • September 24, 1967

THE ESSENCE OF GREATNESS

The drive and desire to excel is in all of us. Some like to talk about it all the time to everybody and anybody who is willing to listen, like Cassius Clay, later known as Muhammad Ali, the boxing champion, while most of us are more modest about it. This basic drive is due to the natural craving for recognition which is a human characteristic. The more we excel, the more recognition we get, and the one who excels the most gets the most attention!

Jesus' disciples were no different. They even argued among themselves as each wished to be considered the leader of the group. Jesus was aware of the contest taking place and faced it squarely, saying, "If anyone would be first, he must be last of all and the servant of all." This may sound like double talk but a closer look will reveal its wisdom.

Jesus did not condemn the desire for greatness as being wrong. On the contrary, he recognized it as legitimate, and in his answer tells us how to attain it: True greatness is manifested by a spirit of involvement in the needs and lives of others, or an awareness of people, their lives, their problems and doing all we can in service of others. This is the essence of greatness.

Bragging either with our mouths or our actions succeeds in making us not great but obnoxious. The quiet life of committing ourselves to each other in service is not a sign of weakness but divine strength!

(Read Mark 9:33-37)

No. 64 • September 24, 1967

HUSBAND AND WIFE

Has your marriage which began with a starry-eyed romance settled down to being a life of humdrum existence of two individuals under the same roof, with the vitality and thrill of real living made impossible by the anesthetic of the routine?

Husband, how well do you communicate with your wife? We do not mean just talk, but response with real feeling, or even better, feeling with her about things to which she is sensitive. Teenagers call it "tuning into the same channel!" How much do you participate <u>with</u> her in affairs of the home? Do you have clear lines of demarcation marked "His" and "Hers?" You know the house, the children, their education, PTA, etc. is marked "Hers," and the shop, or what men proudly call "bread winning," the club, etc. is marked "His." And where does church fit in? We know men who mark that "Hers," but we are thrilled to see many who mark it "Ours."

And how about mutual respect? Men, terror tactics may have worked years ago, but now you must work at it with more finesse if the wife and children are to look up to you with stars in their eyes! And wives, this "equality, or 50 – 50" bit just does not work. If the man is not or cannot be the head of the home, then there is trouble or abnormality.

Happy marriages result from conscious effort, concentration, and work. THEY NEVER JUST HAPPEN.

(Read Ephesians 5:21-33)

No. 65 • October 1, 1967

PARENTS AND CHILDREN

Children can make or break the home. The home can make or break children. We often talk of broken homes, meaning the separation and divorce of parents, but have you ever talked in terms of "broken children?" A look around will show us how starkly real this problem is.

There are thousands of localities in this country where broken and rebellious youth express their hostility and cold hatred of modern organized culture which includes within it the home, the church, the school, the law and government.

What has happened? What has gone wrong in the lives of these young people? Dare we seek clues as far back as when life began for them in the home? We dare and we must, for there is the critical point in the development of their personality.

Children in many a modern home today are being manipulated more and more and being loved less and less! Manipulation means using something as a tool to achieve one's wishes and purposes. The child is "loved" only if he acts in conformity with the parents' wishes. And our wishes are those which will place us parents primarily in positions of comfort and security! So the child is crowded into a narrow box, the dimensions of which have been dictated to the parents in turn by their society, community, church and nation. Soon the child learns that the word "Love" is a tool used by parents to gain their own ends, and begins to react negatively. The child, like all people, learns early to seek the dignity of individual personality, and when this is denied to him, he fights his environment and "dies" internally. What we are seeing in the world of adolescents is the tragic consequence of a chain of events that began as early as infancy.

True love seeks for the child his/her physical, mental, spiritual and social development, and fundament to this growth is training in <u>decision making</u>. Parents, we cannot train our children adequately unless and until we are willing to allow them the possibility of making mistakes. Children have this right which is inalienable. Mistakes will hurt and hurt they must if children are to grow. If, fearing loss of face in the community, church or society, we deny our children this right, then we do them great wrong. This will result in either gradual rebellion or the breaking of their spirit—in the loss of creative spirit, and in the gaining of a no-initiative, uninterested and uninteresting personality which really is the absence of life itself.

(Read Mark 9:36,37; 42:13-16)

No. 66 • November 26, 1967

FAITH—DEAD OR ALIVE?

James is a practical down-to-earth book in the New Testament. It is written with the obvious motivation of deep love and concern and yet it hits hard and is often goading, disturbing and even hurting. The desire is for action! It attempts to stir sleepy, contented Christians and pushes them out into this bustling world of ours which is insensitive to the vital needs of its down-trodden, hungry, and suffering.

In presenting his message, James invariably is confronted by the smug self-satisfied-church-member who says in effect, "What people need is a deeper belief in God! Now, take me, I believe, and see how God has blessed me! I am a man of faith, and that is all it takes!" And to the poor brother who comes to him for help he gives him a tract and a pat on the back saying, "Go in peace, be warmed and filled." To such a person James thunders, "Your faith is dead!"

Did you know that demons not only believe in God but also have emotional feeling about it? Read verse 19 of chapter 2, "You believe that God is one; you do well. Even the demons believe and shudder." Obviously, it takes more than theological orthodoxy to have a vital faith—it takes good old-fashioned WORK. Our faith was never meant to make us lazy and insensitive to human need, but on the contrary, to quicken our consciences to making ourselves available as God's instruments of love. Now that's something demons cannot be, as hard as they may try!

(Read James 2:14-26)

VARTKES M. KASSOUNI

No. 67 • December 3, 1967

A GLORIOUS INHERITANCE

If a legal notice were delivered to you informing you that you were the heir to a great fortune left by a distant relative, would you be excited? Why certainly! And you would follow the announcement up with immediate inquiries concerning the identity of your benefactor, the <u>amount</u> of money involved in your inheritance, and the <u>time</u> when you could take possession of it. No one in his right mind would ignore to do this, and much more, in grateful acknowledgment of his blessing.

The Bible announces to us that we have a "glorious inheritance" which is immeasurable by human standards. Your benefactor is God and listen to His word as He expresses His will that "you have the eyes of your heart enlightened. That you may know what is the hope to which He has called you, what are the riches of His glorious inheritance in the saints, and what is the immeasurable greatness of His power in us who believe." (Ephesians 1:18, 19)

Now, how willing are we to follow up <u>this</u> announcement as well? Will we say, "Oh those are just words," or else apply all our faculties to the understanding and experiencing of its meaning in our life? There is a <u>Who</u>, and a <u>What</u>, and <u>When</u> of this legacy too, but only those who seek it with all their heart will ever find it.

(Read Ephesians 1:15-23)

No. 68 • December 17, 1967

THE HUMANITY OF GOD

During the season of Advent, the spotlight is on the child of Bethlehem…
"born of the Virgin Mary." What is the significance of this event? Our
instinctive response is: "That Jesus was <u>divine</u>, for was He not born of the
virgin, conceived by the Holy Spirit?" All well and good, but does not the
Bible approach it from the other way around—that in Christ, God became
<u>man</u>, taking on <u>full</u> humanity?

What is the difference? Plenty! In Jesus' day many religions
believed their gods often paraded around on earth in human appearance only
(something like a disguise), but never really assuming total humanity—
that could not be possible! But now in Christ, affirmation is strongly being
made that God has come to <u>man in every respect</u>. In his humanity God is
participating in our human predicament of sin, suffering and death. Only
humans can feel how it feels to be human! Apart from the human Christ
even God cannot reach us at the point of our deepest needs. And so we have
Jesus the <u>MAN</u>—"His name shall be Immanuel—meaning God with us."

"He became a man… It was imperative that He should be made
like His brothers in nature, if He were to become a High Priest both
compassionate and faithful in the things of God, and at the same time be
able to make atonement for the sins of people."(Hebrews 2:17,18 Phillips)

(Read Hebrews 1:1-4, 2:14-18)

No. 69 • December 24, 1967

WHICH CHRISTMAS WILL IT BE?

Harold Begbie, in <u>The Life of William Booth,</u> said "The Christian ideal, it is said, has not been tried and found wanting: It has been found difficult, and left untried."

How true! This Christian ideal is based on the life and claims of One who was born in a stable, was a refugee, owned no property, had no formal education, wandered all over the land, was misunderstood by His friends, betrayed by a disciple, and killed by His people.

Dare we surrender our will and our life to Him? Of course not, everybody knows how impractical and even suicidal His ideas are! But I tell you what we will do—we will improve, change and reshape them so that they will become attractive, acceptable and enjoyable. So, instead of a smelly stable, we will have an idyllic pastoral scene. Instead of a hard-eyed revolutionary, we will have a pudgy jolly red-cloaked Santa with his eternal "Ho, Ho, Ho!" Instead of hearing the plaintive cry of the hungry, the wounded and the clash of war, we will broadcast out of every radio beautiful music which will always sing of "peace" and "joy." Then we will all turn to each other and in a thousand commercially glorified ways say, "Merry Christmas and a Happy New Year!"

Now, <u>that's</u> a lot better than the way they did it in Bethlehem 2000 years ago. It takes American ingenuity you know.

No. 70 • December 31, 1967

TOMORROW WITH GOD

Predicting what our tomorrows will bring us is a fascinating game. Projected statistics concerning all phases of life on this earth sound like fairy tales! Can you imagine, for example, one big city from San Francisco to San Diego, in a state with 100,000,000 people? How about inter-planetary space travel as common as a Sunday afternoon ride? Or, how about "made-to-order" babies with exactly the complexion, color of eyes, height, build and intelligence which the parents wished for? All these things are predicted as being in our not-too-distant future.

And how about God in all this? Will there be any place for Him? Will our tomorrows be so neatly made to our personal order that God will, if not blotted out of our consciousness, at best be placed on the shelf as a priceless yet useless antique? Accordingly, science will provide everything that modern man will need to have a satisfying and happy life.

"Lord, thou hast been our dwelling place in all generations. Before the mountains were brought forth, or ever thou hadst formed the earth and the world, from everlasting to everlasting thou art God." We may well make this the reaffirmation or our faith, as the Psalmist did centuries ago. God will not die, but on the contrary, He will be waiting to manifest Himself to those who in their megalopolises and megalomanias will have megalo problems defying the solutions of self-centered man.

(Read Psalm 90)

No. 71 • January 21, 1968

WHEN WORK CALLS

Moses was a reluctant worker. Contrary to the popular ideas we have of him he did all he could to remain uninvolved in the needs of his people. True, he had tried once but was so rudely rejected even by his own people that he had left the country and vowed never to bother again.

When God called him he was ready with his excuses:

1. "What shall I say?" In other words, "I have no authoritative message."

2. "They will not believe me." In other words, "I know that I will do no good. Have I not tried once already? I tell you God, It's no use." This is the pessimist speaking. In other words, "I have no authority."

3 "I am not eloquent." In other words, "I cannot express myself too well, and you know it takes a person with a smooth tongue." He is playing dumb here!

4 "Send, I pray, some other person." He is playing humble here! It's the attitude which says: "I agree with you—it is a great cause, and someone should do something about it BUT I'm not the right man."

Have you ever made any such excuses when God calls on you for service? The games we play with each other to wiggle out of involving ourselves in the mission of the church are nothing new —they are at least as old as Moses and that's about three thousand years.

(Read Exodus 3 and 4)

No. 72 • February 18, 1968

GOD WANTS ALL

"You shall love God with all your heart, soul, mind, and strength." Jesus summarized all of God's expectations (or laws) with these words, and called it "the first commandment." How much more absolute can one get? Can things be put any more clearly than that? God wants all of me!

Emotionally, our reaction is two-fold: First, disbelief and second, anger. We begin to rationalize by saying in our mind. "Now, I am sure 'all' does not really mean 'all'! It couldn't be… that kind of commitment is just not possible." But when the point is pressed that things could not be any plainer or more literal, then our reaction turns to anger. "Who does God think He is anyway? How can I give all and still survive? Anybody would be crazy to respond literally to such a command."

And so we hang back, our life is too precious to entrust to anyone, including God! We either rebel openly and quit the church completely, or else we play games in our minds, saying "I am doing more than many others I know. When they do more, then I'll do more too, but I'll wait until times are a little better…"

Soon things get back to normal, back to the comfort of the rut we have all dug out for ourselves, which is also the coffin of our souls.

(Read Mark 12:28-34)

No. 73 • February 25, 1968

FREEDOM OF WORSHIP

Among the several inalienable rights guaranteed for its citizens by the Constitution of the United States, the freedom of worship and religion is wisely included. Even a simple study of past history clearly shows that when freedom of worship has not been guaranteed, persecutions, wars and tyranny have resulted. How easily some religion or other has in the past, when in league with the state which has recognized it as the only state religion, created havoc in the land.

Such was the case in the 5th Century in Armenia when the Persian Empire recognized only one religion-Zoroastrianism, and forcibly tried to make the Armenians, who were their vassals, give up their Christianity and revert to this religion. Rather than give in, our people under the leadership of Vartan, fought the mighty empire of Persia to preserve their conscience and freedom.

Vartan and his men died, but the principle was preserved. Our little country, even though it continued to be a vassal of the Persian Empire, continued to practice the Christian faith, and today we have inherited this treasure from them.

America is free today because the meaning of that word has been dearly learned by its citizens — the least of which are the Armenians.

(Read Hebrews 11:32-12:2)

No. 74 • March 3, 1968

A MAN CALLED JOB

During Lent the subject of our study and messages will be the book of Job. We will divide these into five parts climaxing with Easter. We urge our readers to follow along with their own personal study to the very end so that they may receive total benefit.

Job has always been a fascinating character-study because people identify with him so easily. We see in his trials and tribulations our own experiences and empathize with him.

This book is not a "nice" book! We cannot find sweetly sentimental thoughts or words here but the expression of anguished and tortured beings. We are lowered into the fires of hell and feel the heat scorching our bodies and souls…

This book is an honest book! It speaks man's thoughts about himself, his fellow men and his God without reservation. When Job sits on the ash-heap of his world, he has no reason to be polite any longer. He reveals his emotions unashamedly.

This book is a glorious book! It is the record of a journey from death to life, from tragedy to triumph, from despair to renewal of life and faith, and what a journey that is!

(No. 1 in a series of Lenten messages on Job, read chapter 1)

No. 75 • March 10, 1968

WHY GOD, WHY?

These senses, O these senses of man!
His eyes, his ears, his hands, his heart!
He sees and hears with distinct clarity,
and how he feels… my God what passion!

Notice the way of a child with a toy,
or the way of a mother with a baby,
or the way of a man with a maid!
But his mind, O God, his mind…
That's the catch, the spoiler!

While senses feel, his mind betrays,
failing to meet feeling with understanding,
abandoning man to frustration and misery!

Why the fight of love — "eternal love"—
And then the sudden death of a beloved?
Why the power to see but no power to see meaning?
Why tears, and pain and death?

And why choose silence for your speech,
O God?
Why, God, why?

"Why is the light given to a man whose way is hid,
whom God has hedged in?"

Job 3:23

(Read Job 2 and 3 for the second in our Lenten series)

No. 76 • March 17, 1968

WHO SPEAKS FOR GOD?

"I would speak to the Almighty, and I desire to argue my case with God."

Pat answers and clichés are bad enough, but when they are given by people who presume to speak on behalf of God, they turn into weapons of torture! Such was the case with Job and his so-called "friends." In desperation he cries out for silence, seeking a direct confrontation with God. His self-assigned spokesmen are doing a miserable job of arguing on His behalf.

How like these people we are too! We give answers for questions not being asked, and ask questions concerning needs that are not being felt. And to top it all off, we do it all in the name of God Almighty! Have we ever dared to stop and listen to ourselves? No wonder the apostle Paul likened us to "noisy gongs and clanging cymbals."

God chooses His time, His place and His method to speak and to act. He did so with Job, and after He did so, He also spoke to these friends. But His message to them was one of rebuke, calling on them to make restitution to Job in apology for their wrong advice. Think of that!

If we gave people our hearts before we gave them our tongues, maybe God would use us more effectively. For, you see, the heart feels, the heart loves with a language which the tongue cannot glibly verbalize. Only then can communication on the deepest level take place. Only then do we enable God to speak.

(No. 3 in the series on Job, Read Job 13)

VARTKES M. KASSOUNI

No. 77 • March 24, 1968

A PURIFYING FIRE

A philosophical answer to the question, "Why do the innocent suffer?" is not possible. After all, the agony he passed through, Job is never given such an answer. In the discourse he has with God there is no elucidation of the mystery, and obviously no design of God is offered whereby He is vindicated or His dealing with Job justified.

But there is an answer of a different nature, a personal and real experience of the presence of God in the midst of suffering, a Presence which reassures strengthens and purifies. It makes Job say, "I have heard of Thee by the hearing of the ear; but now mine eye seeth Thee." Job acknowledges with humility that he is incapable of understanding the mystery of the universe and of human existence and ceases to struggle over this issue. The result is an inner peace which takes over. This is the purifying effect that his tribulations have on him.

Thus, all our sufferings also can serve to fortify us spiritually. In the midst of pain, we can learn to relax and to accept the circumstances surrounding our problems. It is not the elimination of the source of suffering that brings peace, but reconciliation with it.

The cause of suffering remains a mystery. But thank God its effects needs not be a mystery. Spiritual maturity in self-knowledge is made possible in a relationship of abiding trust.

(No. 4 in the series of Job, Read Job 40:1-8, 42:1-6)

No. 78 • April 4, 1968

MY REDEEMER LIVES

"If a man dies shall he live again?" Here is a question that expresses the inner quest of every man and woman on earth. It was asked by Job thousands of years ago and is still being asked by mankind— It is the universal question.

And what answer can we give? From what corner of the human brain can we come up with anything that will even begin to satisfy our craving for immortality? Some people turn to nature and in the glory of spring they see evidence of immortality. How valid is such evidence? Not at all. Others use their imagination profusely and come up with fantastic ideas such as "reincarnation," whereby one form of life at death passes into another, and so on forever. What evidence is there for this belief? None whatsoever.

The only evidence which forms the basis for our belief in life after death is the resurrection of Jesus Christ. It took place in time and space; it has been recorded in a book which cannot be proven to be a hoax; and it has produced results in history— the establishment and continuation of the church. "Because He lives, we too shall live," is the affirmation of the Bible. Christ is the sole basis of our living hope. This is not the evidence of intellect but the response of faith!

(No. 5 in the series of Job, Read Job 49:23-29; John 20)

No. 79 • April 7, 1968

TEARS BEFORE TRIUMPH

"And when he drew near and saw the city he wept over it."

As Jesus rides onto Jerusalem, he is wildly acclaimed as the Deliverer, who comes "in the name of the Lord." Jubilant crowds press in close, waving branches and spreading garments before Him in a gesture of great respect. And soon they arrive at the brow of a hill overlooking the great city of Jerusalem. Behold the object of their desires — the city that they know Jesus will capture and make his royal capital.

But a strange thing happens— Jesus weeps over the city! This the crowd did not and could not understand. (Tears are not fit for a King, and they are commonly interpreted as a sign of weakness). Then Jesus rides on into the city to be engulfed by the conflicting events that drive him to his destiny of death.

And do we understand Jesus today? We who so glibly assume to be His interpreters to modern mankind! Where do his tears fit into our own experience of him?

Maybe we have to learn to weep again— to be willing to be vulnerable to the extent that we allow the agony of human existence to get through our thick skins and touch us at the deepest levels of our personality. How strange that we use our religion to insulate ourselves from each one instead of sensitizing us to an awareness of each other…

(Read Luke 19:28-44)

No. 80 • April 21,1968

STIR IT UP

Church folk "come alive" on Easter but most of them die within a week— if church attendance the Sunday after means anything! We are like the ground-hog who comes out of his hole, sees his shadow and runs back in again.

"Stir up the gift that is within you," admonishes the apostle, speaking to Timothy— and this young man was no ordinary run-of-the-mill person, but the pastor of a church! And if pastors need it, and believe me we do, how about the members of the church?

"God has not given us a spirit of timidity but of power, love and self-control," continues the apostle. We have this gift already, now put it into use! We have within us these divine energies ready to be harnessed, but we act lethargic, helpless and listless. Is it not fantastic that in proportion to such great and magnificent beliefs Christians affirm that they produce so little in practice? We claim the world but are scared of our own shadows— God have mercy on us!

God's power in us is not that of brute force as the world appreciates and uses power— but that of love, which is a force far superior to that of hydrogen bombs. And under the discipline of self-control and sound thinking it can and must be put to use. This is the exciting promise of victorious Christian living.

(Read 2 Timothy 1:3-14)

117

No. 81 • May 5, 1968

WHY CHURCH?

It is becoming popular to criticize the church and those who attend its services, and to find justification in staying away from it and withdrawing support. One says, "It is full of hypocrites." Another says, "it disturbs me." And so on, and so on.

That the church has hypocrites, no one doubts, but it is equally true that to use them as cover for our own indifference is double hypocrisy! And furthermore, it is pride which really says in language that is heard even though not verbalized, "I am good enough. I have no sins and if I did I could confess them directly to God. I do not need the church!" And this attitude of self-sufficiency prevents us from both fellowship with each other and with God as well.

Either with sophisticated language or with outright crudeness, we express feelings which give ourselves away. Man has always tried to shape the church to be what he would like it to be, but God always reforms the church to be what His will is for it to be. And God's will is never <u>naturally</u> enjoyable. Hence our feeling of "disturbance" or "irrelevance" or "boredom." It may well be that if the church conformed to be what our natural desires would make of it that we would ruin it completely. The question is not "Is the church alive," but "Am I alive to God?

No. 82 • May 12, 1968

THE CHRISTIAN FAMILY

The basic unit of society, the family, is being threatened as at no other time before in America, and may well be facing extinction. Many people who are well known in public are saying things about marriage and the family that is indicative of this danger. Marriage and faithfulness to one mate is being considered quite archaic. As one popular movie star said, "I can think of nothing more boring!" and the "sequential polygamy," or a series of marriages and divorces, as envisioned by this same person as the normal pattern for the future, may provide much diversion and variety for men and women, but it means the death of the family. Can you imagine what would happen to children in such relationships? They would become neurotic wrecks! So, instead of allowing them to grow in their homes, they will be placed in collectives where they will be cared for and opportunity will be provided for their parents to visit them whenever their magnanimous spirits succeed in tearing themselves away from their diversions!

The Christian family stands out in the midst of such devastating darkness as a haven of sanity and happiness. The effects of commitment to Christ are faithfulness and joy, love and concern for members of the family, ability to relate to each other and the absence of a restless search for diversion. These which the Bible calls "the fruit of the Spirit" are the ingredients that go into the making and maintaining of a happy home.

(Read Colossians 3:12-25)

No. 83 • May 26, 1968

"I PRESS ON"

These words belong to Saint Paul who writes in Philippians: "Forgetting what lies behind and straining forward to what lies ahead, I press on toward the goal for the prize of the upward call of God in Christ Jesus."

The expectation of the thrilling future, and the hope of an ever-brighter tomorrow with Christ, far outweighed anything that this amazing man had ever experienced in the past! He chooses the unknown future over the familiar past!

Is it not amazing that in the cause of "faith" people constantly urge us to look back into history? As if we somehow have outdistanced God and He is back there several hundred years trying to catch up with humanity! ON THE CONTRARY, GOD IS AHEAD CALLING US TO PRESS ON AND NOT TO FALL BEHIND IN PESSIMISM AND FEAR! Faith makes us claim the future, not the past— for if "We walk by faith and not by sight" that is how is must be. The past is the seen; the future is unseen.

It takes courage, stamina and discipline to press on. Just when we sink to the ground seemingly exhausted from the exertions of life, we are beckoned on to renew our efforts. Our call is to the ends of the earth and to the end of time itself. And our Lord assures us, "Lo, I am with you always."

(Read Philippians 3:12-21)

No. 84 • June 2, 1968

ONE MIND, ONE PURPOSE

"Stand firm in one Spirit, with one mind, striving side by side for the faith of the gospel." Philippians 1:27

Unity of purpose and action is mandatory for effective ministry, either for a church as a whole or any one or more organizations within it. Mechanics tell us that the engine of an automobile which has several pistons in it must be synchronized to work in split-second timing according to a pattern set for it. If this is not done, then the engine will work quite erratically and tear itself from the body. Sheer power is never enough!

In any given church there is always a certain amount of human, financial and spiritual resources that its members possess. Unfortunately, too often they go to work with no set purpose or agreed upon pattern. And before you know it, the result is not smooth and effective production, but working at cross-purposes, disagreements, tension and trouble.

Unity of purpose and mind comes always as a result of all members bending their own personal wills to that of Christ. If our motto also became "Not I but Christ" then we would discover a higher purpose than anyone of us could ever have imagined. Thus, we discover "the faith of the gospel" and work for its fulfillment. Only then can the church realize its goals as set by its Lord.

(Read Philippians 1:27-2:11)

No. 85 • June 9, 1968

DEATH OF A MAN

The news of Senator Bobby Kennedy's death was broadcast early this morning, and as I sit down to write this article, conflicting thoughts fill my mind with turmoil! What can I say? What should I say? What must I say?

This Sunday was to be a Youth Sunday in our church. Young people lost a man they admired and instinctively turned to. Our personal feelings about the man's political stance is not the issue here, but implications of the assassination are.

We adults have made a mess of this world because we have allowed the poison of personal, social, religious, political and every other kind of prejudice to permeate the totality of our existence. And out of such a social climate, individuals continue to emerge with blazing guns in their hands. Now, how about you, young people? You who react so strongly against adult values, which are "sham and hypocritical." Are you adopting a way of life that is any different? I pray to God that you are! But, often among young people exists the same kind of apathy, irresponsibility and tendency to anarchy that we deplore. If you advocate violence as the means of acquiring ends youth deems vital, then let us not be surprised when many more assassinations take place.

(Read James 4)

No. 86 • June 30, 1968

INEDIBLE BREAD

The word Bread represents all the necessities of life. It means health and security, for without it we die. All this is a truism, universally accepted by mankind. And so without a second thought we seek bread just as the body instinctively seeks oxygen.

The popular concept of religion in that it tries to separate man from his bread with other worldly enticements which are commonly called "spiritual." To be spiritual means to be so involved with the non-physical that the body is considered secondary, unnecessary and even evil. It must be suppressed, ignored and finally removed, so that the spirit may be free (in death) to realize its full potential.

It may come as a surprise to our readers that the concept of religion, as outlined above is not Christian, but pagan! The Bible holds to the position that the spirit without the body is a meaningless concept, and that the body must be fed, nurtured and sustained if the spirit is to flourish too.

But the Bible does make it very explicit that "bread" can and often does become man's chief idol, or false god. It is necessary for life, but when it is seized upon as being the most important thing in life then it becomes a slave-master! God created bread, and man who accepts the bread but rejects God is going to find out that bread will not feed him, but choke him to death!

(Read Exodus 16:11-22)

VARTKES M. KASSOUNI

No. 87 • August 4, 1968

ON TO MATURITY

There is a time in the life of a baby when all he can do and should do is drink milk. Then a time comes when if milk is all he drinks, his growth is arrested and tragic consequences occur if his diet is not changed.

There are people in our churches who are so much in love with their spiritual milk-bottle that even feeble attempts made to take them away causes them to put up a fuss accompanied with all kinds of irrational accusations. They interpret these attempts as being a denial of fundamental truths without which they cannot survive. The irony of it all is that their very attitudes reveal basic insecurities which are the marks of spiritual immaturity. They see themselves as spiritually superior to others but are in reality people in whom spiritual growth has been arrested, and unless their diet is changed they will be permanently stunted and deformed!

The author of Hebrews says, "Let us go on toward perfection; leaving behind the basic teaching about Christ, and not laying again the foundation: repentance from dead works and faith toward God, instruction about baptisms, laying on of hands, resurrection of the dead, and eternal judgment." (6:1-2)

Some people have never been spiritually born yet; others are babies in Christ; others should be mature but are still babies; and other are growing healthy into maturity. Where do we fit in?

(Read Hebrews 5:11-6:8)

No. 88 • August 25, 1968

POWER OF PERSONAL WITNESS

Someone else's experiences, as fantastic and wonderful as they may have been, are not strong enough to satisfy us unless we too experience them ourselves. Stories of other people's travels, for example, bore us — especially when accompanied with interminable and mediocre slides or pictures— unless we too have been to the same places.

Borrowed or hear-say Christianity produces the very same effects. A past generation's exploits of faith, as great as they may have been, are not capable of keeping our faith alive, unless we too respond in our own person and lives. How tragic it is that people like the Armenians, who have rich heritage, often end up doing exactly this kind of thing. For example, the fact that the Armenians happened to be the first nation to adopt Christianity as a state religion is nothing more than a point of historical antiquity. And people who have nothing more than this fact to point to as the significant factor of their Christianity end up being fantastic bores! The difference between "I have heard it said," and "I know by personal experience" is the difference between night and day.

Peter says in his letter, "We did not follow cleverly devised myths when we made known to you the power and coming of our Lord Jesus Christ, but we were eyewitnesses of His majesty." God, give our churches eyewitnesses of your power in their daily lives instead of mere story-tellers.

(Read 2 Peter 1:16-21)

No. 89 • September 8, 1968

BLOCKED VISION

Jesus asked a question worth repeating in our day, "Why do you see the speck that is in your neighbor's eye, but do not notice the log that is in your own eye?" And he prefaced this question with the admonition, "Do not judge, so that you may not be judged." (7:1)

It is a cruel and devastating thing we do when we tend to locate the center of the problem that plagues us always in other people, never in ourselves. You see, it is a neat trick we play whereby we convince ourselves that since the trouble is with "them" then we remain blameless and therefore without any guilt at all. This spiritual and mental "buck-passing" is bad enough, but we go even farther... Since we know the source of the troubles (we tell ourselves), we now go around playing God! With a "holier than thou" attitude we seek recognition as spiritual leaders. And so it is that the blind lead the blind and they both fall into the pit of destruction!

Blessed is the man whose attitude is not that of satisfaction but of need. This person recognizes his faults, knows his limitations and always reaches out not in judgment but support. Jesus said, "Ask... seek... knock..." (v.7) Herein lies the essence of a growing and true spiritual faith.

(Read Matthew 7:3-5)

No. 90 • September 15, 1968

DARE WE TRUST?

The ability to trust is a learned skill. It does not come naturally or instinctively. A child will naturally be hostile to a stranger unless or until he learns that person loves him and means no harm. We naturally draw close to those who are our friends and in whose presence we are comfortable and happy.

When God makes His claims known to us, we just as naturally turn away. First because those claims always seem to demand from us things which are dear to us, and from which we derive our sense of security. It is the very essence of sin to depend on ourselves alone, our own insights and values.

One's own insights then, unless brought under the learned discipline of a trust in the goodness and wisdom of God, will mislead and ultimately destroy us. As painful as this process may be, we know how necessary it is. And how ironic that we know this to be true in every area of our existence except the spiritual, but if the spiritual is neglected then every other area of life fails to experience the right kind of growth and maturity! We work hard at everything else, but assume God loves us and all is well in our relationship with Him. This nostalgic view is deadly!

And trust entrusts— In other words, it is not afraid to let God take and use our resources. It is the source for joyful and ready giving, knowing that we can never outgive God.

(Read Proverbs 3:1-12)

No. 91 • September 22, 1968

THE UNREACHABLES

"Do not reprove a scoffer, or he will abuse you... Give instruction to a wise man, and he will still be wiser." Proverbs 9:8,9

Teachableness is the essence of wisdom, without it, we are dead!

It is the essence of death to have neither the desire nor the ability to change and grow. Senator Dirksen says, "Only two kinds of people do not change— the dead and the mentally ill." Why do church people often become so set in their beliefs and ways that they are no longer teachable? A certain kind of spiritual smugness settles in which says in a silent voice "I have arrived. I know all that needs to be known. My destiny is secure, therefore leave me alone!"

When people ask me about church, I sometimes jokingly say, "What bothers me is that a great number of church people are invisible during the week and impregnable on Sunday!" There is a lot of activity, talk, commotion of course, but what are we accomplishing? The lines from the song "The Sound of Silence (Simon & Garfunkel) come to me saying:

"In the naked light I saw
Ten thousand people, maybe more.

People talking without speaking;
People hearing without listening..."

How true this is of us, for all we seem to do is echo the sound of futility and complete chaos around us. But what is so horrible is that we claim to be in communication with God.

(Read Proverbs 9:7-18)

No. 92 • October 20, 1968

RAGING HEARTS

"When a man's folly brings his way to ruin, his heart rages against the Lord." Proverbs 19:3

There was a time when man hid from God among the bushes and God went after him calling out, "Where are you?" (Genesis 3:9) Today we have it completely turned around. We believe that God is hiding somewhere from us and we are out looking for Him, crying, "God where are you?"

After a thorough search (or so they say) some have found a dead body. And they now claim with great lament "We have found God, but alas He is dead!" Others are a little more modest and say, "We are still looking for Him, but have no idea where He can be found!" Others have given up the search and say, "God is lost for good!" And others still unfortunately claim His marks are all over, but alas only in the tragedies of existence. They blame God for everything that goes bad saying, "If he is a good God, why does He allow such things?"

God is not lost— but man is! God is not dead— man is! The dead bodies we find are our own! The folly of human rebellion against God has separated us from our Creator, and we have been abandoned to our own folly. "Since they did not see fit to acknowledge God, God gave them up to a base mind" says the apostle Paul (Romans 1:23,24). Maybe if we raged at ourselves a little, we would call on God to save us instead.

(Read Proverbs 19:1-16)

No. 93 • October 27, 1964

REFORMATION SUNDAY

Today we recall reformation movements which form an integral part of our heritage. Without these, we would be a decadent and lost people. Such reform movements have periodically renewed the church and brought it into position of effective ministry and action in society.

In the Bible we have the reformation movement of King Josiah for example, which brought the nation of Israel back into obedience and faith after they had drifted into religious idolatry and social decadence. Every prophet sought these same results as well and their books are messages calling for reform in the fabric of personal and national life.

In our history, beyond Bible times, we have significant reform movements too. Out of all these, two have uniquely given us our distinct identity as Armenian Protestants. The first is the Armenian Evangelical reformation which in 1846 created the first Armenian Protestant Church. The second (although first in time sequence) was the reformation in which Martin Luther played a key role in the early 1500s. In this movement, Protestantism emerged as a distinct and powerful arm of worldwide Christianity.

Today we have new fresh winds blowing through our churches again. It takes sensitivity to the guidance of the Holy Spirit to differentiate between forces that would build up and renew the church and others that would tear it down and destroy it. This is all the more reason why we must as members of God's church remain personally committed to Him in such a dynamic way that we seek out and perform His will. But at no time must we make the fatal mistake of confusing spiritual sterility with piety and traditionalism with spirituality. The God of the church is a God of action who claims the future with confidence. We dare do no less if we would allow Him to use His church as an effective instrument in meeting the needs of people in our day.

No. 94 • November 3, 1968

GOD AND POLITICS

This week we choose the president of the United States of America. Politics is the topic which keeps us in its hypnotic grip these days, and with much anxiety we discuss the destiny of this nation of ours.

The Bible states that the head of any nation is "God's servant for your good." And consequently calls us into responsible citizenship by stating, "Let every person be subject to the governing authorities." Here then is the formula for good government and good citizenship: On the part of the public official an awareness that his office is a trust that is not to be misused for private privilege (either for himself or for any one segment of society), but for the good of all citizens; and on the part of citizens an awareness that loyalty to the government is a divine expectation.

It is most vital that we understand the issues, know the candidates as much as possible, and also that we seek not only our personal advantage but the good of the total country. For whom shall we cast our vote? For the man who has convinced us not only by words but also by actions that he has a conscience sensitive to the needs of all segments of our society, and with humility and not arrogance accepts his office as a trust from God and the people. Who is that man? Let your conscience under the guidance of God's Holy Spirit give you his name!

(Read Roman 13:1-7)

No. 95 • November 10, 1968

LISTEN, PLEASE!

"Don't just stand there. Do something!" The instinctive desire to save ourselves by doing something, no matter what that may be is a feeling we all know so well.

Wise judgment, however, compels us to stop, listen, and think before acting in panic. Immediate action often is the worst and most destructive response to a need that we can make. Like throwing water on burning oil for example, we can easily compound the problem rather than alleviate it.

Human relations are more volatile than physical objects, and the consequences of our actions can create havoc vast in scope. And yet, we, who have been trained carefully by our environment to think before we act in adjusting to the physical world around us, are most careless and destructive in adjusting to the world of people or society.

We have our opinions made up already about people, young and old, about governments, about issues and about a million other things. And we express those opinions instinctively, never stopping to evaluate the harm we cause and the pain and suffering than ensues. While people around us say to us "Listen please!" we violate their dignity by closed minds, open mouths and nervous hearts. We try to cover up our own deep insecurities by appearing knowledgeable. But instead, all we succeed in being is judgmental. He who learns to listen, learns to understand the meaning of grace. "A fool takes no pleasure in understanding, but only in expressing his opinion."

(Read Proverbs 18:1-10)

No. 96 • November 24, 1968

WHAT PRICE PROSPERITY?

In a land where the American teenager alone is today a billion dollar annual market, and at Christmas time alone (1966) they spent over two billion dollars on gifts. It's Thanksgiving time again!

Prosperity is the identifying mark of our culture. And the trend is to better, bigger, more expensive and more beautiful articles which make up the components of that culture. One is afraid to buy any item lest it already be obsolete due to another item on the market of which one is not aware… Our wants, stimulated by cunning psychology of the manipulators of mass communications media are never satisfied. And our goals seem to recede ever farther from us like elusive shadows.

Thus it is inevitable that a very logical and yet deadly companion of our blessed prosperity be our cursed anxiety. Precisely because we never seem to be satisfied with what we already have achieved and do possess, we reach out with renewed energy for something else. And we wonder all the time, "Will I make it? Will I earn it? Will I achieve it?" And with the quest come the uneasiness, the fears and the competitiveness that eats us up like acid!

How ironic and futile is our religion if it cannot rescue us from such a deadly spiral. To top it all off, it leads us into church on Thanksgiving Day to sing "Praise God from whom all blessings flow."

(Read Matthew 5:19-34)

No. 97 • December 1, 1968

FAITH DARES

This age is not for the timid. All one has to do to scare oneself is to pick up any day's newspaper and read the headlines. The urge to run, to hide, to forget it all is a feeling quite familiar to us all.

The courage to live comes from faith, and in times such as these, living does not come easy. Without faith we run from life, but with faith we welcome it for faith dares to live!

Faith dares to adventure. When others around us try to conserve their resources and become overprotective, faith steps out into the unknown with confidence.

Faith dares to dream. Thank God for dreamers. They are so "impractical," so "vulnerable" and so "nonsensical." But without them, we would still be in the stone-age tilling the soil with our bare hands.

Faith dares to love. The courage to reach out and touch someone else comes from faith. The timid ones who protect themselves are incapable of love because they cannot give, or are afraid to give.

Faith is the key to life because by it God becomes real to us. By faith we experience His presence and His power. He is the great creator Spirit.

(Read Hebrews 11:1-3: 8-12)

No. 98 • December 8, 1968

JOY UNSPEAKABLE

"JOY"— is a magic word that reminds us of a bright ray of sunshine breaking through swirling fog. What a refreshing sight that is— especially on a typical fog bound winter day in Fresno.

Joy in human experience is a precious and real element of Christian commitment. To be a Christian means to discover the source of joy. How ironic that most people believe the truth to be the other way around— that to be a Christian means to be joyless and rather dour.

The Christian is not sustained in joy by feelings he manufactures, but by a trust that he sustains in Christ, come "hell or high water!" Our feelings, based on circumstances are fickle, transitory and completely untrustworthy. One day things go "our way" and we are happy, but another day things go contrary and we sulk. This kind of inconsistent emotional life is a sign of spiritual short-circuiting which has separated us from a genuine relationship with our Lord.

Thank God for a faith which insists that I am not my own savior but He is, and that my salvation depends on His faithfulness to me, and not vice versa. And God is the only eternal constant that his universe or a billion others can ever find.

(Read 1 Peter 1:1-9)

No. 99 • December 22, 1968

GOD WITH US

The great affirmation the church makes at Christmas is that in Jesus, God became man. In doctrinal terms this is called "The incarnation of God." In Latin <u>carne</u> means "flesh." So incarnation would mean "the taking on of human form."

The astounding and paradoxical truth is that deity could be found in the form of a baby, born of a common peasant woman in a stinking barn! Now, no amount of romanticizing can possibly eliminate this fact from the truth of the nativity. But how artists try to make this scene appear angelic, peaceful, beautiful and attractive.

And these circumstances of His humility became a stumbling-block to many people. Precisely because He consistently refused to assume the trapping of pompous royalty, He was rejected and eventually killed. And today one disturbing thought keeps needling us as we think of His presence in our time— "Since He is of such nature, precisely where would He go today for His abode?"

Certainly not cathedral thrones or exalted places recognized by the world's great. But on the contrary, He would seek the slum, the poor, the rejected of society and identity with them! And where does that leave us?

And what of our worship? Does the Christ of Bethlehem accept the worship of those who turn their backs on the poor, the dispossessed, the hungry and the rejected? How can He, for He is one of them.

(Read John 1:1-9)

No. 100 • December 29, 1968

WELCOME THE NEW

John Oxenham, in his poem "New Year's Day-Everyday," speaks of life's "mightiest possibilities" awaiting us in the New Year. How true this is! And what a dramatic demonstrations of this fact we have been having during this week as Apollo 8 has been blazing fantastic trails through space.

A new age, a new era, opens up before us. This age is not for the timid, or for the proud. Timid people, who with wistful longing, look back to the familiar and the cozy, will find more and more reason to be threatened by much that will happen in this new age. Proud people, who with arrogance, appropriate all things around them for selfish use, will find and abuse much in the new age. While the timid will not act, the proud will overact with destructive energy!

Christian faith is not for the purpose of running away from life, but for the purpose of shaping personality and character for right conduct and action in any age. So, with confidence and joy we welcome the new. And how fitting it is that this Sunday we gather around His holy table to partake of Holy Communion. We do so as an act of commitment to Him whereby we call on Him to be our energizing Lord of all life—as He has been in the past how much more shall He be in the magnificent future.

No. 101 • January 5, 1968

HUNGER NOW

In Jesus' time His disciples were hungry and lean and restless. Today, the picture is quite different— we are overweight, over fed and pampered! Jesus said, "Blessed are you that hunger now…" But we do not know the meaning of hunger anymore. Especially so after Thanksgiving and Christmas food festivals when we worship belly-gods of modern society.

Churches today have to resort to all kinds of "gimmicks" to get people to attend. Just like trying to force another item of food on those who have already had too much. Like night-clubs that have to change their variety shows regularly to keep their crowds, so churches keep their "shows" always dazzling and attractive.

Is this Christianity? No! It is paganism. People who are genuinely hungry do not have to be enticed this way. How wonderful it would be if we came together because we instinctively sought spiritual food.

We have no sense of spiritual hunger? How sad! This may be a result of feeding on the wrong kind of food, keeping us under–nourished while we actually feel no hunger. Sick people have no appetite for food either. And the sickness of the soul has gripped many of us. We are outwardly well-fed but inwardly starving! We laugh outwardly while inwardly we weep! How pitiable is our condition.

(Read Luke 6:20-31)

No. 102 • January 26, 1969

ENCOUNTER WITH CHRIST

The highly fictionalized Hollywood concept of Christ is that of a man who looked like a Nordic noble in the midst of dark-skinned Easterners, wearing shimmering white robes with a magical fluorescent quality to them. As he walks, although one could call that trance-like walk more "floating" than "walking," kind of mysterious music fills the air and people turn toward him, as if mesmerized by a psychic phenomenon. This concept of Christ is pure bunk! Maybe all that Hollywood is doing is giving people what their religious institutions have already given them—a dehumanized, highly sentimentalized version of the true person.

Jesus was an ordinary-looking man, who remained ordinary for all people, except for those who discovered His divine nature, mission and powers by a personal encounter and involvement with Him. Such was the case of the Samaritan woman at the well for example. This personal encounter takes place today in the real-life demands of our existence. The person who is willing to face himself, and accept what he sees there and seeks guidance will come to the point where Christ will meet him at some previously undetermined point. And His face today will most probably look no different than any other human beings.

(Read John 4:16-30)

No. 103 • February 2, 1969

TO WHOM SHALL WE GO?

This question was put to Jesus in direct response to His question wherein He asked His disciples, "Will you also go away?" People deserted Jesus in droves after being disappointed in Him because He had refused to feed them.

To whom do we go? Modern man pathetically stumbles from one person to the other with hopes shattered, impoverished in body and spirit. It is fashionable today in academic circles to say, "I go to no one but myself!" but how easily myself betrays and defeats me... In reading Count Leo Tolstoy's biography, for example, (*Tolstoy*, by Henry Troyat) one is struck with His attempts to master himself by putting down stringent "rules of life," and how repeatedly he failed, driving himself into despondency and moral chaos.

Others very glibly say, "Come to Christ." Easily said, but what claims Christ makes! Many people today "Come to Christ" for exactly the same reasons they came back then —to find easy bread, comforts and influence. Christ refuses to feed such people! And they soon depart, seeking in someone else fulfillment of their desires. Their excuses are many, such as "cold church," or "wrong theology," or "poor preacher," or "wrong denomination." But they are really saying "I refuse to be made over by Christ, so I will seek a church and a Christ that I can make over" But gods made in the image of man never have been good, and serve no purpose other than household decoration.

(Read John 6:22-71)

No. 104 • February 9, 1969

TO BE ALIVE

How sweet the word "life" is! How much sweeter it is to contemplate the meaning of real living which goes beyond a mere existence. We all work hard and seek fine health with the constant hope that this kind of living will be our lot too. Most people, if you ask them, will confess that they are reaching into the future to claim such a life for themselves, but that it is not quite in their grasp yet.

Such a "place in the sun" cannot possibly result from the accumulation of more wealth than we already have, or more leisure time that we now have, or any other thing that we keep hoping will be ours someday. Getting things never brings true joy, but giving does. Giving is participating in the creative forces that God exercised to bring forth heaven and earth. Giving is the secret of loving. Giving is a sign of inner peace and security. Only people who feel threatened or are plagued by anxiety wish to hang onto what they have and are. Giving is the only tangible evidence of a genuine faith and trust.

Only diseased and dying trees stop bearing fruit. By giving fruit, they fulfill their purpose for existence. People, who do not give, have lost their right to be called healthy human beings in the true sense of the term.

(Read Acts 2:37-47)

No. 105 • February 2, 1969

WHEN GOD GIVES

When God gives, He <u>creates</u>. We read, "In the beginning God created…" For God, existence or being, cannot be separated from action. In other words, to be, is to act. Life without movement cannot be. Think of our bodies, for example: if no part within them moved at all, would our bodies be alive? Absolutely not! And action with meaning and progression is creation. Movement with no product is worthless.

When God gives, He <u>loves</u>. Love means a personal relationship with the object of one's attention. Young people are said to "love" their cars, for example. This, as stupid as it may sound, is so because for them the car almost breathes and lives in response to the attention it gets from them. God created us to become personally involved with our life; to give us of Himself primarily and not to merely to give us life.

When God gives, He <u>suffers</u>. To create and to love the object of one's creation invariably means suffering to sustain the life of that creation. "God so loved the world He gave His son…" and that Son ended up on the cross! The ultimate creativity of God is the product of that suffering —the new man in Christ! And that new man lives to become in our contemporary life the creating, loving, suffering God with us.

(Read Genesis 1:1-5; John 3:16-17; Philippians 3:8-11)

No. 106 • March 2, 1969

YOUTH DAY

It is somewhat tragi-comical that a church should condescend to have a "youth day" once in a while. It seems that every day is getting to be "youth day" in our society, with young people making headlines of all sorts!

Power is like strong wine —when imbibed in large quantities, it goes to one's head and the consequences can be quite destructive. Young people today have found out that they have tremendous power in their ranks. And they are asserting that power in every segment of society.

Ah, sweet, sweet power! We have "Black Power," "White Power," etc. The other day one of our church school pupils had taken chalk and scribbled in bold writing on a black-board, "Armenian Power!" (As a copy on all the other "powers" of course). But power released without restraint, discipline and positive purpose is nothing more than indulgence in the insane activities of the pyromaniac! Flames may be dazzling to watch but create havoc when unchecked.

Years ago, Saint Paul cautioned, "Let no one despise your youth..." Today, the church calls on its youth to exercise its power in responsible participation in its life. We too wish to make every day a "youth day" here, but let the results be life and not death.

(Read 1 Timothy 4:6-16)

No. 107 • March 16, 1969

FROM RICHES TO RAGS
(A LENTEN MEDITATION ON THE PRODIGAL SON)

Three statements trace for us the decline, fall and rising again of a young man. They may well be the story of "Any man 1969" also, because our journey through life is no different.

First: "<u>Father give me the share of property that falls to me</u>." With hot impatience this young man sought immediate fulfillment of his desires without stopping to analyze them first. He wanted a good time and was going to have it regardless of consequences. How popular the claim "NOW!" is with us too. We seek with compulsive force satisfaction of needs and easily break relationships with God and man in the process.

Second: "<u>I perish here with hunger</u>." The playboy has turned into a pauper! His moral degeneration reflected in his compulsive ways has brought him to a point of total ruin. Hunger due to natural causes is a terrible thing, but when it is due to the moral bankruptcy of the person, then the heart and not the stomach is in need of treatment.

Third: "<u>Father, I have sinned</u>." Here he begins his journey back, his moral regeneration. Before he passes the point of no return, he takes a good long look at himself. Taking stock of the situation, he acknowledges his mistake. With repentance and change of heart, he resolves to "come home." The waiting father receives him with open arms, calling him "my son"—no vindictiveness, but joy in seeing a boy now grown into a true man.

(Read Luke 15:11-24)

No. 108 • April 11, 1969

BUSINESS AS USUAL

Peter was a fisherman when Jesus called him into His service. Fishing is a wonderfully relaxing hobby and many among us turn to fishing to take our minds off our troubles when we wish to "get away from it all!" It is not surprising then that after the fantastic events of Holy Week, Peter said, "I am going fishing."

It's back to "business as usual," for almost everybody in our churches too, on the week after Easter! Attendance drops like the temperature in mid-winter in Alaska, and our memories of Easter Sunday are good enough for the time being: "Wasn't that a fantastic attendance last Sunday, and the way those darling children sang! God bless them."

The Risen Christ, however, did not allow Peter to go fishing and forget it all. He went after him all the way to the lake and kept after him until Peter finally (he did tend to have a thick skull) realized that Jesus was calling him to a full time work. He wanted Peter to be His ambassador to men —what a noble calling! And for us too, Easter is not the end but the beginning of an exciting life with our living Lord if we are willing to let Him get through to us as well.

(Read John 21:1-8)

VARTKES M. KASSOUNI

No. 109 • May 18, 1969

A FAITH THAT COMPELS

What good is faith?

Faith is no good at all if by it people resign themselves to a life that has no frontiers. To use faith as the means for preserving the familiar is to abuse it for the purpose of becoming smug and complacent.

Faith is no good if it is used for the blind acceptance of dogmas and ideas which need definition and clarification. For without the use of reason, faith turns into superstition.

Faith is no good if it is used to hide in the shadows of daily existence that is drab and colorless. To evade challenges because one is afraid to deny the essential meaning of true faith.

Faith places us in the arena of life unafraid, for faith means trust; it means a "plugged-in" relationship with the root-source of all life— God Almighty!

Faith believes; faith dares; faith leaps into the dark; faith lives.

(Read Romans 1:8-17)

No.110 • June 29, 1969

TENSION— CALL TO CREATIVE LIVING

Would it not be just wonderful if we had no conflicts and problems which "get us down," and depress us? We dream and hope for such a trouble-free existence, but most of us continue to have it hard in life. So, we either continue to exist with rugged determination in the face of hardship, or else we feed ourselves a steady diet of self-pity and become more and more miserable every day.

"Chew, chew, chew your troubles away..." so goes a commercial on TV, which claims that all it takes to solve problems is the right chewing gum! This oversimplified approach to problem-solving exemplifies the wishful thinking we all indulge in, hoping to find some quick answer to the hard questions that crop up. Such methods will sell products and make merchants rich, but they will not solve people's problems.

Problems are solved only when we learn to live with them and use them creatively. A right approach to an issue which seems to be an obstacle in our way, may well mean a breakthrough to a higher level of understanding and a deeper appreciation of life in relationship with others— those "others" being people we have conflicts with and whom we would ordinarily reject as enemies.

Learning to live within tension may well be one of the most precious gifts we could receive from our Heavenly Father.

(Read Matthew 6:25-34)

No. 111 • July 6, 1969

AMERICA, AMERICA!

Today we celebrate your birthday,
And in doing so, we celebrate our own birthday,
For life began for us within your boundaries.

Some of us were born and others were reborn here.
We came with hopes and dreams and visions, leaving behind the starved,
the wounded and the dead.

While others came reluctantly, victims of human greed.
Here we are, America.
In the year nineteen hundred and sixty-nine.

We are white and yellow, brown, black and red.
"A melting pot" they used to call you,
But a "Boiling Pot," would be more like it!

Maybe we have been too naive,
and so are not prepared for the troubles that now beset us.
We have loved you dearly, America.
But that love has merely used you for our selfish needs.

We have taken and taken and taken.
But have not been willing to give in return:
We have exploited you terribly while singing.
"Thank God for America!"

America, America, God shed his grace on thee,
and crown thy good with brotherhood, from sea to shining sea.

No. 112 • July 20, 1969

GLORIOUS HEAVENS, AND MAN

"When I consider thy heavens, the work of thy fingers, the moon and the stars, which thou hast ordained, what is man that thou art mindful of him?"

Here is not an astronaut talking, but a shepherd-boy thousands of years ago. And man's fascination with the glorious expanse of the universe is infinitely more intense today. This weekend a man will be actually walking on the moon!

The more we explore space, the more puzzling the meaning of human existence becomes. This little speck of dust, called man, has the capacity to reach out in innumerable ways and investigate what is in him, around him, and beyond him. And it is only natural that man be overwhelmed with the meaning of his own person as he contemplates his relationship to all these celestial bodies.

Why does God bother with man, when we are nothing compared to all else in this vast universe? The poet realizes that man has been placed "to have dominion over the works of Thy hands." Herein lies our ability to rise above our environment. All other creatures are tied to their environment, but man has the God-given ability to overcome natural limitations. Modern science then discovers tools that God has intended for man to have in his mastery of his environment.

"O Lord, our Lord, how excellent is Thy name in all the earth!"

(Read Psalm 8)

No. 113 • July 27, 1969

"PEACEMAKERS"

Jesus said, "Blessed are the peacemakers; for they shall be called children of God." We say. "Blessed is the fighter, for he shall be called 'Our Hero'."

God give us peacemakers!
We need them in our homes;
We need them in our churches;
We need them in our cities;
We need them in the world.

God give us peacemakers!
Fighting comes naturally.
It is so easy to twist a word here and a thought there:
To claim hurt, offense or injury.
And to spring for the jugular vein of our opponent!
Then to stand over him and gloat in victory!

God give us peacemakers!
We are a restless breed,
Chased by shadows and hounded by self.
We smile with the mouth and hate with the heart.
God, we are miserable people!

God, make me a peacemaker!
Quiet my heart;
Make me feel secure in your love.
Then I can make others feel secure in my love,
And thus bring peace to my neighbor.
God hear my prayer.

(Read Matthew 5:1-11)

No. 114 • August 3, 1969

THE OTHER CHEEK

Jesus said, **"Do not resist one who is evil. But if any one strikes you on the right cheek, turn to him the other also."**

Aggression, justice denied, freedom violated, and safety endangered poses a real problem for the Christian—how is he to cope with it? Or, how do we reconcile justice with love? The secular world denies that it is possible to be true to both. Either blind justice is applied and judgment is meted out against the aggressor as power is exerted against him, or else he is allowed to have his way completely and love is powerless to stop destruction and ruin.

Which way shall we go? Many groups are protesting the war in Vietnam. Our government is cast in the image of an aggressor, and in the name of humanity objection to its foreign policies is openly upheld. On the other hand, these same groups are beginning to advocate aggressive policies in meeting their goals in America! "As a means of last resort," they say, "We do not rule out the use of violence." This contradictory stance reveals the confusion and garbled valued which are emerging out of our chaotic times.

Is the Church going to help us today to "turn the other cheek," or as some would have it teach us to throw Molotov cocktails and ransack offices in the name of justice? The Church which uses power effectively could lose its soul in the process and may well turn into a monster far worse than any we have seen yet. Power used violently in the name of God is the most destructive kind!

(Read Matthew 5: 38-48)

No. 115 • August 10, 1969

"PRAY LIKE THIS"

Jesus taught his disciples how to pray by saying, "Pray like this…" and the prayer that followed is commonly called "The Lord's Prayer." It should really be called. "The Disciples' Prayer." Because Jesus taught this prayer for their use.

This prayer is not to be only a prayer memorized and then repeated over and over again until it loses its meaning with overuse. On the contrary, Jesus expressly forbade the use of words in superstitious repetition. And yet this prayer has turned into a spiritual exercise which we indulge in without hardly thinking about its meaning anymore.

This prayer contains the germinal truth which is the significant content of all our prayers. It begins with the acknowledging of God as our Father, and gives Him due honor. It then seeks the fulfillment of the Father's will and kingdom on earth— so far from our usual thoughts in our prayers! Then and only then does it mention our own personal needs, such as food.

Forgiveness of sin is then sought, but the genuineness of our request is made evident by our willingness to forgive those who have sinned against us. God does not dispense "cheap grace!" and finally, guidance is sought in our perpetual struggle against evil forces. Our guard must never be dropped because the battle for the minds and lives of people continues. He who prays and lives this prayer lives victoriously.

(Read Matthew 6:5-15)

No. 116 • August 17, 1969

THE SOUND EYE

"The eye is the lamp of the body. So, if your eye is sound, your whole body will be full of light."

Split loyalties and conflicting interests create havoc in one's personality. Singleness of purpose and simplicity of desire is what Jesus called "The sound eye." The King James Version translates it as "the single eye." Wanting too many things all at one time because we are insecure throws our whole life off balance. Being content with what we have because we are at peace within our own selves is the secret of happy living. Double vision can make life miserable!

In Proverbs we read: "Better is a dry morsel with quiet than a house full of feasting with strife." (17:1) To the person who is content, that dry piece of bread tastes as great as cake; while to the person who is in emotional turmoil, cake loses its taste for the appetite is gone!

The thing to do, then, is to stop long enough in this busy schedule of our daily life and ask ourselves, "Have I a single all-including purpose in life? And is that purpose a high enough one to demand and get all the energies that I can generate?"

(Read Matthew 6:19-24)

No. 117 • August 31, 1969

PROPHETS ON TRIAL

From a thousand different directions today we hear voices saying, "This is the way, follow us!" Whether it be political philosophy or religious commentary, many are the prophets who would lead the modern-day wanderers in the deserts into the promised land of tomorrow.

Church people are being inundated with all kinds of literature campaigns, radio programs and even personal home visitations. They are all quick to point out what is wrong with our own church or accepted way of life, and urge us to shift our traditional loyalties. Often this introduces conflict and controversy within our ranks, turning brother against brother and sister against sister.

Put your prophets on trial! Test them, see if they are of God! We carefully choose our doctors, for example, checking their credentials before we entrust our lives into their hands. But how foolishly we hand over our eternal soul to the smooth-tongued self-proclaimed prophet who comes along! Jesus said, "Watch out for false prophets."

We need to challenge established institutions of the land and to claim the future with selfless dedication to the real needs of human beings. But we must shun hotheads like the plague! Prophets we need; zealots we must reject.

(Read Matthew 7:15-20)

No. 118 • September 7, 1969

THE FATHER'S WILL

Jesus teaches us to call God, "Our Father." Thus, He who otherwise would be known by the cold and impersonal term of "Supreme Being" only, assumes in the term, "Father," a relationship with us which is warm, love-centered and personal. He no longer is just a force "out there," but He is a real presence who cares and sustains.

Jesus teaches us another truth which is closely associated with the first and without which the Fatherhood of God would be meaningless— that the Father reveals His will to us and calls for obedience to it. Ah! This truth is hard to live up to. How easily we grasp at the idea that God loves us, and how just as easily we ignore the fact that such love calls for a response of love and commitment! To receive love without returning it is the height of arrogance and presumption. Even doing mighty works "in His name," which are not sanctioned by Him are rejected by Jesus as utterly worthless.

The final worth or worthlessness of our actions will be determined by God and not us. As correct as our works may seem to us, we are cautioned to place them under His scrutiny and direction. It is not just living a life that counts, but living a life in tune with the infinite, to have a heart that beats in tune with our Father's— that is true living!

(Read Matthew 7:21-28)

No. 119 • September 21, 1969

I APPEAL TO YOU

Someone has said, "When you have found a purpose worthy enough to die for, then you have found a purpose worthy enough to live for." When the Bible calls us to be willing to die, it is simply challenging us to think hard about our priorities in life.

We are called upon to "present our bodies a living sacrifice, holy and acceptable unto God." God is asking of us exactly what is being demanded and exacted from us anyway! Our lives are being taken from us bit by bit by all sorts of masters daily as we live and labor "in the pursuit of happiness." How ironic that the world offers us life and in conforming to its values and ways we find death instead. We shrink away from God because we are afraid he asks too much from us, offering us death in self-sacrifice. But those who dare in faith to try Him find life with a big L instead! No wonder the apostle cries out in ecstasy, "O the depth of the riches and wisdom and knowledge of God!"

Only he who limits his God or shrinks Him down to his own size, will have a god who will fail. People who create their own gods, create puny little powerless gods. And this is what we all do with our lives, our religion, and our church as well. Because of fear, pride or plain unbelief, we do not respond to God's call in full and complete commitment. But those who do, even though they may be little people, end up being giants in life.

(Read Romans 11: 33-12:13)

No. 120 • September 28, 1969

HOW TO BUILD FOR GOD

For 70 years the Jews had been exiles and captives in Babylon. Their land was desolate. Jerusalem, God's city of peace was in ruins. Its walls crumpled. The few misfits and aged who had not been exiled were discouraged and had intermarried with exiles from other lands. It was a sad and dismal state of affairs.

Over in Babylon things had also changed. The proud conquering king Nebuchadnezzar was dead. His successor, king Belshazzar was a "playboy" ruler. Much more interested in feasting and drinking than in the affairs of State. Because of his profligacy, both his life and kingdom came to a sudden end. While he was feasting and drinking with a thousand of his lords and desecrating the holy vessels from God's temple, Darius, king of Media, tunneled beneath the walls of the city, captured it and slew Belshazzar.

Darius was followed in power by Cyrus. king of Persia. He was sympathetic to the captive Jews and issued a proclamation which in effect released all those in exile to return to their homeland and rebuild their cities and walls. There wasn't a "mad rush" to return. Many of the exiles had prospered. They were comfortable here. Babylon was their homeland now. Why should they be uprooted and be concerned about their past heritage, worship and homeland? In Romans 11:29 we read, "For the gifts and calling of God are irrevocable." Simply stated this means that what God has purposed to do, He will fulfill. It was never His purpose for His people to remain in exile or bondage. This was purely a disciplinary measure for a season, but now it was His time for them to return to the land He had given them for an inheritance. To fulfill His will and purpose God has always had "His Man." There was a succession of men He used in this instance. First, (in 533 BC) Zerubbabel, who with a few returned and laid the temple foundations. Then it was Ezra who restored the law and ritual. Then came Nehemiah with a company and restored civil authority and built the walls.

It was not easy. There were enemies. There was fear, but a man "sent of God" with a mission had great persuasive powers. In response to his pleas, "they said, 'Let us rise up and build'" and build they did. It was a great achievement. It wasn't a "one man" production; it was the combined product of ALL working together. "We rebuilt the wall… for the PEOPLE had a mind to work." (4:6)

(Read Nehemiah 2:17-18)

No. 121 • January 4, 1970

IN COMMUNION WITH CHRIST

Communion is the declaration in dramatic form of the content and meaning of Jesus' mission to humanity. We have observed or participated in this dramatization so often that in the familiarity of the form we have possibly lost the message. We must again ask the question, "What is Christ saying to me in this divine act?"

In this act Christ is offering me forgiveness and acceptance. In a day when condemnation and rejection of one another is common practice, how welcome is His voice saying, "Come unto me all who labor and are heavy laden..." He is including me within His circle; we are sharing bread and wine together!

In this act Christ is dramatizing the extent to which He has gone to bring us within His circle—suffering and death. Wow, what can I say? I can merely gaze at the Man on the cross while a million thoughts race through my mind in tangled sequence. And with reverential fear and awe I reach out to touch Him.

In this act Christ commissions me to think His thoughts, speak His words, live His life, die His death and celebrate His resurrection. "As my Father has sent me, so send you," he says to me. What a magnificently exhilarating and beautiful thing His working in us can be! Come, let us gather and feast together around His table.

(Read John 17:1-19)

VARTKES M. KASSOUNI

No. 122 • January 11, 1970

THE BEAST AND MAN

While in the city of Amsterdam on September 27th, I visited "Anne Frank House." Ann Frank was a young Jewish girl who was taken by the Nazis and killed in a concentration camp. Her diary was later discovered by Professor J. Romein among a pile of books and documents at the Government Institute for War Documentation. In commenting on the life of this girl, as reflected in her own diary, he wrote on April 3rd , 1946:

> "The fact that it was possible that this girl has been taken away and killed, has proved to me, that we have lost the fight against the beast and man. And we have lost it because we have not put anything positive over against it. And that is why we shall lose again, in whatever shape the inhumanity may waylay us, when it appears that we as yet will not be able to put something positive over against it."

Lest we glibly reply, "But the Gospel of Christ is the answer to this man's search for 'Something positive,'" as I instinctively did while reading his words, let me say something else about the Ann Frank House. As you look out of the kitchen window, you see one block down the street a huge Christian church! I wonder what comfort the pealing bells of that church ever gave to that family. And suppose that church had been ours?

No. 123 • January 18, 1970

CHALLENGED CONFESSIONS

"I believe" is a confession of faith which is the hallmark of Christianity. To affirm belief is to declare allegiance to Christ and to the Church.

Our declarations of allegiance are being challenged today as never before, making it harder and harder for us to remain comfortable in the pews. It is becoming increasingly clear that to say, "I believe" is no longer a sufficiently meaningful confession. One must answer the more basic question, "WHY DO I BELIEVE?" One can believe in the right thing, or in this case, the right Person, for the wrong reasons. This challenge was first worded by Jesus himself who always questioned motives before accepting people's worship.

Modern man is an inventive genius. Among the many gadgets which he creates to serve and pamper himself, we find churches whose voice is merely a play-back of man's tape-recording of his own voice. To cry, "I Believe, I believe," then becomes an expression not of faith but of fancy. When self is worshipped in the name of God, what a wonderful and satisfying feeling this can create!

Such challenges that question the motives behind our confessions are good and necessary. They help create faith which is not escapist or "pie-in-the-sky" variety, but a relevant, vibrant and truly godly faith.

No. 124 • February 8, 1970

OUR LIFE IN GOD'S WILL

Patterns, blueprints, and designs, are most essential in planning. Whether it is buildings we erect, clothes we assemble or engines we invent— it is mandatory that they first go through the pattern stage. Thus the completed product is carefully constructed to conform to the design just as it was conceived in the builder's or inventor's mind.

Jesus is the prototype of a new breed of man, and he forms the pattern for our life also. He is called "second Adam." We who by faith have committed our lives to the hands and direction of the Master-Builder then must simply trust Him to fulfill the job. The process which God chooses to use often seems strange, painful, and even unbearable, but we simply must allow Him to continue the work He has begun in us. Through all the blood, sweat and tears will emerge the kind of person who reflects the strength, beauty and majesty of the life of Christ!

"All things work together for good to them that love God... who are called according to His purpose... to be conformed to the image of His Son." Trust Him to complete the work He has begun. But in the meantime accept all things that come your way as being part of that divine process. This is the secret of inner peace.

(Read Romans 8:28-34)

No. 125 • February 22, 1970

GREAT EXPECTATIONS

Mothers are known to want the best for their children, but what the mother of James and John wanted for them could not be topped— to sit at the right and at the left of Jesus in His glory! A request such as this makes us blush in embarrassment, and had we been around at the time, we would have been disturbed and angry also. Partly so because her openly expressed request was the secret desire of everyone else.

Mansions on hilltops, crowns with glittering jewels, streets of gold and bliss forever— with such great expectations we entice ourselves and others into Christian discipleship. And we are no different from this poor mixed-up woman.

She wanted a crown but Jesus offered her a cross. How ironic that immediately preceding this incident, Jesus talked to them of His passion and death in Jerusalem! And they did not even hear him, for their pre-conceived ideas of what His "kingdom" meant kept getting in the way. Even when He asked "Are you able to drink the cup that I am to drink? They naively said, "We are able."

He who claims to believe in Christ should first learn to listen to what He is saying. As Jesus said, "He who has ears to hear let him hear."

(Read Matthew 20:17-28)

No. 126 • March 1, 1970

MIRROR, MIRROR ON THE WALL

"Please, mirror, tell me I'm the fairest of them all!" is fairy tales mirror speak, and as long as they give the right answers they are cherished dearly.

Reality has its mirrors too. Take the church for example. Have you ever thought of the church as being a mirror? In his letter in the New Testament, James thinks of it in that way. The church, by way of its Gospel preached and taught, is geared to show us "our natural faces."

But how unflattering and downright ugly that natural look is. So we go to work on it— No, not the look, but the mirror! Some people build elaborate mirrors, so prettily decorated. Others are so disturbed by what they see in the mirror that they do something about it— they change mirrors! Others are so righteously indignant at what they see they act decisively, and smash the mirror! Others being afraid of what they may see close their eyes and refuse to look into the mirror. But the great majority of us are much more positive —we accept what we see in the mirror, have emotional reactions and even shed a tear or two, tell each other how true the picture is that we see, and then, oh so quietly, we ignore the whole thing!

But thank God, once in a long while we do meet people who have quietly gone to work, not to change the mirror, but themselves…

(Read James 1:19-27)

No. 127 • March 8, 1970

GIVING— FOR WHAT PURPOSE?

This Sunday, being Stewardship Day in our church, we are again going to emphasize the place of our commitment to Christ and His Church in tangible terms— money and life. Why give? Because giving is the only way we can show love. Try to love your family without giving of yourself to them, for example. It is just not possible to do so.

The measure of our giving is the measure of our love. Giving which is done in cold calculation, measured not to bother our pocket books but to ease our conscience, is not giving at all. If you would considerer the blessing which true giving in love can mean in life,, consider the following true story.

A Kyoto University student, having heard a missionary speak on 1 Corinthians 13, asked what he meant by LOVE. "I'm Communist," she explained. "We don't need love. But I'd like to know what you mean by it. Could I live in your home to find out?" The busy missionary couple agreed to admit the Communist girl to their household. There she did discover the meaning of Christian love, became a Christian and was baptized. In the process, the student committed the "Psalm of Love" to memory. When after graduation she was married, the young convert asked all the guests at the ceremony to read 1 Corinthians 13 in unison. All human ideologies are but demons that can be exorcised by the love of God when it is shown forth in the lives of Christ's followers.

(Read 1 Corinthians 13)

No. 128 • March 22, 1970

THROUGH GATES OF PASSION

"He comes, He comes, the Master comes!"
Fling wide the gates!

And then He came and NOW is here,
and Fresno must answer the question,
"What will you do with Jesus?"

We will fling wide our temple doors
and shout with lusty voices, "Hosanna!"
Or some other memorized cliché.

We will compete for positions closest to Him,
and mouth words of loyalty "I Believe!"
I have always believed—My Savior, my Lord.

Today we declare Him King.
And tomorrow? Ah, tomorrow is different.
For when Jesus calls us hypocrites and smashes
our sacred idols that are monuments to our own vanity…
Then, we will CRUCIFY him!

We will do Him one great favor though.
We will continue to worship Him and say,
"He died for us. Isn't He wonderful?"
"Yes He is; Yes He is!"

And in temples built "for Him"
His glowing Cross will dominate the scene.

Hallelujah Amen.

No. 129 • April 5, 1970

THE AROMA OF CHRIST

"For we are the aroma of Christ to God among those who are being saved and among those who are perishing."

Whereas in different Scripture references, the Christian has been likened to light, salt, and leaven; in this one he is called "an aroma," we are to so permeate society that people are drawn to Christ through us.

Aromas are usually associated with pleasant experiences—such as delicious food baking in the oven. And fragrance is usually associated with perfume— a scent which pleases, intrigues and invites.

However, a Christian can be not only pleasant, but on the contrary, obnoxious and unpleasant. People such as these, are not a fragrance but a smell! They do not invite, but reject. They repeal so strongly that one mutters to oneself, "Never again!"

We must so live and act that people who respond to our witness will make a genuine response to the claims of Christ. When our offensive attitudes get in the way of effective witness, then we have no one but ourselves to blame when our witness is rejected. The aroma of Christ must never come across as a revolting stench!

What a joy it is to see people through whom Christ comes across— beautiful, loud and clear! May their number increases.

(Read 2 Corinthians 2:14-3:3)

No. 130 • April 12, 1970

I AM FREE—YET A SLAVE

"For though I am free with respect to all, I have made myself a slave to all so that I might win the more often." (v.19)

The search for freedom is becoming increasingly a consuming passion. The tensions generated by an over-organized society with its myriad demands, is almost too much to bear. And many who think it is too much to bear have become "social dropouts." The urge to "get away from it all" including business, church family, and even self is being expressed by many who in all honesty are no longer satisfied to hide their inner feeling of frustration.

To me, in the midst of such a quest on the part of members of modern society, the meaning of "Christian freedom" holds increasing fascination. What did Jesus really mean when He said, "The truth will make you free." What does Paul mean when he says, "I am free from all men?"

It may very well be that Christians who have really discovered the dynamic meaning of Jesus' saying have something of utmost importance to communicate to a world hung up on itself! Show us how to be truly free!

Only the one who is and feels truly free can relate to others in a wholesome, genuine way. The free can relate and interact freely! The unfree keep running away. Jail cells have one thing in common with self-made utopias—solitary confinement!

(Read 1 Corinthians 9:19-27)

No. 131 • April 19, 1970

A HARD SAYING OF JESUS

"If anyone comes to me and does not hate his father, mother, wife, children, brothers and sisters. Yes, and even his life itself, cannot be my disciple." (v25)

Immediately, on hearing this saying of Jesus, we respond. "Who then can be a disciple of Jesus?" Furthermore, we look into our own hearts, and knowing that we have not literally fulfilled this demand, we feel quite hypocritical about our profession of Christian faith.

Like most other sayings of Jesus that do not conform to our ideas, we probably rationalize it away by giving it some bland interpretation. For we have mastered the art of fitting Jesus' saying to our own style of life, rather than changing our style of life to fit Jesus' guidance and control. We call Him "LORD" but make Him our servant. This is evident in the discussion of today's issues in which the church is involved. A soon as our own comfort is challenged by the church, or any declarer of God's Word within it, we bristle with hostility and say, "What concern is it of the church?"

Jesus is seriously cautioning us to "count the cost" of Christian discipleship. He is calling people out of a hostile society into full commitment to Him. And the situation is no different today in Fresno, even though our fair city has over 300 churches, each bearing His name.

(Read Luke 14:25-35)

169

No. 132 • June 7, 1970

THE CHRIST OF THE CROWDS

"When he saw the crowds, he had compassion for them because they were harassed and helpless." (v.36)

I don't like crowds. People pressing in on me make me nervous and uncomfortable. Crowds are noisy, unruly and demanding.

Crowds are turning into mobs these days, shouting demands that scare me to death. Talk of riots and even revolution make me wonder whether I may be having a nightmare! And I ask with thousands of other people equally confused by the crowds —"What has happened to America?"

But a more important question keeps breaking through my thoughts —"What am I willing to do for America now?" Shall I in anger lash out at the crowds because they have taken my peace and my security away? Shall I curse them and then tend to my business, hoping they will somehow disappear?

How can I turn my back to the crowds when I see in them faces that I recognize? And the most disturbing fact of all is that among those faces is that of Jesus Himself! He is among them with compassion and understanding, not in anger but love. He is not there to agree with them but to save them.

"Then He said to his disciples, 'The harvest is plentiful but the laborers are few...'"

(Read Matthew 9:35-38)

No. 133 • June 14, 1970

LET US CELEBRATE

"In Thy presence there is fullness of joy; in Thy right hand are pleasures for evermore." Psalm 16:11 (KJV)

While attending General Assembly in Chicago (PCUSA) two weeks ago, I had an experience which made a profound impression on me. One night, shortly after I had gone to sleep, I was awakened by the sound of singing in the street. I looked out and saw an amazing sight: A group of youth delegates to the Assembly were walking down the street holding hands and singing, "He's got the whole world in His hand." And as they walked along, they prevailed on others to join the group. They marched to the hotel several times, and each time they passed by my window I would see how the group had grown in numbers. Thus they kept celebrating with open and unashamed enthusiasm their exuberant faith.

These young people reminded me most dramatically that the Christian faith is a thing of joy, and that its celebration is the primary means of its proclamation. I am convinced that unless we are able to reinstate this spiritual exuberance into our personal and corporate life as Christians, we are doomed to sterility and death.

You and I have a fascinating job to do in our church— finding ways and means of making such celebration possible in all different areas of our life together.

(Read Psalm 16)

VARTKES M. KASSOUNI

No. 134 • June 28, 1970

WALLS AROUND OUR CHURCH

Walls serve to protect, separate and keep apart, making those inside feel comfortable and secure from the stranger beyond.

In religion, walls exist also. In the temple at Jerusalem, there was a wall that told gentiles— "Stay Out! From this point on, only Jews are allowed." Thus, a wall built to protect the purity of their worship eventually served to segregate and separate. It felt great to be a member of an exclusive people called "God's chosen people."

"He (Christ) is our peace, who has broken down the dividing wall of hostility…" Here the crucial role of Christ in breaking down walls is affirmed. The faith we confess is meant to remove walls, not to build them! A church that builds walls in the name of sustaining the purity of whatever it cherishes better watch out, for sooner or later such protectionism degenerates into selfish exclusivism. And a church with such a mentality contradicts the very Gospel it may claim to be affirming.

The church's mission is to develop disciples and not a clientele. The former reaches out; the latter keeps itself aloof. In one, love is the dynamic force active in the spirit of Christ, but in the other, there is fear protecting pride! Walls eventually crumble into dust, but a life without walls goes on forever.

(Read Ephesians 2:11-22)

No. 135 • July 5, 1970

MY WAY, OR ELSE...

There is a wrong way to do things.
There is a right way to do things.
And of course, my way is the right way.

There are convictions that are genuine.
And others that are artificial.
Can't you tell how mine are from the heart?

My doctrine is right doctrine:
I am sorry yours is false.
It's really a shame you are not enlightened.

My country is the greatest.
Of course, we make mistakes,
But "my country, right or wrong!"

And furthermore,
I am dedicated to my cause!
I promise to help you come my way.
I'll love you, and I'll woo you.

Then I'll pull and maybe push you.
But if you insist on your way,
I will call down heavenly fire
to annihilate you.

So that right may rule with might!
For God is on my side.

(If we want to know what Jesus though about this kind of mentality, read Luke 9:46-56.)

No. 136 • August 2, 1970

GIVE US A MIRACLE

In the Greek language the same word that is used to mean "a sign" is also used to mean "a miracle."

One day people came to Jesus saying, "We wish to see a sign from you," meaning, "We wish to have you perform a miracle." This extraordinary event would then be proof of Jesus" divinity supporting the claim that He was the Messiah.

Jesus gave a startling reply: "An evil and adulterous generation seeks for a sign, but no sign shall be given to it except the sigh of Jonah…" And then He referred to His death and subsequent resurrection as the one and only sufficient "sign" necessary.

The fact that God works miracles in <u>not</u> in question here at all. The fact of the matter is that Jesus was working miracles all the time, but He refused to use this power of His to attract converts to His movement. How well He knew the fickleness of followers gained by such means.

Today, there is a disturbing trend growing in Christian circles, and that is the seeking of "miracles," as the only proof for authentic faith. "Give us a miracle," is the growing demand on the part of people who use this as the test of true Christianity. Hearing of fabulous happenings in some church circles, they expect the same from their own as well.

Most basically of all, followers of Christ who are miracle oriented don't develop a cross-centered faith at all. A cross means death and death is the very negation of miracle. Remember Jesus' words, "If any man would follow me, let him take up his cross and follow me." A sensationalism that feeds on the spectacular does not develop the ability to suffer pain and tribulation in patience. On the contrary, that very same pain and suffering is considered the fruit of lack of faith! Thus, in a very subtle way, the very people who claim access to a faith centered in miracle-power are the very ones who lose their balance and flounder in confusion when the going is rough.

Sensation-conscious Christians who carelessly dismiss ministries or churches in which "miracles" do not take place as being dead or powerless, should remember that at the cross all His disciples and followers, except one, had abandoned Him. There was no power in evidence there at all! Undoubtedly they were deeply disappointed that He had failed to demonstrate His divide powers.

(Read Matthew 12:38-42

No. 137 • August 9, 1970

SCARECROW AMONG THE CUCUMBERS

When the gods of people are considered as powerless as scarecrows in a cucumber patch, it is about time that people took a fresh look at their religion.

Jeremiah the prophet calls the idols of the nations "powerless scarecrows," and points out an amazing thing —that the people of Israel who have seen the hand of the Living God at work so mightily in their midst, in the past, are now turning aside to imitate their neighbors in the making and worship of hand-made scarecrows.

The art of idol-making is not as ridiculous as it may sound however. For there is something in us that compels us to keep trying to be creators instead of creatures. To acknowledge that we are created beings is to acknowledge the existence of a higher authority, a Lord, to whom we are answerable. Ah, this must not be! We must assert our freedom over everything, including a supreme God. The only way we can do that is to make our own gods! What sweet feeling we can then have, for thus man becomes the Creator. Having tamed his gods, man then proceeds to use and abuse himself, his neighbor and his earth without twinge of conscience.

And so modern Adam continues to eat of the forbidden fruit, seeking to become as God himself. And in our blasphemy we destroy both ourselves and nature's beauty and resources. Seeking divinity, we find folly, judgement and death. "Claiming to be wise, they became fools, and exchanged the glory of the immortal God for images resembling mortal man…" **(Romans 1:22)**

(Read Jeremiah 10:1-10)

176

No. 138 • August 16, 1970

ONE IN TEN

"UNCLEAN! UNCLEAN!" Lepers were required by law to cry thus, as they wondered in aimless dejection, warning people to stay out of their way, lest they too be contaminated with the dread disease.

"Jesus, Master, have mercy on us." One day ten lepers appealed to Jesus for healing with these words. They had heard that he cared, he loved, and he saved. Here was at least one man who did not avoid them like the plague.

And Jesus healed them! Even though it sounds that easy, showing love to the scum of the earth never is easy. To stand with a leper is to risk condemnation and isolation too. That's what happens to champions of unpopular causes and unpopular people!

One would expect all ten of them to worship the ground Jesus walked on in inexpressible gratitude. But no, only one remembers to say, "Thank you." And he was a foreigner, or an "Odar," as we say in Armenian.

In Fresno we are a different breed. We have built Him beautiful churches in thankfulness for escaping from massacres, and famine, and all kinds of spiritual and physical pestilence. But how ironic that from our community of people just about one in ten worships regularly in these very same churches?

And Jesus said, "Where are the nine? Was no one found to return and give praise to God except this foreigner?"

(Read Luke 17:11-21)

No. 139 • August 23, 1970

WRITING, WRITING ON THE WALL

Babylon and Jerusalem—
Two cities far apart.
Babylon was great and powerful,
its king, the ruler of the earth.
Jerusalem was ravaged and fallen,
Its people, slaves in exile.

The God of Jerusalem— what a laugh!
Where was He when the city fell?
Or when the people cried for help?
When murder, rape and pillage
reduced the "chosen race" to a
demoralized and broken rabble?

How about the Temple itself?
Why did not God stop the desecration,
when in blasphemy the holy vessels were
taken into Babylon?
"Their God is dead!" in ridicule
Belshazzar spoke, then cried,
"Bring out their vessels,
Let us drink wine from the golden cups!"

And as he partied in drunken stupor,
the hand of a God long considered dead
wrote words of chilling judgment,

"Your days are numbered:
You are weighed and found wanting, and
your kingdom divided."

That very night Belshazzar died,
his kingdom conquered by Darius, the Mede.
And somehow God keeps reaching through
Our walls built high and long.
Just when we think we're far enough
Beyond His range and hold,
He makes His presence felt,
In judgment and in grace;
calling us to new decision:
to laugh in derision and die; or else
to live from faith to triumphant faith.

(Read Daniel 5)

No. 140 • August 30, 1970

MY NAME IS LEGION

"I implore you, do not torment me!" Read this line over and over again. Listen to it as if your ears were actually hearing it. Allow your mind to picture the condition of the person uttering this pitiful plea.

It is the voice of a mentally deranged person, given up by society as completely hopeless. It is the plea of a man in solitary confinement among the caves used as tombs. It is the cry of a poor soul tortured by his fellow men—adults fettered him in chains, and youngsters gazed on him like a beast in a cage…

And when Jesus came near, he instinctively though that another of his tormentors was drawing near. "Please, do not torment me!" he cried, wishing to be afforded at least the comfort of solitude.

"Leave me alone!" Tormented children cry this to children, children to adults, husbands to wives, wives to husbands, students to administration, citizens to government, teenagers to parents, people to people, people to God! Our name, my friends, is "LEGION!"

By God's grace, in the midst of our shouting and our hurting and our wondering, some do manage to hear the quiet voice of Him who comes to heal and not to hurt. It takes an awful lot of loving to bring a tormented soul to the point where he is willing to trust again. Thank God, Christ has all the patience and the love it takes!

(Read Luke 8:26-39)

No. 141 • September 6, 1970

WORK, MAN, WORK!

"Give us jobs!" This is the cry we hear people uttering all around us. In an inflation/recession kind of economy we are currently trapped in, many people who have been working for years have lost their jobs, swelling the ranks of the unemployed.

To be lazy and to have no desire to work is one thing, but to be trained and to be willing to work but to have no job is something else. To the first kind of person, the Bible says, "If anyone will not work, let him not eat. For we hear that some of you are living in idleness, mere busy-bodies, not doing any work." But what does the Bible have to say to the second kind of person? Strangely enough, very little. But it does say much to those who have jobs about sharing their income with the needy. Within the fellowship of the early church, those who needed special attention, such as the widows, were given support from the central treasury of the church. But nowhere is there mention of able-bodied and trained people who simply would not find adequate work. It is inevitable that in a population that is growing geometrically, availability of work will not keep pace with the increase of people. This is what is happening today—a situation possibly not foreseen by any writer of Scripture.

Therefore, "Only lazy people do not work," is no longer a valid statement. On the contrary, Christians with consciences sensitized by the love of Christ for one's fellow human beings must be willing to share the proceeds of their work willingly so that the unemployed may be benefited as well. We must continue to create the kind of government in this country which is able in justice to spread the wealth of the employed for all to benefit.

Paying taxes to such a government could then be an act of commitment as serious as that initially made to Jesus Christ as Lord and Savior. For after all, Scripture does say, "Bear one another's burdens, and so fulfill the law of Christ," and also "Pay all of them their dues, taxes to whom taxes are due, revenue to whom revenue is due…"

Happy Labor Day Weekend!

(Read Romans 13:5-7; 2 Thessalonians 3:3-13)

No. 142 • September 13, 1970

HOW OFTEN SHALL I FORGIVE?

Most of us don't have to even ask this question because we don't believe in forgiving. "An eye for an eye and a tooth for a tooth" is our way of settling accounts. And if we can get two eyes for the loss of one eye, better still! We know that being soft toward those who slight us is no way to do things.

"Would you want God to settle His account with you then as you wish to settle your account with others?" Jesus replies.

"What do you mean?"

"Well, your sin in His sight is so great that it is actually not possible for you to ever pay Him back what you really owe Him."

"Well…" we hesitate, sensing what He is leading to. "We could not possibly pay for our sins committed against God. Without His mercy we would perish in Hell!"

"Aha! You hypocrites!" He startles us with the severity of His words. "You wish to be forgiven, but you do not wish to forgive. It is fine with you to receive grace but you refuse to give grace to anyone who sins against you. Your double standard condemns you!"

"That's something to think about…" we stammer as we get out of His presence fast, feeling most uncomfortable.

(Read Matthew 18:21-35

No. 143 • October 11, 1970

THE TEST OF SACRIFICE

"Nice" Bible stories no longer seem that nice when we are faced with the same challenges people in these stories faced. We admire people of faith and seek to develop the same spiritual muscle and sinew that they had, and we pray to God, "Lord plant my feet on higher ground…"

And then the test comes. It does not come nicely announced on an engraved and perfumed card saying, "The presence of Mr. and Mrs… is requested at a sacrificial event at which time they will be requested to prove their faith in blood, sweat and tears!" On the contrary, it hits like a lightning bolt and in the process shakes the foundations of our very being!

"Take your only son whom you love, and offer him there as a burnt offering." This astounding command comes to Abraham. An only son through whom God's own promises could be fulfilled is now being taken from him.

"What a contradictory, cruel and amazing God this is!" Abraham could have easily thought, but instead he obeyed, as painful as it was to do so.

Can we, dare we, trust such a God today? Our answer will determinate the nature of our faith—whether it will be a pietistic nicety or a thing of power. The test of sacrifice will tell the difference.

(Read Genesis 22:1-14)

No. 144 • October 18, 1970

JOURNEY INTO THE UNKNOWN

Films and stories like "2001" fascinate us because they are journeys into the unknown. New machines, new times and new worlds fascinate and challenge, beckoning to adventure and discovery.

In a very real sense the Christian life to which we are called is no different. It is a challenge calling us to experience the new and the unknown with a faith and a resolve no less than that of astronauts!

Unfortunately, the Christian faith is traditionally presented as being a resting place for the weary, the tired and the defeated. If such a gospel had been preached to Abraham, he would never have left his comfortable house in Ur and struck out "not knowing where he was to go… for he looked forward to the city whose builder and maker is God."

Woe to us who cherish comfort above challenge, whose churches are not training schools for life but old-age residence for the retired, whose gospel prepares not for life but for death, whose God is not energy incarnate but an old man with a long white beard sitting on a throne with rocking chair legs!

(Read Hebrews 11:8-16)

No. 145 • October 25, 1970

THE CHURCH RE-FORMED

On Reformation Sunday, which is today, we would focus attention on the need for the church to be re-formed, to be changed and put together again by the Spirit of God.

Why is reformation so necessary? Obviously there are many who are very satisfied with the way things are. Seeing, hearing and doing the familiar makes many feel good and cozy inside. To re-form the church would place such people in a very vulnerable position emotionally. We have to remember, however, that the church does not belong to people but to God, and whenever the church has settled down in lethargy He has seen fit to stir it up, to shake it and then to renew it.

A church that cherishes tradition over truth is in dire need of reformation.

A church that cherishes ideas <u>about Christ,</u> as fundamental and orthodox as they may be, over <u>Christ Himself,</u> is in need of reformation.

A church that spends thousands of dollars on itself but balks at the very word "mission" is in dire need of reformation.

And the church that openly confesses its weaknesses and seeks reformation is not weak but truly strong. Let us become this kind of a congregation of believers. "The time has come for judgement to begin with the household of God…"

(Read 1 Peter 4:12-19)

No. 146 • November 15, 1970

THE URGE TO QUIT

**"It is enough, now, O Lord, take away my life;
for I am no better than my fathers."** (v.4)

Who could ever guess that the magnificent Elijah, the miracle-man of Israel would ever come to this low point in his life? This sense of complete frustration, this feeling of utter loneliness, however, is not unique to the life of Elijah, but common to all who seek to be vessels in the service of God. Elijah had his cave, Jesus had his Gethsemane experience, and we all have our own times of dejection and gloom.

"It is enough, I've had it!" The urge to quit comes sweeping in when seemingly insurmountable odds pile up against us. We cry to God and the heavens seem to shut up hiding a silent God who seems to have completely forgotten us.

Using stillness as His medium, God finally speaks. Why so? Why not use fire and lightning? Why the small voice of stillness? Maybe because when we are at our lowest and all hope is shattered, and all is still around us, we are finally open to hear what we otherwise could not because of all the noise we were making. Maybe this is how God teaches us to shut up and listen for a change!

How true that the very moment we quit may be the moment of opportunity lost forever.

(Read 1 Kings 19:1-10)

No. 147 • December 6, 1970

PREPARE THE WAY

Television began advertising for the Christmas trade months ago. I heard "Jingle Bells" at a department store weeks ago. Two weeks ago, I saw a Christmas tree being carried home on top of a car. I suppose all these happenings we can assume were done in preparation for Christmas! I think in the pseudo-Christian culture we have concocted in America, Thanksgiving is really celebrated as "Thank God we can start pushing Christmas sales week!"

The Christian church does in an authentic way make preparations for Christmas. The season is called Advent, and covers the four Sundays preceding it. During this period prophetic scriptures fore-telling the coming of Christ are read, studied and with prayer and meditation preparation is made for a fresh commitment to Him as His birth is celebrated again.

Before Christ began His ministry, John was sent to "prepare the way in the wilderness." And he preached, "After me comes He who is mightier than I… I have baptized you with water, but He will baptize you with the Holy Spirit."

Let's not let Christ be lost under piles of cards, ribbons, paper, toys, cakes and all that stuff this year. May Christmas be a refreshing time of renewal rather than a pain in the neck and pocketbook!

(Read Mark 1:1-8)

No. 148 • December 13, 1970

GOD OF THE FUTURE

"The created universe waits with eager expectation… to be freed from the shackles of mortality and enter upon the liberty and splendor of the children of God." (Romans 8:23ff NEB)

This is Advent faith—to claim the future with confidence for God is ahead of us. In this sense true Christianity must always be prophetic if it is to be a "light unto our feet."

But when the future is seen as a continuing series of changes, upheavals, new styles of living, unfamiliar cultures, realigning of power structures, we are filled with apprehension and fear. Dare we claim God is in all that? Aha, at this crucial point, our faith is painfully put to the test, either to act in accordance with our declared faith or else to react to all change and seek to turn the clock back to have things as they used to be.

And what about the church? Will it continue to be an institution seeking to recreate the past (especially the Armenian Church with its emphasis on tradition and heritage?) or will it claim the future as its exciting heritage? Institutions organized to recreate the past are called museums, but the church is the people of God on a holy pilgrimage seeking a city of the future "whose builder and maker is God."

(Read Romans 8:18-25)

No. 149 • January 10, 1971

I AM
(A DIALOGUE WITH MYSELF)

I am.
"You are what? I mean what is your function?"
Why do you ask?
    "Because your worth depends on it."
Please explain.
    "You are acceptable if you provide some service."
And that successfully, of course.
    "Of course, if you fail, I and others will reject you."
Then my worth depends on my satisfying you.
You love me only because you want to use me!
    "I had never thought of it that way before."
When worth depends on function rejection follows,
sooner or later. I can never produce enough to make
either myself or others completely happy. Demands
grow with service and success eludes me.
I reject myself in contempt and so do others around me!
    "What do you base your worth on then?"
On just being me and accepting me as I am.
Now, production is the result of spontaneous joy
celebrating my life, not dependent on quotas at all!
It is done out of genuine creative spirit. But when it is done
to buy dignity I become a slave and no longer free.
    "I wish I could be free too."
    You can, you will!

(Read Romans 5:1-11)

No. 150 • January 31, 1970

WHERE IS YOUR FAITH?

Here is a penetrating question that startles us. And our answers may well go something like this:

"My faith… well, what is faith?" some answer with these words, hiding comfortably behind pseudo-intellectualism that smiles with smugness.

"My faith… I wish I had faith like my parents did." So replies someone else. His faith is in a memory guided by imagination.

"My faith… it is in myself," answers still another. "I believe in my mind, my arms, my work. God helps those who help themselves, you know." So answers the self-worshipper.

"What good is faith?" sneers another. "Why is there so much suffering in the world? Why does God do nothing about it?"

Actually, it is not we who ask this question but Jesus. He asked it to a group of scared men who were desperate during a storm. As he asked it, he stilled the storm. That's faith.

(Read Luke 8:22-25)

No. 151 • February 7, 1970

SERVICE IS A PLEASURE

Recently I was asked by the Volunteer Bureau of the Fresno Community Council to help choose the Volunteer of the Year. I joined a number of other judges in the difficult task of determining who should be so honored. In the process of doing this, I was deeply impressed by the truly great work volunteers are doing in this city of ours. They are all donating their labor freely and many of them sacrificially.

The man who won the award this year, Mr. Harold Young, "almost single-handedly recruited volunteers coaches and managers to build the Junior Soccer League to its present size of approximately 90 teams and 1,800 boys." And he did it during prime business hours because he is an insurance salesman!

Service is a pleasure: Ask Mr. Young, or ask Mrs. Dollie Long, age 81, who rides a bicycle every day to Valley Medical Center to be the chaplain's aid, or ask Mr. Sarkis Paparigian who has contributed over 1800 hours over the past 2 years to the Youth Conservation Education program, or to Mr. George Rodriguez, who has organized extra-curricular activities at Roosevelt High, such as marimba band and student trips. Or ask people in our own church who are quietly doing so much all over this city in our schools, hospitals and playgrounds.

Jesus said: "It is more blessed to give than to receive." Our volunteers know how true that is!

(Read 1 Corinthians 13)

No. 152 • March 7, 1971

FORGIVENESS AND FREEDOM

True freedom springs from forgiveness. Forgiveness springs from grace. Grace springs from love. And God is Love. A person who has experienced forgiveness is a free person, and a free person is he who has experienced God.

Obviously, we have many among us who glibly claim to have experienced God but are not free people. How free am I? This haunting question grips me because I am learning to love and that is not easy to do! So do I know God? Yes, because I have accepted His forgiveness and that is the crux of the matter.

Now I am learning to accept people in the openness with which God has accepted me. And you know something? It is a beautiful thing to experience… it is like learning to appreciate all kinds of food after I have for years been eating just one item. What a fantastic world of people God has created!

We are not free because we are afraid, and fear is the denial of faith. Ah, to walk ahead even when the destination is not revealed to us yet —that is faith. It is faith that dares to be different.

"Perfect love casts out fear"

(Read 1 John 4:18)

No. 153 • March 28, 1971

WHY JESUS?

"We want to see Jesus" said a number of Greeks who had come to Jerusalem for the Passover feast.

In the pulpit of the Fresno Rescue Mission there is this verse written in bold letters, big enough for every preacher using that pulpit to read, "Sir, we would see Jesus."

Young people are rediscovering Jesus today. Lapel pins, bumper stickers, posters, slogans and banners declare "JESUS POWER," with boldness that thrills some and scares others!

So, Jesus is a live topic again, just when the secular world thought that God was dead and buried once and for all. Dare we, however, go beyond the names, the topic, the idea, to the person of Jesus himself? Do we who use and bear his name know who He really is? Once having come to know Him, will we want to be like him?

"Why do you want to see me?" Jesus said, in effect, as he heard the request of the Greeks. He refuses to be a tourist attraction! And those who really get down to the business of "seeing Jesus" find out how different He really is than what they had imagined Him to be.

(Read John 12:20-33)

No. 154 • April 18, 1971

WHEN A CHILD LED THEM

The futility of it all has overwhelmed us all, at some time or other, when we have been faced with needs too great and challenges too strong. "It's just too much!" has been our response as we have withdrawn from the challenges confronting us.

This was the feeling that the apostles had when they were faced with the monumental task of feeding 5,000 people, when they were not even prepared for feeding 50!

What kind of ministry inside and outside the church are we being trained for as we present ourselves regularly in the church for worship and study? What kind of ministry are we giving our time and money for as we consider our stewardship?

The apostles, from whom one would expect generosity based on true faith, claimed complete inability to serve in the vast multitudes gathered before them. But a child, who is supposed to know nothing about such things, led them by committing his lunch to the Lord! It's as simple as that—willing to dedicate what we already have, never what we wished we had!

(Read John 6:1-15)

No. 155 • May 16, 1971

GOD'S SELECTIVE SERVICE

When Gideon was trying to gather an army of fighters to fight the Midianite invaders, God told him to narrow the number to a mere 300 men! This is God's selective service. (Judges 7)

And when Jesus sought messengers to be his proclaimers to the land, he narrowed down the field considerably as well, and we have a record of the rejects! One wished to follow Him, without first counting the cost involved. He though being a follower of Jesus would bring him prosperity, health and popularity —after all, had not Jesus worked all these fabulous miracles and the crowds were following him? To him Jesus said, "Sorry, Charlie..." Another wanted to attend his father's funeral. Sounds like a legitimate request, but when it is used to delay one's full response in obedience to Jesus marching orders, Jesus says to him too "You're not really with me yet, sorry..." and still another threw in the one excuse that usually works. "My family comes first!" And Jesus answers him, "In that case stay with your family, but do not claim to be my messenger either!"

You see, it's honesty that counts. To say, "I want to follow him," when in truth we don't really care to do so is the hypocrisy Jesus condemns the most.

(Read Luke 9:57-62)

No. 156 • May 23, 1971

AN EXPRESSION OF WONDER

"When I look at the heavens, the work of Thy fingers, the moon and the stars which Thou hast established; what is man….?" (Psalm 8)

As children, we stand out in a field and gaze at the stars in wonder and amazement. As adults, we build spaceships and travel to the moon, and probe the planets with satellites. Whether child or adult, we do essentially the same thing —seek to unravel the mysteries of the earth and the heavens. And all along, the feeling that we are masters, with the ability to dominate nature, thrills us to no end!

That man has special powers above all other creatures in relation to nature, there's no doubt at all. But as to what is to be our role within nature is in serious question today. We are learning, after painful lessons that we are not to be the dominators but stewards of nature, answerable to the God who is its creator. We have no right to indiscriminately use and abuse nature. It is God's gift to us, and one's use of a gift always reveals the true love and loyalty we have towards the gift giver. Faith in God may well be demonstrated by careful and loving use of earth and all its resources.

CHAPTER IV

UNITED ARMENIAN
CONGREGATIONAL CHURCH
LOS ANGELES, CA, 1978-1983

No. 1 • May 1978

WHAT GOES ON HERE?

Several years ago, in my former place of ministry, I came upon a prominent man in our Fresno community walking up and down the corridor of our education building carefully reading all the notices and posters that were displayed. "What a pleasant surprise, Bill" (not his real name) I said. "To what do we owe the honor of this visit?"

"Somebody called me, saying that you had a controversial banner on your wall," he answered, "and I came to see for myself." "Well, what kind of banner, and did you find it?" I asked somewhat shocked.

"No," he answered, "but what goes on here anyway?" That was the clue I needed. Having ascertained the fact he had really been misinformed, we proceeded to discuss our various programs and the purposes for which our building was being used. When we were through, he expressed his satisfaction and urged us to keep up the good work. The point I am seeking to make is this. When the unusual, the creative and the imaginary programs take place in the church, the curious are attracted and they come in, when otherwise they would never do so, as was the case with this friend.

What is going on here? Is there anything really exciting, or is the usual being carried on in a routine and humdrum way? Is what we are doing bold and beautiful enough to get people talking about it, arousing their curiosity and attracting them to come see for themselves?

Centuries ago, the believers got so filled with the Spirit of God that the whole city came pouring out to see what was going on in the church. They were accused of being drunk! On another occasion their spokesman was accused of being crazy. On many occasions they were accused of turning the world upside down! That's the kind of church I am talking about. That's what can go on and is going on here. Open your eyes, look around you and then see what wonderful things God is doing.

No. 2 • December 1978

A PASTORAL REFLECTION ON FIRE

Fire! Last month we were again jolted into full awareness of its awesome power as we witnessed the devastating brush fires which consumed thousands of acres and burned several hundred homes. In the days following, we read the sad details of many losing their houses in the holocaust with all their possessions. All of these events have provided me with much food for though. Let me share some of these thoughts with you.

It is quite ironic that natural disasters, such as flood, mud-slides and fire, seem to hit the wealthy around L. A. they are the people who are often looked on with envy for having succeeded in getting out of the crowded urban scene and having relocating in choice hills and canyons. No, there is no ultimate security is there? I have been amazed at all the talk going on now about making sure that it does not happen again. But, can we ever become so secure? I do not think so. Having escaped the crowded city, a brush fire can get us. Having escaped the fires, a flood or earth-slide can get us. Having escaped the flood, and earthquake can jolt us. We may escape all that and the crash of a stock market can ruin us. We can escape all that which is material calamity and our families can fall apart… Remember Jesus who said, "Do not lay up treasures on earth where moth and rust can corrupt."

Stories of the conquering spirits of those who were caught in the fires have truly amazed me. Here is a woman who forgets her heirlooms and wastes time looking for her cat until it is too late. There is a man who forms a caravan and carefully leads people through fire and smoke to safety. This is my favorite: the man who said, "Insurance will pay for the mortgage on our house now totally gone, then we will have one dollar and ninety eight cents to rebuild with!" I think he should name his new home. "The house that $1.98 built." Belief in oneself, determination, imagination laced with a sense of humor, will help us surmount any obstacle no matter how high! I know this man will succeed in re-building his home, as difficult and even impossible as it may seem now.

When all is said and done, could it be that God is reminding us that apart from Him there is no security? Or putting it another way, he who accepts life in the wisdom and purposes of God is never caught by surprise and demoralized by the sudden twists and turns of life. To that person, the affirmation, "Yes, though I walk through the valley of the shadow of death I will fear no evil," is a reality immeasurable in worth. That is laying up treasures where no fire or water or thief or depression can touch. That's heaven.

No. 3 • February 1979

THE CULTIC MIND

Ever since the Jonestown tragedy that took the lives of nearly 1000 people, cults have been very much in the news. Recently, the troubles of the Armstrong Empire and the breakup of the cult known as the Worldwide Church of God have been accented. Several weeks ago, the L.A. Times carried an article on another cult known as the Local Church with a leader name Witness Nee.

It is disturbingly apparent to us that most cults are religious in nature, and in this country Christian in origin. Do you know what happened to many young people in the 1960's who "turned on" to Jesus? Many of them were taken over by cults and led very far from the Christ they so wildly acclaimed. A classic example is the group known as "The Children of God" What does all this say to us who are serious followers of Jesus Christ and seek to maintain His church responsibly? A lot indeed!

There is a major difference between Christians who take the teachings of Christ seriously and those who have a cultic mind. The person with the non-cultic mind takes them and applies them as an individual who is free to direct his life according to his best understanding of Christian truth. The cultic mind, however, attaches itself to one or more leaders who claim special powers and authority and seek to organize believers into tight-knit communities, allowing no deviation of belief and conduct.

The normal Christian mind seeks guidance and fellowship within the community of Christ, the church, but never allows his conscience and his judgement to be ruled by others. Interdependence within the independence of individual members is the key to normal Christian fellowship. Utter dependence is the key to the cultic fellowship. Pastors, teaches and leaders with the non-cultic mind so minister that members are encouraged to ask questions, to prove. to investigate, to grow, hopefully, even beyond the statutes and knowledge for the leaders.

Jesus said, "The Kingdom of God is within you." He warned us to shun self-appointed messiahs and gurus who lay claim to the souls of their followers. The most precious gift of the Gospel is a mind and body free from fear and in control of oneself. "The truth shall make you free," said Jesus, and not slaves to people who seek to lead others in His name. It is a sad and most disturbing thing to see Christians today, many of them evangelicals, handing themselves and their money over like children to self-proclaimed apostles who then proceed to abuse them and violate their trust. This is not discipleship. It is sheer stupidity.

It would be a very good thing indeed if we were to analyze our own attitudes to see if our beliefs are leading us toward a healthy and growing faith or towards the development of a dependent and cultic approach to truth. One approach leads to life, and the other to death.

No. 4 • April 1979

DEATH AND RESURRECTION

There is a very popular song being heard among Armenians these days titled, "Where Were You God?" It asks the questions with a terrible sense of anguish, recalling the black and devastating days of the Armenian holocaust of 1915. It is a song that makes me shudder because it expresses with full force the latent sense of alienation from God felt by vast numbers of our people as a result of forced marches into deserts, torture and death, and finally dispersion of the remnant few to the four corners of this earth.

The question having been asked, the charge of silence and abandonment having been made, we wait for an answer. No, God will not speak through the clouds like some intergalactic messenger, but speak He does. His medium of communication is the person of Jesus Christ. He is the Word. For the Christian there is no other voice but His. When we turn to Jesus, it is amazing what we hear Him say. His is also a deep cry of anguish uttered on the cross, "My God, my God, why have you forsaken me?"

If we really believe what we claim, that Christianity got a firm hold of our nation in earliest of times, and if we affirm that the Christian faith continues to be our guiding light then, for God's sake let us try to understand this cry of Jesus. It may very well be that it holds the clue to our own suffering and death. By His own deliberate choice, Jesus confronted evil and took upon Himself the sins of the world, allowing it to have its full effect on Him. He had to accept the consequences of drawing unto Himself the sins, prejudices, hatred, and the evils of mankind. Evil kills, and Jesus had to die. For God to intervene and prevent His death would have meant a drawing back from the implications of His declared mission. Hence, the silence of God and Jesus' extreme sense of alienation. He was totally and completely alone on the cross!

Jesus told His followers: "In this world you shall have tribulation." He called upon them to "take up your crosses and follow me." Paul says, "I die daily." The Scriptures are full of similar statements spelling it out for us. Hence, we too must come to grips with this same profound truth: that when we, or any other people, stand for righteousness, for faith and highest standards of morality and human dignity, we too shall be opposed, resented, and efforts will be made to remove us from the scene. This happened to the Armenians in Turkey, and our people died indeed. The result of noble, truth-centered living is never tolerance, acceptance and honor, but bigotry, rejection and death! It can never be otherwise, whether it be in the experience of Jesus, the Armenians in 1915, the Jews twenty years later, or any similar case anywhere else today. When light threatens darkness, darkness must seek to kill it or else it will be overcome. Truth and love do not win by persuasion but by allowing themselves to be killed. Those who are caught in this great cosmic struggle, but have no personal faith themselves, are left confused, demoralized and bitter. Hence, their expressions of alienation and confusion.

If death meant the end of things, then I too would join the ranks of the bitter and the apostate. But it is not! The resurrection of Jesus stands for all time as the supreme expression and demonstration of this fact. Truth cannot remain dead. It rises from the ashes of history to haunt mankind in every generation. Evil cannot seal the tomb of Christ, for He comes forth with power to claim His own! Easter has basic meaning for us because it points to our own resurrection as well. Not only the resurrection of individual believers, which we have always believed and proclaimed, but of the people, as the corporate body of God's people on earth. Scripture teaches that the "Kingdom of our God and of His Christ shall reign forever and ever!" Evil can kill but can't hold its enemy in the grave. "It was not possible for death to hold Him." Peter says of Jesus. We too, as Armenians in the diaspora, have begun to live again and to experience the meaning of such resurrection truth. All that we have lived and stood for is being affirmed today in new power. We are sprouting like desert flowers in the very nooks and crannies of the world to which we have been dispersed. We too can't die; we shall not die because the God or our soul is with us yet!

No. 5 • November 1979

A SEED IN THE EYE

The other day I read an amazing story about a boy in South Africa who complained of constant eye ache. Upon close examination, the doctor found out that there was a seed imbedded in the eye, and it had already started to germinate. It had struck roots an eighth of an inch long and was beginning to grow! Actually, he would have gone blind if the seed were not removed, which the doctor proceeded to do.

While shaving this morning, I began to think of this story and about what Jesus said of specks and beams in people's eyes. There is a difference, however. The seed was a living organism, a growing thing full of life and vitality, while the speck Jesus talked about was a piece of dirt or dust. Therefore, this story opened up for me new ways of looking at Jesus' teaching.

The eye is not meant to receive only one impression, in this case the seed, and allow it to lodge and grow there. If it did, the eye would die and the body would be darkened. The eye is meant to keep on receiving impressions as a gateway to a healthy and functioning body. Taking it spiritually, I see much truth here. Our spiritual eyes are also meant to keep taking in sights, ideas, visions of reality for the purpose of maintaining healthy and productive lives. Some people, however, go blind because one key concept, doctrine, belief, idea is received exclusively as a seed and is lodged in the eye and begins to grow.

Growth is received with joy, for it means life. It strikes roots and grows deep into the person, tapping vital sources of energy. But alas, it kills the eye in the process. It is no longer able to see. The mind goes dark and light can no longer penetrate. And eventually, the person dies!

Keep your eyes clean. Don't allow any seed to lodge and grow there. For one seed in the eye will prevent you from seeing a billion seeds germinating and a hundred thousand trees growing in God's beautiful nature all around you!

No. 6 • December 1979

THE MIRACLE BUS

Traffic on Fairfax Ave. was backed up, and I was getting quite edgy. I had to get to my appointment and this was no good. As we inched along, we finally came to see what the problem was. There in the middle of the street was a broken-down bus and a truck was trying to push it out of the way for the rest of us. As I drove by, I couldn't help read in amazement the big sign painted on the side "MIRACLE TABERNACLE!" How about that? So I got to thinking about the word "miracle' and how it is used so much these days by people and churches seeking to lure people into their influence and orbit. It is "miracle preaching" for "miracle healings" and "miracle success." If you only follow the Rev. Mr. Miracle who has had some miraculous experiences that have lifted him from failure and poverty into a fabulously successful ministry, where thousands are now finding the miracle way out of their own problems... But alas, the miracle bus does break down after all, and it has to be pushed out of the way to let ordinary people in ordinary cars on their routine rounds get through to accomplish their very common tasks.

Jesus was tempted to follow the miracle road to the accomplishment of His mission, but refused. On the temptation mountain, He was urged to turn stones to bread, throw himself down the tower and float down to earth on wings of angels, to command the attention and loyalty of the kingdom in one grand gesture. He turned this all down for the way of the Cross! Ah the Cross... that lonely, bloody, excruciatingly painful instrument of execution! He said He could call on heavenly legions to come to His rescue, but He refused.

When "miracle buses" break down, it is Christ-centered people bearing their crosses who come along and gently push them aside so that you and I may get through to experience and to celebrate life within the reality of God's love and presence. Yes, be careful of those bearing miracles, and may the Christ of the Manger — a common ordinary stable, help us this Christmas Season to turn our stables into the dwelling places of God.

No. 7 • January 1980

IN THE NAME OF GOD

God is making headlines these days. That's quite unusual because religion is usually relegated to the back pages of our newspapers and magazines. At first, we who are involved with the church may be glad of this turn of events, but on closer scrutiny one is dismayed and even frightened by it all! This morning I listened to "Good Morning America," and on it was the ambassador of Kuwait, who was one of two Muslim members of the United Nations Security Council voting on the matter of American hostages in Iran. He was asked. "Is there a Holy War being declared against the West in the name of God?" Events in Iran have created what would have been a totally unbelievable thing only six months ago —a 20th Century theocracy with a priest as absolute ruler controlling everything in the name of God. And in the name of that same God, our Western culture is being branded the dwelling of Satan himself!

We cringe in dismay and unbelief at all of this, but it is happening right before our eyes. What is even scarier is to read, for example, in Los Angeles Magazine an interview with the former Cassius Clay, now Mohammed Ali, who says, "I want to serve God and do something spectacular in that effort. I am the greatest in boxing, and I want to be the greatest in this regard too." If this kind of zeal were expressed in the name of Christ, we would all applaud, but it is being done in the name of Mohammed and God.

Religious zeal can and does easily deteriorate into a vengeful and consuming passion that destroys innocent people. Islam has demonstrated this to be true time and time again. Who more than the Armenians can attest to that? But, what I wish to point out is that even Christians can and at times have lowered themselves to such depths of infamy and abhorrent behavior, all in the name of God! We are not above such devastating explosion of passion.

My personal recourse is to the person of Jesus Christ Himself, who reveals to me the essence of God's being. He reveals a God of grace, mercy, love and forgiveness. His supreme demonstration of power is the CROSS. Nothing has ever superseded that expression of God's essential nature and will, and nothing can ever replace it. Let us beware of Khomaini-type Christians who may someday arise to lead Christendom in a crusade to regain the lost rights and privileges of Christianity.

VARTKES M. KASSOUNI

No. 8 • April 1980

I HAVE TOUCHED HIM

"I have touched him with my own hands. He is God's message of life."
1 John 1:1 (The Living Bible)

Life without the possibility of touch is an absurdity and impossibility. After all, the scholars and the scientists, philosophers and theologians have spoken on the topic of the meaning of existence, whether personal or cosmic. It all comes to this simple and yet most profound and exhilarating word, "TOUCH!" Touch is where subject and object make contact, and within that one single act, reality breaks through with magnificent clarity. Everything without touch is mere theory and anything with touch is fact. Having read all about electricity, for example, we take wires and bulbs and generators and put them all together. But that one final act of touching one wire to the other by way of a switch is what it takes to illumine the room and demonstrate the correctness of the system. It is called contact!

Touch means discovery for a little boy exploring his universe. Touch means love for a man and a woman as they timidly allow the hand to follow the heart as the two become one. Touch means food to the farmer as he reaches into the good earth to plant the seeds of an abundant harvest. Touch means life to the mother as her new-born baby is gently placed into her arms. One can go and list a million daily occurrences, so common and yet so profoundly beautiful, as touch after touch bring home to our minds and hearts that we are alive indeed.

After all the books have been read, and all the sermons have been preached and heard; after all the traditions have been observed and

212

all formulas correctly followed, the truth of what we proclaim at Easter becomes reality in that one word, "TOUCH." We are talking of that fantastic moment when reaching out with trembling hand our faith makes contact with reality. When fears have subsided and doubts have dissipated, we begin to understand and to celebrate. Whispers of timidity turn into shouts of joy… it is the Lord! "And He walks with me, and He talks with me, and He tells me I am His own. And the joy we share as we tarry there, none other has ever known!" Christ is risen; He is risen indeed!

VARTKES M. KASSOUNI

No. 9 • Summer, 1980

THE CHRISTIAN AND POLITICS

For months we have been hearing of primaries and caucuses and elections of all sorts. All this is preliminary to the big event — the November presidential election. Our country seems to be forever involved with political events and elections. It seems like every other month, we are called out to vote or to register our feelings about local, state and federal issues. In all of this the question rises up again and again. "What is to be the relationship of the Christian and his faith to the politics of the land?"

"Religion and politics do not mix." This is the well-known maxim we have all heard, and to some extent, followed as absolute truth. We have believed and worshipped in our churches and have been careful to leave politics outside the church doors before going in. We have expected our religious leaders to leave out issues concerning politics when it comes to their preaching and teaching. Social issues were not to be discussed, only matters concerning personal salvation. "Stick to preaching the gospel" used to mean. "Preach only about our personal sins and how through Jesus Christ we can be saved and go to heaven when we die." Now, we do sense a change coming over the religious scene and politics seems to be gaining legitimacy in the church.

It began with liberals who usually stress what has in the past been called "The social gospel." During the sixties, they stressed anti-war sentiments, for example, and espoused social justice, minority rights and helped people organize so that the government would hear them and respond to their demands. Conservative and evangelical Christianity reacted to all this as being wrong and distracting from the main business of the church

— personal salvation and proclamation of the Gospel only in evangelistic type rallies. Now, a very interesting and significant shift has taken place. Conservative and evangelical leaders are urging Christians to get involved politically and they are organizing them into political action groups. So, there is now a growing consensus that Christians must get involved in politics, and that our religious faith must address social and political issues, if we expect our governments to be sensitive to social as well as private morality. I welcome all this as good and proper. I think that Christians, whether liberal or conservative, must stand up and be counted, and they must leave the safety of church environments and seek the platform of the public square to proclaim their beliefs. After all, we are the inheritors of the tradition of the prophets, who were people raised by God to confront kings and governments and the public at large with the word of God. They sought justice and they sought righteousness in high as well as low places. It is the cry of Amos being heard in the land again. "Let justice roll down like water, and righteousness like an over-flowing stream." (Amos 5:24)

No. 10 • October 1980

OF WEEDS AND FAITH

I like gardening. I've been at it since I was a little boy. From those early days, I have always had to contend with weeds. They are a nuisance, a bother, and most certainly deadly to our gardens. We work hard to eliminate them, and we invest all kinds of time and resources to make sure they are eradicated. However, I have developed a tremendous respect for weeds. While on the one hand, I too see to it that they stay out of my garden. I still think they are beautiful. You know why? Because they teach me so much about life and the meaning of faith, they are silent messengers of God Himself! Let me give you just a few reasons why.

Weeds have tremendous power to resist the exterminators. After battling Bermuda grass, for example, I have often given up and allowed it to grow at will. Christians should have that kind of strength and ability to "keep coming back" after defeat and disappointment.

Weeds survive and even thrive on little or seemingly no water at all. I marvel how, after watering my plants and carefully feeding them, many still die, but the weed? No such chance! It will grow anywhere and under all kinds of deadly influences. Christians, very often fed and overfed, still complain that "they are not being fed." My response tends to be when such a claim is made in my presence, "What did you do with the food you've been given all these years?" or "How much food do you need to grow?" The weed needs very little, but the pampered petunia never seems to have enough.

Weeds are beautiful. Years ago, as I was traveling through the desert of Arizona I looked up and saw a beautiful white flower growing out of a crack in a rock. I photographed that plant… it was a weed. But you take it and place it in your hot-house and of course, it will be ignored and even killed. Man carefully nurtures and multiplies plants and flowers he wants and calls them "beautiful." But that is exactly the point. A Christian is not chosen by man but by God. That which is a reject for man is a chosen vessel for God. We are anxiously trying to copy man's standards for beauty and success, and in the process, I am afraid too often we are creating nothing better than hot-house plants which wither and die as soon as they are exposed to the heat and cold of the outside world. Not so the lowly weed!

When all is said and done, it is the weeds which keep nature's balance and ultimately help us survive on this planet. Wild vegetation is, after all, the chosen and vital means of maintaining our human lives. No, I am not advocating "wildness" and the lack of refinement and finesse in matters cultural and spiritual. I am saying that when God does his mysterious work of creation, some of us turn into roses and orchids, others into Bermuda grass and milk-weed. Let each thank God for what he is, for in the last analysis the weed may play a much more essential role than the mighty rose. Happy Gardening!

No. 11 • November 1980

EVERYTHING... WITH THANKSGIVING

"Have no anxiety about anything, but in everything by prayer and supplication with thanksgiving let your requests be made known to God, and the peace of God which passes understanding, will keep your hearts and minds in Christ Jesus." Philippians: 4:6, 7

We are ready to give thanks for our blessings, which by interpretation are those things that make us feel good or add to the good things we are required to maintain a comfortable and happy life. But give thanks for our calamities? Now, there's a novel and unusual idea! To accept the negative things that happen to us does not come easy, and most of us reject the thought outright. But let us take a moment or two to think about this matter and consider whether it is not a good thing to do.

We know that whether we like it or not, the destructive and negative things will come our way sooner or later. We can pretend that they will not, or we can work hard to ensure nothing but health, wealth and happiness will be our lot. Sure enough, in least expected places and times, the bad will happen anyway! What do we do then? We become confused and demoralized. We call the faithfulness of God into question, and we begin to doubt the need or practicality of having faith in God. The grand result is loss of faith and loss of peace of mind and of life. This need not be our experience at all.

The alternative is to accept the realistic view of life which acknowledges that we will have calamity, sickness, business reversals, family problems and finally death itself. We eliminate anxiety by accepting these as facts of life. We do not evade them, but we seek to overcome their destructive emotional effects upon us when they do strike. We do so by developing a belief in God which is not imaginary. We do not confess God as our Lord only as the result of some cosmic deal we make with Him — "God I'll be a good boy or girl. I'll go to church, and I'll give my money to the missionaries, and I'll read my Bible and pray every day. You, God, give me in return a healthy life, a good family and a good business. Take care of me, God, when all other safeguards fail."

Whether we want to agree or not, deep down this is the religious faith most of us have adopted. It is however pure superstition! God does not operate that way. We are urged to bring our requests to Him with confidence and thanksgiving without anxiety. That is, we thank Him for everything. Prayer is used for the purpose of calling on God to help us accept all experiences. The result is our emotional and spiritual balance with a maturity which rises above circumstances after accepting them as part of life itself. The grand result is that the peace of God will be ours. Ah, yes… wonderful mysterious peace. "It passes all understanding," says Paul. In other words, logic can't explain it. But the heart and the soul will understand it and celebrate it! That is the secret of true thanksgiving.

No. 12 • December 1980

...AND ON EARTH PEACE

Christmas 1980 finds us in a world no closer to universal peace than the world in the year Jesus was born. The once-popular belief that the progress of civilization had brought humanity to the threshold of final and lasting peace is now no longer held as a possibility in our lifetime, and only a scattered minority of people throughout our world still hold on to this belief like cherished myths. With our nuclear arsenals increasing daily, even the possibility of maintaining an armed truce is quickly receding from the realm of probability.

All of this consequently forces us to ask the obvious questions, "Where is the peace promised by the angels the night Jesus was born?" It is right that we ask this question again. People in Jesus' day expected that Jesus would establish the eternal Davidic Kingdom and rule forever. They were disappointed. We will be too, unless we study Jesus' own teachings about "peace." What did He say, and what did He mean by it?

Jesus taught that we can experience peace on a level of consciousness quite apart from the political world to which we easily refer when this question is asked. He made it clear that within such an outside world of turmoil one can have an inner world of peace. He offered us this world in His person. When He was confronted by Pilate He did acknowledge that He was the King, but refused to identify His Kingdom with this world. The Pilates, and the Caesars and the Hitlers of this world will not be stopped from working their hellish schemes. What Christ will do is to neutralize the effect of these devils among us by preventing their power from reaching into our inner person and destroying our soul.

That is where the Kingdom of God exists and no one can disturb the peace put there by the Spirit of God. A most significant statement He made once was, "The Kingdom of God is within you." The inner world of man orders his external world, and the external world made chaotic by people who have chaos in their hearts can't prevent those with inner peace from continuing to live lives in the calmness of God's presence!

More significant than the peace we normally seek in inter-human relationships is the peace we can have with God, Himself. The peace proclaimed by the angels must refer to the most basic of relationships, that of the creature with His Creator… "Justified by faith, we have peace with God." Paul proclaimed. How true! All religions of man have one thing in common — the desire to appease their god or gods, and to find acceptance in their eyes. Jesus addressed this issue squarely. It is no longer fear and dread, but love and joy that describe the believer's attitude. Not only is his daily relationship one of peace, but his destiny of eternal life is also settled in Christ. So it is that the challenge is flung, "Who can separate us from the love of God?" The answer comes bold and clear, "Nothing in all creation!" All forces of man and devil marshalled against the believer can't defeat him. Here is the secret of our peace.

So, ring out the bells of Christmas! While people may turn to all kinds of political, military, economic and nationalistic programs in pursuit of peace, we will turn to the Manger. There is One who is truly the "Prince of Peace." Let our prayer be that He be born in us today.

No. 13 • January 1981

TIME

Just the other day, I remembered the time in my early youth when my mother taught me how to tell time by reading the clock. It seemed so complicated! Yet I was most anxious to learn because it would help me to join the world of "grown-ups." On another occasion, when my mother was in the hospital, the babysitter gave me a toy watch to help cheer me up. I was most unhappy to discover, after the initial thrill of owning my own watch had passed, that this was a toy watch with no working parts. I got hold of a hammer and quickly smashed it to pieces! I could hardly wait to grow big and act like all the big boys and men around me.

So it is that we wish to be part of "the action" going on all around us. We want to move with the times, to experience growth, creative and ongoing activities; we want to be in control of things, to take the wheel of life and drive on to newer and greater things. We welcome the new, and we make it ours with joy. So, welcome the year 1981. It is here!

But then, as time flows by like the swift waters of a mountain stream, it brings with it reminders of our passing on along with them, and we become sad. The same rushing stream that takes a boy's toy boat and gives it exciting movement soon takes it out of his sight, and it is gone! How sad, and yet how unavoidable as well.

Time, therefore, brings us the thrill of life and eventually takes it away from us. Nothing is given permanently. We grow old, and we look back with nostalgia at the good old days. "Lord, make me to know my end, and what is the measure of my days... how fleeting my life in" (Ps

39:4),. Here is a strange request that the Psalmist makes. The secret of a calm, contended and fruitful life is found in this request — to accept our limitations and to work within those boundaries for the short time we are on this earth. No, not to seek more and endless time — only God can have that. But to accept what we have as a precious gift which we are privileged to enjoy for a period and then we move on.

VARTKES M. KASSOUNI

VICTIMS OF OUR OWN ILLUSIONS

The story is told of a railway employee in Russia, years ago, who accidentally locked himself in a refrigerator car. He was unable to escape or to attract the attention of people outside. As he felt numb, he recorded the story of his approaching death in sentences scribbled on the wall of the car. "I am getting colder ...still colder, nothing to do but wait." "I am slowly freezing to death." ... "Half asleep now. I can hardly write." And finally, "These are my last words." When at length the car was opened, he was found dead. But an amazing thing was also noted. The temperature was only 56 degrees! The refrigeration mechanism was not working at all. There was no physical reason for his death. He had not frozen. He was the victim of his own illusion!

Our own illusions about ourselves, about our friends, about our church, about our society so easily distort our own attitudes also and so easily prevent us from living normal, peaceful lives. A young person gets the idea the he or she is not "attractive" or "smart" enough to get along with friends. Soon he or she begins to withdraw with feelings of inferiority and rejection. You can't convince them that they are acceptable to their friends. "Nobody likes me!" is their terrible anguish, "Society is out to get me" is the paranoid feeling of so many people. The government is slowly killing us... such feelings abound among many church people also. Years ago, in another church which I pastored, a woman actually confessed that the reason she was cool towards me, her pastor, was that I had ignored her during a church social and that was proof that I did not care for her. In reality, she was a person I admired as being one of the most able and helpful people in the church!

Last week I received two letters: One (unsigned) stated how disappointed this person was in my sermon. "I got absolutely nothing out of your sermon today," was the sad confession. I was feeling most dejected and sorry for myself when a day later another letter arrived. This one said, "I thank God for your sermon last Sunday. It met me exactly at my point of need. Thank you indeed." "How could the same sermon affect two people so differently? One was already under the power of an illusion. That illusion was a blinding and distorting force. The other person came with a hungry heart and an open mind. God fills empty cups with his blessings. People with cups full of their own ideas and illusions can't have God do any gracious work for them. "Blessed are the hungry" Jesus said, "for they shall be filled."

No. 15 • April 1981

DEATH CANNOT HOLD HIM

In his famous Pentecost Day sermon, Peter made a central point about the resurrected Jesus: **"God raised him up, having loosed the pangs of death, because it was not possible for Him to be held by it."** (Acts 2:24) It was not possible then, and it is not possible now, to hold Christ in a state of death. He was pronounced dead, and buried and over with. He was put away for good, left to the sentimental feelings and memories of friends. History need not deal with Him any longer… nothing left but ointments to cover the stench of rotting flesh! That's what they all thought, including his closest friends, but "death could not hold Him!" Shocked and thunderstruck disciples were rebuked for their lack of faith. They looked for a body wrapped in grave clothes, but they met a living and triumphant Lord with instructions for moving on and out into the world with a message of life.

The church of Jesus Christ, including our own, sometimes acts like keepers of the cemetery, rather than witnesses to the resurrection. We think that dispensing the sweet ointments of respect and appreciation over the body of religious tradition is just about all we can do in an age of empirical science. Jesus, the central figure of our faith, is not alive among us. He is back there wrapped up in all the vestments and the shrouds of holy history! While we are thus respectfully tiptoeing through the corridors of his sepulcher the Lord of Life suddenly confronts us today, for "Death can't hold Him!" He calls us by name and whispers "Peace!" He opens blinded eyes, awakens agnostic minds, loosens atrophied muscles, puts action into limbs weakened by inactivity. He sends his church out into the world to be his witnesses! No more staying within the safe confines of religious faith cloistered in the hallowed halls of familiar lore and tradition. Out, out to the shores of Galilee, to the streets of Jerusalem, to the jails of Rome, to the marketplace of Athens.

Out into the open to take our stand before the scoffers and the unbelievers. Let those who would again bury our Christ and proclaim, "the death of God," see Him alive in our day as well!

Let us today maintain a church whose message to the world is exactly this: "We serve a risen Savior!" let us have a ministry that matches that message with an outreach program bringing life to people in His name. There is no better way than this to proclaim, "He arose, He arose, Alleluia Christ arose!"

VARTKES M. KASSOUNI

No. 16 • May 1981

"PLEASE PRAY FOR MY SON"

A prayer request was made two weeks ago. It was received by World Vision International from a well-known supporter and Christian business man, John Hinckley of Greenwood, Colorado. Two days ago, his son, John Jr. tried to assassinate the President of the United States! A deeply disturbed young man, lonely, drifting, confused and alienated has resorted to horrible violence! What makes it so troubling and paradoxically exasperating is that he does not fit the stereotype we so easily assume is the image of a criminal. Here is a young man from an outstanding, wealthy, evangelical Christian family living in a beautiful suburb of Denver! One wonders what really ever went wrong in that home. Why did John drift away from all the values, the security and the faith of this family into anarchy and violence?

There are a lot of homes like that of the Hinckley's in America today. Recently, for example, the Best Picture of 1981, Academy Award, went to "Ordinary People." It is the story of a typical middle-class white home in which a deeply disturbed son attempts suicide. "Please pray for my son" is a prayer request being repeated by many parents within our society, and Church folks are by no means exempt!

All indications are that these are not isolated instances, but are indicative of a malaise spread throughout our society, and we need to do more than "pray for our sons." We need to get more deeply involved with them to understand what their hopes, dreams, aspirations, problems and needs are. We need to be open and honest with them, and we need to be open and honest with our spiritual leaders as well, so that adequate help may be provided while there is yet time. Often spiritual leaders' own children develop critical problems as well. We all need each other in times like this. Jesus' story of the Prodigal Son is as contemporary as today's headlines. He has something for us which needs to be accepted and appropriated in our homes. The message is not needed only by the one son, but all the other members of the family and the parents as well. God is ready to hear our prayers, but we must be ready to hear and heed His ways! The words of the old spiritual song comes to my mind, and how appropriate for our time: "It's me, it's me O Lord, standing in the need of prayer…"

VARTKES M. KASSOUNI

No. 17 • October 1981

THERE GOES A MOUNTAIN

All month I have been fascinated with the incessant movement of giant earth-moving machines working the hill across the freeway from our church. At first, I thought they were merely widening a dirt path already existing to open a new paved road to Universal Studios. But as they worked on and on, it became evident that they were onto something really big. They are actually moving the whole hill! At this date, I have no idea why they are doing it, but obviously it is a huge project. I marvel at their vision, the dedication, willingness to put in long hours, the vast investment of funds, the rallying of forces, the securing of proper equipment and learning of skills involved in the execution of such intricate and complex plans.

Jesus said: "You will say to the mountain 'move from here to there," and it will move." (Matthew 17:20) Do we believe that? Actually, I have seen the opposite to what Jesus said to be the case, more often than not: Mountains remove our faith. We "believe" until the obstacles rise before us, and the refusals pour in fast and furious. Jesus said that "children of this world" were often more wise that "children of the kingdom," How true, and yet how tragic.

Our church has been put here by God for these days of challenge and opportunity. I do believe that we have the people, and we have the resources to do whatever God directs us to do. One thing will prevent us from accomplishing our task, however, and that is our lack of faith. Our faith has not been given to us to keep us secure and comfortable in our tight little circles, it has been given to us to remove mountains. I want people who watch us work say over and over again as they comment on our ability to do things, "Well there goes another mountain."

230

No. 18 • November 1981

CAN WE STILL FLY?
(A THANKSGIVING MEDITATION)

During the stern and terrible days of the first winter spent in New England by the Pilgrims, food supplies were so depleted that only five grains of corn were rationed out to each person at a time. A journey begun in England had ended in America. They had dared to affirm a conviction, a faith, a dream, of freedom to worship God according to the dictates of their conscience. They had dared to leave the comforts of their homeland and travel by faith into the vast unknowns. They knew how to fly!

The famous Danish Christian philosopher, Kierkegaard, sought to awaken the church with his biting satire and incisive logic and faith. Once he likened the Christians of his day to a flock of geese living in a barnyard. Once a week they gathered in one corner of the yard and one of their articulate number mounted the fence to speak of the wonders of geese. He recounted the exploits of their forefathers who mounted upon wings and flew the trackless places of the sky. He spoke of the goodness of the Creator who had given the geese the urge to migrate and the wings to fly. And as he spoke, the geese would nod their heads and wonder at these things. What a heritage was theirs!

All this they did, but one thing they no longer did — they never flew again! They went back to their waiting dinners where the corn was good and plentiful and the barnyard secure.

Before we too easily thank God this Thanksgiving for our plenty and for our security let us think for a minute. Are all these "blessings" making it impossible for us to fly anymore? Are we more anxious to maintain our peace, comfort and belongings, than to strike out in faith, to risk losing our "blessings" in the service or Christ? Can WE still fly?

Armenians have known how to fly. Our history is full of stories of how our forefathers dared great odds to come out of hostile environments and to reestablish themselves in this free land called America. But how about us now, their grandchildren? Will we be reduced to telling stories of their exploits while we enjoy stuffed turkey, candied yams and football on T. V.? No, there is much more for us than this. We will not be confined to the barnyard! We will be concerned with much more than keeping the fences strong and the yard clean and our stomachs full. We will spread our wings and fly in God's blue skies and discover His great universe.

No. 19 • January 1982

VISIONS AND DREAMS

Dreams of wonderful days long gone…. visions of great times ahead. Good bye 1981 and Hello 1982!

Visions replace the dreams, or rather, dreams produce new visions. The old is not just gone, it has become the basis for the new. The root feeds the leaf; the streams, fed by rains long since settled into the good earth, water parched tongues and make the deserts bloom. So it is that we hail the New Year with fresh excitement. We welcome it as the sunrise at dawn. The new day brings with it new opportunities, new prospects, new horizons.

"Your young men shall see visions, and your old men shall dream dreams." Thus spoke the prophet Joel thousands of years ago. His message took on fresh meaning when the Church was born on the day of Pentecost. This truth was claimed for themselves by the band of hardy believers on that eventful day when filled with the Spirit, they broke out in holy exuberance and power. "They are drunk!" was the derisive comment of unbelievers gathered around them. "On the contrary," was the response of Peter, their spokesman. "They are filled with the winds of God!" My how those winds have swept the earth since that eventful day… the seeds of life and hope have been carried by them to all nations, and they have germinated in nooks and crannies everywhere. Visions have been realized and life everywhere has been transformed by the hand of God!

What winds of God will sweep over us in 1982? Will holy visions fire our souls this year also? Will we be caught up with the enthusiasm of divine initiatives? Will we dare challenge comfort, prestige, security and Spirit this year?

Jerusalem was their beginning, but their end was the whole world! They were scattered everywhere because of persecutions in the Holy City. Their adversity became the basis for their victory. They did not give up in hopeless despair, but they pushed on with new vision and hope. No obstacle was too high, no barrier too strong, no place too far, no people too strange. Their vision took in the whole universe. This is the stuff Spirit-filled churches are made of!

Now, how about us in 1982? Will our fears and our dreams overwhelm and paralyze us? Or will we reach out with spirits made free by the breath of God blowing on our souls? Friend, share with me your vision, and I'll share with you mine. Together we will feel the wind; we will move with God.

No. 20 • February 1982

OF GIDEON AND VARTAN

Here is a tale of two heroes. One lived 1000 years before Christ, the other lived 400 years after Christ. One was a Hebrew, the other was an Armenian. We would think that there is not much reason to link their stories. However, on closer scrutiny, we see how similar their stories are. We teach Gideon's story all the time in our churches and Sunday schools, but not much teaching about Vartan goes on. Well, I suppose it is so because the Bible contains Gideon's story, but Vartan's is found in history books written long after the Bible was completed. His story, nevertheless, is just as inspiring and just as necessary as Gideon's.

Gideon led a brave band of outnumbered soldiers in a daring battle against the Midianities. They prevailed and established the cause of Jehovah and his people. He was known as "Jerubbaal," meaning "contender against Baal." He did it with faith in God and with great courage. He weeded out of his army those who had no heart for the battle and those with no commitment to the cause. Today he holds a dear place in all believers' hearts. We even have a society of Christian men called Gideons International!

Vartan led a vastly outnumbered army against the Persians in 451 A D. He too was a "Jerubbaal." In his case, the idol was not Baal but fire worshipping Zoroastianism. The Persians demanded religious conformity from their vassal states and the Armenians were to be no exception. "Give up your faith or die!" was the challenge and ultimatum. The Battle of Avarair decided the matter. The Armenians chose death and went into battle resolved to stand firm on their faith. Vartan and over 1000 of his men died, or did they really? Gideon physically survived his battle, but Vartan did not.

His stand, however, survived and the nation did not bow in subjugation. The people held on and their faith flourished. Fifty years later, Vartan's nephew, Vahan, fought again and this time prevailed. The Persians agreed to let our people live and believe in Christ.

These heroes of the faith have written important chapters in the book of Christianity's life. They must be read not only by Armenians but by all Christians. For 2000 years the people of God have been contending for the faith. It has taken much more than prayer meetings and Bible studies to "pass it on!" So, let us tell the story again. Let our children know about them. Remember: don't stop with A. D. 400, but keep going through 2000 years till today. Every step of the way, "truly, the blood of the martyrs has been the seed of the church."

No. 21 • March 1982

THE IMPOSSIBLE WAY

Jesus, the author of our faith, said a lot of things during his ministry on this earth. He spoke, He taught, He lived effectively enough to create a vast following. Among those who proudly claim being first as a nation in following Him are the Armenians (301 AD).

Most of us have sentimental feelings about what Jesus taught. We remember the words that make us feel good inside, that assure us of God's love for us, that invite us into the shelter of His goodness, that promise us eternal life when we die. However, Jesus taught some things that are considered impractical, unworkable, visionary and impossible. Among these saying of His, we have one on which I would focus our attention: "Love your enemies and pray for those who persecute you, so that you may be sons of your Father." (Matthew 5:43)

Jesus is calling us to walk in the impossible way. By "impossible," I mean that which is contrary to human nature. I cannot love my enemy. When I was a boy in school, I came across a large picture of Kemal Ataturk in a pictorial history book in our school library. I took it to a secluded corner, scratched his eyes out, and then quietly put the book in its place! That was the true, natural me, acting in vengeance for I too had heard all the gory stories of the Armenian massacres in Turkey.

As a grown man, committed to the Gospel, I once had the occasion to have a Turk visit in my home and stay with me and my family overnight. Feelings of revulsion and anger which naturally gripped me I consciously put down, and prayed for the power to share Christ's love with him. In response to our hospitality, he thanked me and then repeated the familiar Turkish position: "We are from the same part of the world. We can live together. Turks never massacred the Armenians' forget all that…" This was my opportunity. I proceeded to assure him that I knew our history quite well, and that we all had family members lost in the massacres. Furthermore, I assured him that my ability to show kindness was not due to ignorance or weakness on my part, but due to the fact that as as a Christian, I was witnessing to him of our faith's ability to overcome evil with good! He hung his head and never said another word. Right there "coals of burning fire" were heaped on his head!

The impossible becomes possible when Christ is allowed to prevail. Paul said, "I can do all things through Christ who strengthens me." We have all kinds of situations which demand His power. I think this is the most crucial one for our day. To overcome evil with good takes courage, it does not come easy. It is not recommended for the timid. Try it some time. Your need for satisfaction in seeking justice and restitution from your enemy will be strangely fulfilled.

No. 22 • May 1982

WOMEN AND THE CHURCH

When it comes to church affairs, women have been very much in the news lately. Women have been active in church circles ever since the times of Jesus. Contrary to the traditions of his day, He allowed and invited the participation of women in His movement.

To us this may not seem unusual, but to students of the times and culture of Jesus' day, it becomes readily apparent that Jesus was most liberal in his approach to this question. The early church followed through with the style of Jesus and included women in all areas of its ranks. We have women active in the inner circle of apostles, then we have women taking the initiative in establishing new churches, women teaching elements of the Gospel to leaders of the church as well as to ordinary members.

This question would be without controversy if it were not for the Apostle Paul who said to the Corinthians: "Women should be silent in church." (1 Corinthians 14:34)   Consequently, people who wish to take these words literally forbid women to speak in the church or to ordain them to the ministry. How sad! Many churches have the double standard of letting, and even directing women, to do practically all the work while the men get all the credit for it. Jesus certainly allowed women to speak in His assembly, and He allowed them to lead as well. What Paul said was understandable in light of the chaotic conditions of the Corinthian church where all kinds of problems were threatening its peace and tranquility.

To take His words to be normative for the church universal would be wrong indeed. For was it not Paul himself who said in Galatians 5:23:

"There is neither Jew nor Greek, there is neither slave nor free, there is neither male nor female; for you are all one in Christ?" That is the normative principle that guides the Gospel and the affairs of Christ's church universal.

All this I have by way of introduction to a big **"thank you women of our Church!"** We owe much to each of you for the hard and often thankless work you do for us all and for Christ, whom we know you love dearly. We men have much to learn from you. One thing I wish you could do a little more effectively and that is to get your husbands as involved as you are. Of course, we have many men and many husbands already active, but we need many, many more.

Oh yes, one other thing: **"Happy Mother's Day!"**

No. 23 • June 1982

THE HUMMINGBIRD AND
THE MAPLE LEAF

Thank God for windows! Have you ever included your windows in the list of blessings God has given you? "How strange…." you say as you wonder what I am talking about. Well, I have received many blessings as I have gazed out the windows of my life. My typewriter sits right by my office window and very often I take a minute and pause during my typing. When I do so, I look out my window and sometimes my attention is caught by the unusual.

Yesterday I was delighted to see a hummingbird flutter around a maple tree right outside. It is a rare treat indeed to see a hummingbird. After a while, I saw it again and once again a few minutes later. Finally, it dawned on me that it was building a nest! Today its plan is clear, for it is back and the nest has taken definite shape. What a delight to be honored by this delicate bird.

Who can fathom the depths of the mystery surrounding this one tiny bird? Here is a lone tree between a huge building, a busy parking lot, and the Hollywood Freeway — a most unlikely spot for a nest…. Then again, why those hours and days taken to build the nest on such a fragile base? Here are reasons why the bird should not build its nest here, but still it works on with resolute plan, untiring effort and careless abandon.

This one solitary bird has been my messenger from God. It has inspired me to work on, for I too am trying to build a nest by the freeway. I too seem so very alone at times, putting in long hours with thoughts of frustration and self-pity that tend to sweep over me. Work on like the hummingbird! It does not know I've been watching. It does not know I've been learning from it. It does not know I will be passing on the lessons it has taught me onto thousands of others. It merely enjoys making and using its nest. That is reward enough!

How about that one solitary maple leaf? There are thousands on the tree, but this one was chosen to bear the weight and the honor of the nest. It can't flutter and dance freely in the breeze like all the other leaves. I can hear it complain. "Why me? Why should I be the only one to be so burdened? Why are the other leaves allowed to be free? Will not its extra weight shorten my life, and will I not drop under the burden of the nest and the bird? It just is not fair!" I believe all the negative points are swept away by this one overriding fact: this one leaf is a chosen, special, extraordinary and blessed leaf. It bears the honor of the hummingbird nesting on it. All the other leaves will be gone, but this one will be remembered. Thus, it has gained immortality. Life finds meaning and joy within this thought.

Happy window gazing.... Beyond the speeding cars, acres of concrete, teeming masses, pause long enough to see the hummingbirds of life, and don't forget that leaf.

No. 24 • September 1982

IS THE CROSS STILL THERE?

For the past 15 years or so, our family has taken a few days off and spent our vacation at Lake Tahoe. Those of you who have been there need no explanation for the reason why anybody would want to keep going back to such a beautiful spot on God's earth. Well, one of the first questions the children always ask as we round the final curve and the lake basin comes into the view is: "Is the cross still there?" We all strain our necks towards the mountains, and we then exclaim with joy, "Yes, there it is. Look!"

Let me explain what this "cross" is. When we first went to Tahoe, we were the guest of Satenig Paloutsian of Fresno. She showed us a spot on the western mountains (Mt. Talac) where the snow deposited in the winter hardly ever melts and is preserved in the shape of a cross. It hangs over the entire basin like a silent, divine sentinel reminding us all of the sovereign providence and watchful care of our loving God. This year the cross was still there, bigger and bolder than ever, for there was still much snow on the mountains.

Hanging high over all of us in the invisible world of God's omnipresence, the Cross is still there! We look up and see many things but who among us looks for the Cross to bear its silent witness today?

"In the cross of Christ I glory, towering over the wrecks of time…" So go the lines of the grand hymn by John Bowring. It is more than a sacred symbol, and more than some kind of sentimental talisman. It is the proclamation of God for all time and all humanity. His love for the world is caught in that one great and overpowering act in history — the death of Christ for us all. All of history is judged by that event, and all people shall give an accounting of their life in accordance with the claims and demands of that cross. What do you say today: "Is the cross still there in your life?"

No. 25 • October 1982

I BELIEVE IN THE HOLY CATHOLIC CHURCH

This affirmation comes to my mind as I begin to prepare for Worldwide Communion Sunday, which falls on the first Sunday in October. It is a statement taken from the Apostles' Creed, which is one of the most ancient creeds of the Christian Church.

The Church, as established by her Lord, is a catholic or as the word means, universal church. We should not confuse it with the "Roman Catholic Church," which is a denomination among the many groupings within the universal church. Just as the word "Apostolic," is taken by some churches to designate their name. It doesn't mean that other churches, such as ours, has no apostolic authority or validity.

When we confess that we are a universal church, we affirm several significant truths, which are now worth remembering.

1. Christ's church is one in the whole world. We are essentially a part of the whole which exists under the Lordship of Jesus Christ. We need to ask ourselves: Are we, and if not, how are we in actual communion with the church beyond our own local congregation? Are we aware that an independent church, such as ours, can easily lapse into isolation and become an island separated from the continent?

2. The ethnic nature of our church, or any church organized along certain specific lines, can prevent it from appreciating and celebrating the inter-ethnic or international essence of Christ's universal church. If our beliefs and our programs make us exclusive, then we separate the

church from the body again. No organ can live when it is separated from the body.

3. An ethnic church can and should provide for the whole body that which it is and contains in a unique manner. Our differences should not be eliminated but shared with others who are different from us. As the first century church contained Jews, Greeks, Romans, and they shared their faith and life together, so can we in the 20th century. Isolation for the sake of preservation means separation, deviation and death! Let us enrich the total body of Christ with the rich heritage, faith, culture and vision of the Armenian Church. Let His be our calling as an Armenian church, with a vision to reach out into the whole world!

"I believe in the Holy Catholic Church," and I so live and work that my presence and participation within that church will bring meaning and joy to her, and to me.

VARTKES M. KASSOUNI

No. 26 • March 1983

THE ILLUSION OF CONTROL

I owe my fascination with an exciting definition of faith and trust to Sam Keen and the book, *"Life Maps: Conversation on the Journey of Faith."* In it, he uses a phrase over and over again: "Giving up the illusion of control." Western man seeks to understand, to order, and then to control himself and his environment. His sense of security and well-being derive from his ability to feel successful in this grand scheme.

However, our failure to do so results in all kinds of conflict, disease, chaos or paranoia. We delude ourselves into thinking that we have figured it all out, and that all things do make sense in accordance with our schemes. Furthermore, we distrust and reject all schemes and people who do not fit into our way of ordering everything.

The healthy person is the one who knows and accepts the fact that he cannot be in control of this world and allows forces beyond himself to influence him which he needs not understand. This is where trust comes in. He gives up "the illusion of control," and lets it go. In my youth, I used to hear the saying: "Let go and let God." That's it! However, do not define "God" in such a manner, either, that He is exclusively shaped and formed by your intellect, religious beliefs, creedal formulas and traditions. For then you will fall right back into the same hole from which you just crawled out! My religious paranoias must not insist that you define Him as I do. Even I cannot always define Him in the way that I have done in the past, either. I must allow myself room to expand my understanding in accordance with the experiences based on trust.

Sam Keen says: "To trust is to believe that in some **unknown sense**, everything in the world is connected and benevolent." Everything is connected so that I am not the center of the world. Therefore, I do not have to control it. I can let go… Trust allows me to tolerate plurality in the body and the body politic.

Emotionally, it means I do not have to be consistent. I can contain many contradictions. Herein lies the secret to freedom and peace! Relax within your world filled with puzzling phenomena, your inability to conquer your enemies, including yourself. Relax, as you do in the seat of an airplane and let the pilot fly it. Enjoy the sensation of flight and gaze out the window in awe as the fantastic sights unfold before you. Faith for Sam Keen is not evidence in the ordered life of a tame pigeon but in the free flight of the wild dove. "Trust begins when we stop putting everything into pigeon holes, and start following the wild dove. A trusting life is like a living sun, not a dead planet. It is made up of a series of explosions." It is to me most pertinent that in the New Testament the symbol for the Holy Spirit of God is a dove.

"Come Holy Spirit, heavenly Dove, with all thy quickening powers…"

No. 27 • April 1983

"WHAT IF...?"
(AN EASTER MEDITATION)

Seven times within the short space of eight verses in 1 Corinthians 15, the Apostle Paul confronts the implications of Jesus' non-resurrection, with the hypothetical "what if..." He is fully aware, as we too are today, that unbelievers refused to believe that Christ was really resurrected. Accepting that argument as a working hypothesis, he develops with incisive logic a series of statements which follow from the main argument and brings us to the inevitable conclusion that belief in a dead Christ is not worth our bother! Follow with me his keen reasoning...

If there is no resurrection of the dead, then Christ has not been raised.

If Christ has not been raised, then our preaching and faith is in vain.

We are consequently misrepresenting God and falsely claiming that Christ was raised.

If that is so, then our faith is empty and our sins not forgiven, their full power is in and over us still.

And all who have died believing have perished; they have no rewards and no heaven to experience.

If, therefore, we are to accept this present life on this earth only as "all there is to it," then we are a miserable lot indeed! People can look on us with pity, and all our work has been for nothing...

Humanistic logic, devoid of faith beyond the power of our minds, brings us to this gloomy point and abandons us there! Sorry folks, that's it… turn out the light and let's all go home and forget all this talk about empty tombs and eternal life. Unfortunately, many have bought this line of thinking and in their desire to be intellectually autonomous they have become spiritually bankrupt!

This event, beyond the power of the mind to define, caught up that tiny band of Jesus' followers, however, and lifted them from the depths of despair to the heights of heavenly ecstasy. At the center of it was the presence of the living Lord. Yes, in person, the man they had watched being placed in the tomb appeared to them and uttered the magic word, "Peace!" It is not logic that convinces Paul of this, but rather, it is his personal experience. It is not argumentation but a personal witness he is now engaged in. For "in fact Christ has been raised form the dead," he declares, adding his witness to that of over 500 people who experienced the post-resurrection presence of the Lord. This is what awaits all faith centered in a living Christ, and not a dead hero. This faith dares to face a world gripped in the terror of holocaust, annihilation, and boldly proclaims, "As in Adam all die, even so in Christ shall all be made alive… for the last enemy to be destroyed is death itself."

No. 28 • June 1983

THE MOUNTAINS OF LIFE

June is graduation month. We are filled with pride and joy as we watch our young people walk in those beautiful commencement processions to receive their diplomas. Most speakers at such events remind our graduates that life is only beginning for them, and that the diploma in their hands is to be a tool whereby they will be able to cope with the challenges of life, and that they are to press on with faith and courage. The song, "Climb Every Mountain," comes to my mind as I write this. It is an appropriate theme for our graduates.

I climbed a mountain recently and the parallel feeling and experiences I had motivate me to share my thoughts with you, especially with our graduates.

Every Spring I get the urge to climb the hills behind our house in Granada Hills called the Santa Susana range of mountains. It is then that the whole countryside is green and beautiful. Yesterday I did it! I put on my boots, took a bottle of water and took off, alone, up the hill starting at Bee Canyon Park. It was a crisp, clear day… one of those days when you can see forever.

Let me share with you my experience, for it was an intensely spiritual one, as well as physically invigorating: "Watch out for the rattlesnakes!" this warning has been given to me by a number of people with whom I had shared my intended hike This thought made me nervous and anxious as I began my climb. Finally, I had to make some mental adjustments so that I could proceed. "I'll cope with it if I have to." I said to myself, "But I will proceed without these thoughts hindering me…" Our fears prevent us from exploring new dimensions of the life God has for us. Dare to step out in faith, and most probably the snakes will never appear. It was so with me. I did see a jackrabbit or two, however!

Sweet solitude in God's nature is an experience little else can match. To hear the gurgling brooks, to listen to the birds sing, to appreciate the bright flowers, to meditate and to listen to your heart, completely alone. Ah, that is something else! I remembered the many instances within Scripture history; how God's special lessons were learned while people were alone. My hike followed Easter by one day: Yesterday, the teeming throngs in our church's services in which God was surely present in a special way, and today His presence is felt in an absolutely different environment! So it is that He comes to us in many, varied and completely opposite ways. They are all beautiful and precious.

An absolutely breathtaking perspective form the vantage point of a mountain was mine as well. I could see all the way from the towers in Woodland Hills to the downtown skyscrapers of Los Angeles, to Glendale and beyond. Before me lay the vast panorama of the San Fernando Valley, what a gorgeous sight! One can't have such perspectives on life unless one takes the trouble to climb. One step at a time, watching out every step for snakes, a sure place to stand and planning ahead for the next series of steps to make sure one arrives at the predetermined spot. But the rewards are worth it. Those who stay within their little boxes and immediate neighborhoods, be they physical, mental or spiritual can never discover or understand the full meaning of life. We argue for our points of view not because of principle or because it is the truth but because our ideas are all we have and we feel secure with them. We have seldom allowed God to give us sights that go much beyond our backyards.

Yes, for a refreshing change, go climb a mountain. I sure am glad I did. Do remember that life has its "mountains" for us every day also. Accept the challenges they present to you. Claim them in the power of Christ who promised us that we would move them by faith.

No. 29 • November 1983

ONE OUT OF TEN

"I did it my way!" This song, popularized by Frank Sinatra, expresses pride in achieving one's objectives without any assistance from anyone. We admire such "self-made" people who can point to themselves with puffed chest and head held high. The great American hero is modeled after such people, and we aspire to be included among them.

This picture of the successful person whether he is a businessman, athlete, scholar, or what-have-you, is an utterly false and unfortunate one. There is no one on this earth who is truly "self-made," and nobody "does it his own way" completely! We are all dependent on each other, and especially on God. The difference is that some people acknowledge this fact with humility and gratitude, and others deny it. Their arrogant pride deludes them into thinking that they did it alone, but the truth is far different. Jesus was once deeply pained and surprised that only one out of ten people he healed bothered to return to thank him. Luke makes the incisive observation that the one person was a Samaritan. In other words an enemy and an outcast as far as the Jews were concerned, and one from whom they would least expect such gratitude.

I would venture to say that the ratio holds true todays as well. Only one out of ten among us in our church, our community, stops to really considerer the meaning of God's grace deeply operative in our lives, so that a thanksgiving of praise in faith is given. We are all guilty of the sin of pride which refuses to express our utter dependence on God for everything we so abundantly enjoy. The original sin of Adam and Eve was their desire to go at it alone so that they could brag about being self-sustaining "You don't need God, for you can be like gods yourselves" was the tempter's enticing words. Who does not want to experience such exhilarating power? Yes, we all do, but it is not possible for we are all creatures; we are not self-created beings. We are all our brother's keepers; we are all each other's burden-bearers; we are all the channels of God to spread to everyone his blessings; we are all parents and children alike; we are teachers and students at the same time; we are providers and consumers as well; we are leaders but followers at the same time; we are successful today, but failures tomorrow. Humility acknowledges this to be a fact. God save us from pride which hides our weaknesses and boasts of our successes and ends up making fools of all of us!

No. 30 • December 1983

THE JOY OF CHRISTMAS

We all have joyful memories of our past Christmases, I am sure. The rising sense of excitement as the Day drew near. The great expectations and hopes about our most cherished gifts, glittering trees, candles, cards, decorations, parties and family gatherings, hugs and kisses, carols and late night church services… all these and 1000 other cherished recollections make up for us the magic of our Christmas celebrations.

"I'll be home for Christmas!" These are the sweetest words parents can hear from children who have moved away. Everyone tries to come together for this Holy Day, for Christmas has no joy unless it is celebrated with loved ones. My mind often wanders to the countless millions in our huge, teeming cities where the lonely huddle in solicitude. For them Christmas has no joy, for there are no loved ones around to hug them. I remembered the old Armenian woman in Harlem, years ago, whom I visited for the first time. "You are a visitor from God," she said. "I have been alone for months. Neighbors bring me food for I can't leave the house and have no loved ones. Sometimes I take a glass of water and a piece of bread and I serve myself Holy Communion because I have not been able to go to church for years…"

God is with us. He hugs us at Christmastime. The name of the Christ child was to be Emmanuel: God's presence in the person of His Son is the central meaning and content of Christmas. "Love came down at Christmas…" says the beautiful carol. And how can we make that love come down again this year? Without the actual birth of a real human being in the person of Jesus in Bethlehem, that love would have had no way of demonstrating itself in actual and real terms. It would have remained a mere sentimental thought. "The Word became flesh and dwelt among us… full of grace and truth." (John 1:14) Ah, that's the joy of Christmas!

Let us all try something new this year. Let us invite some new family in our church, or some foreign student who is away from home, or some elderly person whose family is long gone and departed, to our home for our Christmas gathering. Let us share the joy and thus multiply it for ourselves and others. Entertain strangers, says the Bible, for thus we will be entertaining angels unawares. Jesus was born in a manger around which were teeming crowds of people who had no idea what was going on. Jesus has a way of coming around today also when people least expect it. That's the real miracle of Christmas.

No. 31 • January 1984

THE OLD AND THE NEW

With the ushering in of the New Year, our thoughts turn to all the good things we hope the New Year will bring us. The list could be a mile long, if we were to actually write down all of our fondest expectations. May all your wishes come true, by the grace of God!

The old is always inextricably intertwined with the new. The old provides meaning and substance to the new and the new provides growth and life to the old. We need both and never must so live that either is considered unnecessary. This lesson is an especially important one for us to learn in the church. The old history of any church provides its vital identity. It is the foundation on which the building stands. It is the source of dignity and honor. It must never be forgotten or treated as "old stuff." The elderly members of the church are truly the pillars that hold it up. Their white hair, as the Scriptures say it, provides beauty and honor, just like a house in which a grandma and a grandpa live is full of much love and joy. Children who have had the privilege of relating to grandparents are indeed lucky!

Equally important in the life of a church is all that which is new: new facilities, new programs, new outreach, new members and new staff. All of these add the dimension of growth in much excitement. A house in which a new baby is born is immediately filled with celebration and joy. Even though it means much added expense, hard work, little leisure time, and tons of responsibility, all of that is taken on with no hesitation whatsoever. So it must be in any church in which there is an inflow of the new.

The prophetic proclamation of the Bible is, "Behold I make all things new!"(Revelation 21:5) We say it at every funeral, as the dead are placed lovingly into God's good earth and put to rest. It is done with the belief that God's creative forces will ultimately give new and everlasting life. However, it is this affirmation that keeps us going within times of discouragement and defeat. Let us rejoice. The God of the new life is with us still.

CHAPTER V

FIRST PRESBYTERIAN CHURCH
PALMDALE, CA, 1984

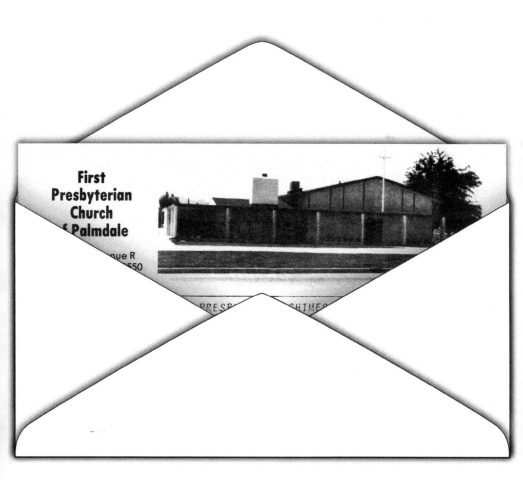

No. 1 • June 1984

THE DYNAMIC CHURCH

We are all interested in having and maintaining a "dynamic church." In the interest of helping us have such a church here, I offer the following suggestions. They are principles gathered from a study of the early church as originally established in Jerusalem. You may wish to check them out, so refer to Acts 2:41-47; 4:32-35:

First, the Gathering Together of people who have made a true and open commitment to Jesus Christ as Lord in response to the clear calling of people into a relationship with Christ, the head of the church. **This is our evangelistic task.**

Second, Participating in Worship Services where we present ourselves to God in thanksgiving, prayer, praise, confession and hearing of the Word. **All else, without worship, leads to pride and arrogance**. Worship places us in proper relationship: To God as the creator and us as His creatures; to God as Lord, and us as His subjects; to God as guide and us as followers.

Third, Studying Together under the guidance of the pastor and others helping him. "They devoted themselves to the apostle's teaching." For all practical purposes, the called and installed pastor of a church is for that congregation God's apostle. Today, church people running all over town to attend all kinds of "Bible studies," without the basic commitment to one's church and pastoral leadership, leads us into eventual confusion and deviation. **All else, without study, leads us into credulity and superstition.**

Fourth, Maintaining a Warm Fellowship. Gatherings whose sole purpose is the introduction of church people to each other as members of the one church family is of great importance. Fellowship has no other objective but the people themselves. The church must show interest in the persons comprising the body with a growing sense of commitment to meet the needs and stand in support of all as brothers and sisters. **All else, without fellowship, leads to isolation and estrangement.**

Fifth, Serving Others in Outreach and Mission. Having developed a keen sensitivity to the needs of all, the early church people gave generously because they cared. Some sold everything and donated the proceeds for this purpose. The dynamic church is a giving church, not because the budget demands it, but because the love of Christians so grips people's lives that they really care for others. **All else, without service and outreach, leads to sterility and eventual death.**

In conclusion we read, "Grace was upon them all." It became obvious that the church operating by these principles by the power of the Holy Spirit becomes a "grace-filled" church.

No. 2 • July 1984

SWEET LAND OF LIBERTY

"My country, 'tis of thee, sweet land of liberty, of thee I sing…"

In July, we celebrate Independence Day. Beyond the fireworks and picnics, beer busts and brass bands, we need to think seriously and clearly again concerning the meaning of freedom in America and of America, for there is nothing more cherished among us than this gift.

The American Revolution was the predictable consequence of a movement which brought the Pilgrims to America seeking religious freedom. Political tyranny had deprived them of their rights to assemble as they pleased, to worship God as they pleased, and to organize their community as they pleased, in accordance with their faith and religion. In America, they found this freedom in the Bay Colony and America was born! Politically, this new land was still under the dominion of England. Oppression and tolerance slowly increased until the colonies realized that the very forces they had fled in Europe had caught up with them again. Eventually, the Revolutionary War resulted in the final and total independence of America.

A very interesting, unique and extremely important item was worked into the Constitution of the United States by the founding fathers, which we must now and always take careful note — the principles of the separation of Church and State. One could ask, "If the Pilgrim Fathers came here for religious freedom, and they succeeded in founding their own country, why then did they not guarantee that the State would perpetuate their own brand of religion?" Actually, there are Christians in America today who say this is exactly what their intention was. In other words, a Christian Republic. They contend that a separation of Christianity from all matters of State is wrong and false. Hence, they are now attempting to establish such a Christian Republic in America! Is this interpretation of American history that many Christian-oriented parochial schools are working into their curricula in the interest of "putting God back in our country's affairs?"

Well, if this were the design of the Pilgrims why then such a shift away from it by the time the country was formally declared independent in 1776? It is because it had become clear in this country that religious intolerance can strike here as well as in Europe. The Pilgrims, themselves, developed a society that began with pure piety but grew into harsh intolerance. Remember how Roger Williams had to flee the colony because he dared to be nonconformist? If caught he would have probably been executed. The result was the establishment of Providence, R. I., and the Baptist approach to Christianity — something not allowed in the Bay Colony.

How about the witch hunts of Salem? Protestants, it was thus revealed, can become just as intolerant as followers of any other religion. Consequently, freedom in America, as defined by the heroes of the revolution, was defined as being the maintaining of a country without the dominating influence, subtle or obvious, of religious beliefs, movements, denominations or powers. Hence, we have a secular state here which guarantees for all people within its boundaries the right to believe or not to believe, to worship or not to worship, as they please, with no fear of persecution or retaliation. America is not a Christian country or republic, but it guarantees Christians the right to live, to grow and to propagate if they please. Thank God for America!

America is not anti-religious. It does not seek to "remove God" from the scene. It lets all such matter towards religious people and groups to pursue as they see fit. It also allows the Church the right to affect the values governing our affairs, not by direct programmatic involvement, but by shaping the values and principles of the people who run our government. By exercising the freedom of choice, our leaders can follow consciences shaped by the ethics of Jesus and to influence legislation so that this government will be loyal to principles of equality, justice, freedom, peace and prosperity for all. This is done not for the partisan advancement of any religion or denomination's fortunes, but for the common good — Christians, Hindus, Buddhists, Jews, Gentiles, Muslims, Theists and Atheists alike. We have no room for "Khomeinis" in American democracy.

Am I downgrading Christianity? On the contrary, I am saying that one of the most precious gifts Protestantism has given to this country is that of true freedom. Freedom not only from the foreign tyrant, but freedom from our tendency to enslave our neighbors in the name of God! This is our noble heritage. We can and must be proud of this fact. For once people in the majority did not do the predictable thing — insure for themselves power and position for posterity. They willingly accepted limitations on themselves that all may enjoy the gift of this great land called America. To deny my neighbor his rights means the eventual loss of my own rights as well. To guarantee him his freedom is to guarantee my own as well. This is the fertile soil in which our faith has been planted and taken strong root. Thus, America is a unique and wonderful country. God Bless America!

No. 3 • August 1984

WHAT IS MY CHURCH?

The Church is a family of people gathered together by the love and grace of God for mutual support, caring and growth. The common bond that binds us together is not nationality, race, social or economic standing, but our being children of God by the love and saving grace of Jesus Christ, our Lord. This family includes adults and children, including tiny babies, as well as grandparents. We are one in the Spirit!

The Church is a home where we gather to grow in our love for each other in a great variety of activities carried on in this spiritual and social center. Yes, I did say "social" because we need to mix together in fellowship activities as well as carry on religious exercises if we are to experience the fact that we are truly a family.

The Church is a school where we receive instruction and training in the Way of Christ. He is the great Teacher who has called us to follow him as his disciples. He spent much of his time teaching his followers. The topics he covered were the crucial issues of life and death. The university he established carries on its program through the church today!

The Church is a training center where we are shown by doing how we can address the issues of life with the truths of the Gospel of Jesus Christ. Beyond talk, action is the key factor here. Leaders of the church, starting with the pastor, including elders and deacons, officers and teachers of the Sunday School must be people who train and equip the membership of the church in doing, as well as, studying the Christian life. Projects of evangelism, outreach mission, caring and support must be carried on so that all can be helped to develop skill in Christian ministry.

The Church is a temple where we gather to worship God and commit ourselves to him as our Creator and Redeemer. We come with our sins to find new life and forgiveness. We come in weakness to receive strength. We come lost and are found by him. We come spiritually dead and are made alive in Christ! We come to pray, to meditate, to sing praises, to share our needs and to seek guidance and support. The Church is where the Holy Spirit abides, for this is the House of God for the People of God. This is where you belong!

CHAPTER VI

TUSTIN PRESBYTERIAN CHURCH
TUSTIN, CA, 1985-1986

TUSTIN
PRESBYTERIAN
PRESS

Tustin
Presbyterian
Church

Tustin,
California

No. 1 • January 1985

MUSING WITH THE MINISTER

"The past is finished and gone, everything has become fresh and new."
(2 Corinthians 5:17)

We welcome the New Year hoping that the mere passage of time could create for us a whole new set of circumstances assuring peace, prosperity and happiness. "Goodbye to 1984 and hello to 1985!" It does not take too long for us to realize that the New Year holds much of the same as did the year before, and that the New Year turns old very quickly. Our New Year's resolutions are soon forgotten or they are filed away to be remembered a year later, maybe…

"What are you giving up for Lent?" a man asked his friend. "My New Year's resolutions!" was the poignant reply.

The Christian's celebration of "the new" is based on the objective and substantive fact of the person of Christ and not on wishful thinking. Christ's coming is the introduction of the new age, and his work results in the creation of the new person.

There is now among us and in us that which is imperishable and timeless: The Kingdom of God. By the work of His grace in us we are all citizens of this "Kingdom" and members of the new humanity created by Him. We are not at the mercy of forces and powers holding people in the grip of fears and anxieties. We live in the midst of present society as representatives of this new age. We are people of peace and of hope, and we pray that the Church of Jesus Christ may make this truth more visibly real for the world to see, to understand and to experience in 1985.

VARTKES M. KASSOUNI

No. 2 • February 1985

THROUGH CHILDREN'S EYES

A few years ago Barbara Murphy, our Director of Children's Ministries, shared with me a delightful set of drawings made by children of our Church School on the occasion of our Church's Centennial celebration. They were asked to draw three pictures: The first of how they though the church looked a hundred years ago, another of how it is today and the third about how the church might be one hundred years from now. I would like to share with you my sense of delight over, and appreciation of their creative insights. I am again reminded of Jesus saying, "…and a child shall lead them."

The sanctuary building dominated their concept of the church. A hundred years ago they see us worshiping in a simple barn-like building, with no stained glass showing anywhere. Today, they see us in a building with a big tower and some stained glass adorning it. A hundred years from now they see us in a building practically covered with stained glass and with two big towers! Now, that's a correct observation that tells the story of the evolution of church architecture. One wonders what our building may actually look like after another century… (How about a "Stained Glass Cathedral" folks?) In any case, it is comforting, or disturbing, depending on how much or how little an "edifice complex" we may have. Our children are right there with us, learning and reflecting our values!

Another picture that really said something to me of how religion is evolving in America is that of the pastor standing at the pulpit preaching to the congregation. One hundred years from now he is depicted as being a robot preaching into a VCR placed on the pulpit! I would make one suggestion to the artist: "You should have placed a VCR in each pew!"

There you have it... robots preaching to robots, with everyone staying home, cozy and comfortable! I wonder if this is not the logical conclusion to which the "electronic church" is leading us! This picture may also be saying to us preachers, "Your presence in the pulpit is like that of a robot. You are not real or human to us..." That gives me a lot of room for thought. Thank God for our children. Their presence among us is not only delightful but prophetic indeed! Woe to the church that dismisses their role among us as insignificant, for God continues to find unusual ways and unusual people in continuing to speak His word.

No. 3 • March 1985

EASY STREET OR MAIN STREET?

We are in the season of Lent. We remember Jesus' suffering and death. We meditate on the meaning of such suffering. We consider His call to cross-bearing as being essential to true discipleship. We are puzzled by this fact, for is not the "good news of the Gospel" that we can now live free of pain, of failure and poverty? This is popular California theology. The Jesus of Gethsemane and the Cross are relegated to past history. The Jesus of today is the successful executive with a mansion on the hill who invites us to his place to teach us motivational techniques in "successful living." He drives by in his limousine while we stand on the side of the road cheering...

Leary's was a famous bookstore in Philadelphia where all kinds of rare books could be located. It was situated on 9th Street, near Market Street. Around the corner, Gimbel's Department Store wished to expand and in doing so approached Mr. Leary with a good offer to buy his shop. The offer was refused,. "You're crazy not to take the offer," Gimbels said. "You could be on easy street!" Replied Mr. Leary, "We want to be on 9th Street!"

We are tempted, as individuals and as a church, to get on Easy Street, sit back and sing, "Let the rest of the world go by..." but we can't. Somehow God frustrates our plans designed to eliminate our need for hard work, our sacrificial giving, our agonizing over our mission here and to the world, over the plight of the unfortunate and the oppressed. God keeps us on Main Street where we are to keep on reaching out to the crowds with the love of Christ. Main Street, forces us to face the issues of life and that is painful. But that's what the Cross is all about. Without the Cross there is no Gospel. Without death there is no resurrection. Without Calvary, there is no empty tomb.

No. 4 • April 1985

TO LIVE AGAIN

"If a man dies, shall he live again?" (Job 14:14). From the depths of his suffering Job asked this question of questions. We ask it again and again today in a thousand different ways. Theist and atheist alike seek to preserve life and maintain it beyond the span logically held possible for the human body. Whether it is by way of the ritual of the priest in the temple or the experiment of the scientist in the laboratory, we are equally obsessed with the desire to live longer and longer. From organ transplants and mechanical replacements to test tubes and clones, we seek breakthroughs assuring us that someday we can live forever.

Into this contemporary scene of our universal quest for the preservation of life steps Christ in person. The Gospel which emanates from him is "good news" relative to our basic quest for life. Hence, should we not give serious attention to what he holds for us? Should our faith not go beyond the mere celebration of festivals and maintaining of colorful traditions? Should we not again ask what it is that our faith holds for us and wherein lies our basis for hope that in Christ "all shall be made alive"?

The Christian concept of resurrection addresses the meaning of death itself. It is the human condition resulting from alienation and separation from God, from each other and from the environment. Tinkering with the human body, trying to extend its life, while the "soul" is dead in self-alienation highlights the real crisis of modern existence. We need Christ more than ever before!

It is not the Christ of memories but the living Lord who confronts us in our quest for life. His victory over death, his resurrection, presents us with a challenge no less than that which faced the disciples. To believe, receive and to act with boldness as witnesses to the fact. We too have encountered the living Lord! We too are called to be witnesses, to be the carriers of the exciting news: "I know that my Redeemer lives…" (Job 19:25) Job came to that point of confident faith in the midst of his suffering. He lived again in the power of his experience. This Redeemer is with us still to empower us also to be a people of hope and abounding joy.

No. 5 • May 1985

ARE WE LIBERAL OR CONSERVATIVE?

To be "conservative" is in and to be "liberal" is out these days, we are told. According to a **Los Angeles Times** religion article recently, Presbyterians are labeled "liberal." That got me thinking, hence this article.

What is a "liberal" and what is a "conservative?" A seminary professor once defined it for us: "A conservative is one to your right, and a liberal is one to your left. But the question is, "Where are you?" Among the Amish, for example, there are liberals who drive cars... that's bad, you know. But some among them drive cars very conservatively; they paint their bumpers black. They are known as "Black Bumper Amish" in contrast to the "White Bumper Amish." Among us common Protestants, we too have some curious practices and beliefs. In Church music Presbyterians use lots of Bach and Handel and are tagged as being "liberal." Other churches play "Gospel rock" with bands that split eardrums, but are called "conservative." The "good old hymns" that many "conservatives" love were written less than a hundred years ago, and the hymns "liberals" enjoy in our churches date back to Luther and Wesley and Watts, written hundreds of years ago. How's that for consistency?

"Ah, but we believe the Bible more than you," says the "conservative." Well, a close scrutiny clearly reveals it is not the Bible but certain parts that we "believe" depending on what our pet doctrines are. Take ordination of women, for example. I have never heard anyone accuse Pentecostals of being "liberal" yet they have been ordaining women for years! Social issues that supposedly mark the "liberal" are themes that come from the prophets and the teaching of Jesus himself. Justice, mercy, rights of all without discrimination, love of enemy, peace and non-reliance on the instruments of violence and armies for security; these all come right out of the Bible. They are conservative, Biblical themes, and dare we call those who refuse to preach or teach them "liberals?"

What and who are we at TPC? We are disciples of Jesus Christ, called by him to be his Church. We have accepted his love and are thriving in the sunshine of his grace. We share his love with others as best we can, and we enjoy our faith immensely. We seek to affirm all people without discrimination and with justice. We pray and work for peace in the world. Are we "liberals" or "conservatives?" I really can't say, and God bless you if you can!

No. 6 • September 1985

ARE WE MEMBERS OF ONE BODY?

Within the churches of Jesus Christ in America today there is a popular movement away from corporate life, mission, witness, denominational responsibility, and towards independence. Ministers and congregations who break away from parent bodies or organize as independent churches act like they have done something really great under the direct guidance of God! Taking advantage of and sometimes creating problems in "mainline churches," many such people design, in contrast, painless, attractive and comfortable programs, carefully sidestepping anything of controversy. They woo and they attract the angry, confused and dissatisfied people out of existing churches into pews, made comfortable by soothing music, safe theology and purely ego affirming preaching and teaching. Their mission causes are "safe," addressing purely "spiritual" and hardly any "social" causes. Often the results are dramatic growth. People point to such growth as evidence that they are blessed of God and therefore justified. I dare challenge this conclusion, and I would offer an explanation which may be somewhat severe, nevertheless in my estimation true.

Dr. Joseph Fort Newton makes a statement which is quite applicable to this point. It is self-explanatory: "Our world is a sick and cancerous world. What is cancer? Scientists tell us. 'It is the unchecked proliferation of cellular tissue by one organ independently of the rest of the body.' It is just cellular selfishness. If cancer cells could talk, they would say, 'We have been injured. Our pride has been hurt… we'll go at it on our own. See what astonishing progress we are making, too!' They separate themselves from other cells and advance amazingly. And what happens? The agonizing death of the body and of the cancer cells themselves."

"A selfish man is a cancer in the universe," said the Stoics, and they were right. Selfishness defeats itself, whether it be a selfish nationalism or religion. "We are one body and members of one of another," said St. Paul. "If one part of the body tries to go it alone, the whole body dies." It is cancer, and that is the fatal malady today.

"Independent" churches may be thriving here and there all over Orange County, California, or in the United States, but the crucial question is, "What is happening to Christianity as a whole in this country?" What is the condition of the body? How well is it functioning? What has happened to our collective witness to the world? Are we seen as servants of Jesus Christ or as ecclesiastical dilettantes and primadonnas, with each doing his or her "own thing?" Will the body survive? That is the question.

No. 7 • October 1985

I THINK IT'S WONDERFUL!

Two emphases come together for our consideration and celebration on October 6th: World Communion and Peacemaking. We take both of these seriously in our church, hence my desire to chat with you about them.

The Church of Jesus Christ, of which we are a part, exists throughout the "whole inhabited earth." We confess in the Apostles' Creed: "I believe in the holy catholic church," meaning the universal church. Don't let that one get by you too fast, for in this fact we celebrate something very precious indeed. We are one with people throughout this earth, belonging to all nations, peoples, languages, tribes, cultures, social and political persuasions. We count them all as our brothers and sisters in Jesus Christ, and they count us as being their kinspeople in Him as well. Thus, according to our Gospel. We bear allegiance to a Lord who is now Lord of all, through all and in all. We have gone far beyond the narrow nationalism of Old Testament times when the "Kingdom" was identified as belonging to one single national entity called Israel. Yes, as Jesus said, "The kingdom is among you" already! Let us celebrate it!

Peacemaking grows most naturally out of the first fact noted above. Since in Jesus Christ we have discovered the secret of being one with people throughout the world, and since in Him is the demonstration of the true meaning of reconciliation and celebration of our essential humanity, do we not have the secret to true peace in the Gospel? We must certainly do! Let us then shout it from the rooftops, pass it along wherever we may be, sing it with gusto, reach out and touch the world with God's Peace. Don't let narrow nationalism or scare political tactics rob you of your birthright in Christ. He said, "Blessed are the peacemakers, for they shall be called sons of God."

"The wisdom from above is first pure, then peaceable, gentle, open to reason, full of mercy and good fruits, without uncertainly or insincerity. And the harvest of righteousness is sown in peace by those who make peace." (James 3:17)

No. 8 • November 1985

CLAIMED BY GOD'S GRACE

Our Stewardship theme this year is taken from 1 Peter 2:9-10, "You are a chosen race, a royal priesthood, a holy nation, God's own people, that you may declare the wonderful deeds of Him who called you out of darkness into His marvelous light."

"Being "chosen" does not mean always being on the receiving end of prosperity, security and blessings. This is the mistake Israel made. They failed to heed God's call to mission in service to others, and rejected God's own Son because they no longer could identify with God's purposes for the world!

What do you do after you "Count your blessings, name them one by one...?" "Blessings Savings Account" to accumulate more blessings as insurance so that we may never run out of divine goodies. Jesus calls on us to take them and invest them in lives, our own and that of our neighbors, so that gifts of grace may multiply. A beautiful example of this is the story of Mr. Foster McGaw, the founder of American Hospital Supply, who recently gave a gift of $8,357,000 to the United Presbyterian Foundation for services of mission and witness. "The surest way to be enriched," he says, "is to share freely what you have, whether it be money, love, appreciation of beauty or devotion to a worthy cause." Most people spend so much of their lives acquiring financial security that they never develop skill in giving money away. Too late they discover that giving is the greatest philosophy. From the beginning of his career, at the age of 25 he started his business with a $10,000 debt!

> "...As children of dust, we are showered with life
> Encircled with love, while made festive and free.
> Empowered as partners, in Christ's fervent quest
> Forgiven, affirmed and claimed by God's grace"
>
> **— Robert Chase**

No. 9 • December 1985

CHRISTMAS 1985

For two thousand years, Christians throughout the world have celebrated the birth of Christ. An exciting variety of ethnic and national traditions proclaim the blessed event. We too plan special activities which bring us together in joyful celebration. All of these customs, however, recall a historically concluded event and tell a story pointing us back to year 1. For it to become real for us, we must seek the birth of Jesus Christ for us in our day as well. In one of our popular carols we sing..." Be born in us today." I've often wondered, "How is Christ born today?" That's the question I now ask.

Traditionally, we answer the question by saying, "Christ is born in our hearts when we turn to Him and ask Him to come in as Savior." That answer, as legitimate as it may be, centers the experience in the inner or subjective person. My reading of the Biblical story places the birth of Christ not inside people but "out there" in public, verified by shepherds and inn-keepers and magi. It was not a "spiritual" experience but a physical one in a real manger in somebody's actual barn, and shepherds walked a real path from the fields and came to a city, on an actual map, called Bethlehem. The doctrine of the "incarnation of God" is this taking on of human and physical dimensions by God in Jesus Christ. That is what we mean by "birth." Well, does that happen today?

The "birth" or presence in a new way in our time can happen in accordance with Christ's own teaching. He said, "When you gather in my name there I am in your midst." Every worship gathering then is one way where we experience in actuality the coming of Christ. The group of people in such gathering actually turns, by God's miraculous act, into "The body of Christ." Think of that and believe it every time you come to a worship service and see if it won't "blow your mind."

Not only in worship but in mission, we experience the birth of Christ in new times. How about seeking the Christ-child in the birth of a new idea that catches the imagination and grips the soul for action in a new direction? Jesus, in a sobering statement in Matthew 25, reminds us that He is incarnated in the lives of the hungry, poor, lost and alienated. Our challenge is to seek for Christ's birth in the mangers of our day, located not in the cathedrals we build, but in the caves and barns of our Bethlehems. Herod and his retinue, filled with pride and fear, looked for the child but failed in their search. In her Magnificat, Mary sang: "He has scattered the proud in the imaginations of their hearts, he has put down the mighty from their thrones and exalted those of low degree."

O God, teach us your language so that we may understand what Mary is saying and then let us join together in a chorus of praise: "Glory to God in the highest and on earth peace!"

CHAPTER VII

CHRIST PRESBYTERIAN CHURCH
HUNTINGTON BEACH, CA, 1986-1987

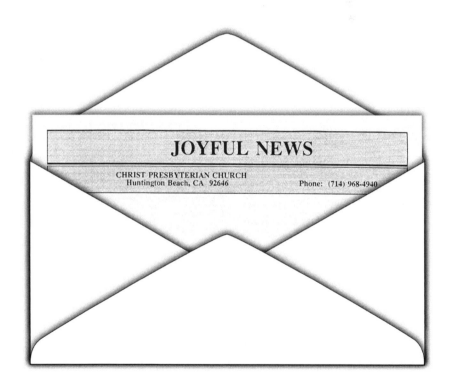

No. 1 • March 1986

A WORD ABOUT LIFE

"Because I live, you shall live also." (John 14:19) These are the words of Jesus spoken to his friends in an intimate gathering. I quoted them during a funeral service yesterday, as I have done a thousand times before, seeking to bring comfort and hope into lives disturbed and often shattered by suffering and death. Today is the first day in Lent. Last night we had an intimate gathering of church people here for Ash Wednesday service. We talked about the seven astronauts who died in the explosion of the shuttle, Challenger. I shared with them the feelings of a four year old girl in our Preschool, who along with other children, was asked to share her thoughts about this great tragedy. "The space shuttle exploded…" she began. "My mom cried because it was sad. You know, my mom used to work for the space people. Mom and dad and the people watching thought they had won, but it exploded instead. The people were saying 'Yeah!' The people in the spaceship were floating then there was an explosion and all the people died."

We too first believe, in all our planning and doings, that we have won, and then things "explode" around us and inside us, and we die! Shattered dreams, lost loves, opportunities gone, associations broken, loved ones separated, businesses bankrupt, and the list could go on and on. Death has a way of striking long before we are laid to rest in a grave. What then? From where will our salvation come? From where will hope spring? How will we put the pieces together again? Shall loneliness ever be replaced by laughter and celebration and warm hugs?

I don't mean to be trite and pious about it, but I do believe that Christ fulfills His promise. To believe Him, to come into the circle of His person,

His communion, His community is life. Easter is celebrated every day, not just on the one day so designated on the calendar. I believe Easter comes every time those who said "never again," are surprised by their ability to take that first step, smile and sing songs thought long forgotten.

"You shall live!" Believe it, say it, repeat it, act on it. There is nothing in the world that can take that fact away from you. The cross in unalterably followed by the resurrection.

No. 2 • April 1986

WHAT NEXT LORD?

You finally came to our city.
For some time we thought you wouldn't dare,
and you'd rather stay in the country.
It's much more quiet there,
and the people believe anything…
But the City, now that's something else.
Well, you came at last, but what an entrance!
You moved right in
and took charge of the Temple,
no one would dare prevent you.
Why then the sudden turn of events?
Why did you give it up?
Why the journey from the temple to the Cross?
After demonstrating such power,
why did you die?
We love you, you know…
We wished to keep your memory alive,
so our women were prepared
to keep anointing your body
and bringing flowers to your grave.
Just when we thought
things had settled to a routine—
Religion becomes so soothing
when the routine takes over
And the predictable prevails —

We found the tomb empty!
Now that really shook us up!
We know what to do with the dead,
it's the living that confuses us!
You really scared Mary and Martha, you know,
walking through that door
when it was closed shut.
Knocked us off our feet indeed!
You seem to be playing "hide and seek" with us.
Where are you now?
"Go to Galilee" you said, and we went.
You met with us
and then disappeared into thin air.
What next, Lord?
Where will you meet us next?
You keep challenging, pushing, surprising us.
So, in our confusion and isolation
we are now gathered in a rented room,
praying, studying, singing, waiting...
You said something about
"being filled with the Holy Spirit" —
But we know you're going to do something BIG
"Jerusalem, Samaria,
and to the ends of the earth,"
you said.
Where's that?
We love our place here.
Please don't disturb us anymore...
What next, Lord?

No. 3 • June 1986

THE JOYS OF JUNE

June holds many joys for us. When I was a boy, it was "kick-off your-shoes-and-go-barefoot-all-summer-long-time" with the ending of school and promises of fun, fun, fun! Children today welcome June for the same reasons, although I suspect parents cringe at the thought of having Johnny home all day long! Nevertheless, it is a welcome change from the routine of school. It is camp-time, and another grand opportunity to enjoy the outdoors and experience the beauty and wonders of God's Nature.

June is graduation time. It is the magic season when boys turn into men and girls into women. With diplomas in hand, our children come home matured and seasoned, ready to step out and fend for themselves. Parents, still filled with apprehension however, wonder if they are really capable of doing that and very fearful that this cruel world will gobble up their darling children alive!

Wedding bells are heard often in June, it is a time for the coming together in marriage of lovers who have spent the winter months discovering, wondering thinking, praying, planning and hoping. At last the time is NOW, and two become one in this enchanted season.

Father's Day is June 15th. Let's not forget good old dad folks, and do something different this year than we've done before to express to him our love and devotion...maybe something different than a tie for a gift? How about two weeks in Acapulco... all expenses paid, of course.

What goes on in the church in June? We too share in these times of joy and celebration. It is confirmation time for our young people. Seven of them will be coming into the communion fellowship of the church as they affirm their baptismal vows and take their place of membership among us. What a time of joy for them and for us! We welcome them and receive them with gratitude and promise them all the love we can have in the grace of our Lord. June is a time for us to celebrate our being one big family. Our Church Family Campout is going to bring us together in a unique and joy-filled way as we gather in the mountains and share the love we have been given for each other in the grace of God. June is a time for us to recognize our church school teachers also. Thank you teachers for carrying on a task so very vital and yet recognized by so few of us. We tend to forget who you are because you are in your classes while we are at worship together. You are deprived of much, but God's rewards are many indeed. Nothing can take the place of knowing that you are channels for God's grace and Spirit as young lives hear and absorb what you share with them, about Christ and His love. God bless you indeed!

Yes, June is a blessed month. Thank God for the Seasons, thank God for the movement and for change in God's time, and thank God for giving us yet another time when we participate in the working of God's grace in and among us in fresh and beautiful ways.

No. 4 • July 1986

COME WONDER WITH ME

When preachers grab headlines, as it happened in Los Angeles this week by praying publicly on the steps of City Hall for the death of several justices of the U. S. Supreme Court, I wonder what's happening to us.

Rosalyn Carter shares the scary experience she had one day when a placard was waved in her face with the message "Jesus does not love you!" I wonder what's happened to the old favorite gospel song, "Give me the Old Time Religion... Makes me love everybody, makes me love everybody... and it's good enough for me." I suppose it is no longer good enough for the new fundamentalists.

How ironic that the key informer hired by the government to build a case against the churches giving sanctuary to South American refugees has a first name of "Jesus!" I wonder if he knows what that name means. I suppose he does and goes to church and even lights a candle or two from time to time... (His full name is Jesus Cruz).

How interesting that last week the pastor of Crystal Cathedral refused to allow the use of his church for a meeting to hear a black speaker form South Africa invited by the church's own denomination while meeting in this same church for their annual meeting. Now I don't find that to be too "positive," do you?

We're due for a word of good news to balance all of this depressing kind of stuff... Last week the Rev. Ben Weir was elected to be the Moderator of the Presbyterian Church (USA) during our General Assembly meeting in Minneapolis. He is our Presbyterian missionary in Beirut who was kidnapped and freed after 16 months of captivity. While in captivity, he created what he called a "Protestant rosary": a chain of 33 links binding him to a radiator and 120 slats on the window blinds — all reminding him constantly that he was surrounded by a "cloud of witnesses." A piece of reinforcing steel in the ceiling reminded him of God's eye, and two covers for electrical connections became a reminder of God's attentive ears to his cries. He prayed constantly, "Lord, when the time comes, I hope to have the soundness of mind to be with your people and share with them." Now, he is with us to share with 3 million of us and the whole world.

May the Ben Weirs among us increase and light the way for days of darkness filled with hatred, violence and chaos. Most especially in the land of South Africa where the faithful people of God are coming under increasing pressure and attack because they refuse to conform to the state and laws that are unjust and dehumanizing.

One last word… Opinions expressed in this article are not necessarily the point of view of others around here, although I sincerely hope I am convincing to all of us! You are free to discuss, debate and even argue with me the points raised herein. However, please do not stop loving me, I feel very insecure when unloved!

No. 5 • August 1986

THE YELLOW BALLOON

Driving down the Santa Ana Freeway, I was encountering the usual traffic… heavy! As it often happens, there was an object on the road. However, it posed no danger because it was a balloon. After having drifted away from its point of origin, it had floated down, for it was too heavy to keep on soaring. However, it was still light enough to bounce around the highway, driven here and there by every tuft of wind stirred up by the rushing traffic. As I drove by, I and other drivers hit it, but all that happened was that we gave it a new lift and for a second or two, it soared upwards again. I watched it all in my rear view mirror, and it kept prancing and dancing and floating and soaring, having a grand time of it! The harder it was hit, the higher it flew, and as far as I could see, no vehicle, including the big intimidating trucks succeeded in destroying it.

All day long, for some strange reason, I kept thinking about that bright yellow balloon. "Good for you!" I mused, "You found the secret of surviving by staying light. Soar with the Spirit! Let every hit, be it hard or light, push you not down and out but up and away. Learn how to use the blows of the adversary to your own advantage."

When Jesus said, "Don't be anxiety-ridden about your life," could He possibly have been speaking of this kind of attitude? I think maybe sparrows and balloons have much in common in teaching us about survival and celebration of life.

No. 6 • October 1986

"CANNED GODDS OF ALL KINDS"

A prayer request from a social services organization caught my eye the other day as I was reading their bulletin. "We need to gather goods... we need you to bring canned godds of all kinds," it pleaded. Of course, it should have read "goods" and not 'godds." It got me thinking: hence this article. What if we were to read it as "canned gods?" then I wondered, "How canned is my god?" well, let me try to define what a "canned god" is. It is the "god" who is made captive to our own desires, our own prejudices, our own perspectives and aspirations, personal, social or national. It is the "God who is not addressed until we have a need, then we go to the shelf, take "it" down, and open it for quick and convenient use. Can-openers are usually provided by the sellers of the cans. They are religious entrepreneurs who offer them free if you will only purchase their cans. They are experts in the field and probably have even written books such as "Can Your God Do It? Yes He Can!"

Candidly speaking (pun intended), such gods are not what we worship, or are supposed to worship. In the Bible, a "canned god" used to be known as a "tribal god." Tribes fashioned gods uniquely suited to reflect their beliefs, culture and aspirations. The worship of Jahweh was a giant leap above and beyond such parochialism. "Who are you?" Moses asked, seeking a definition of the God who revealed himself as being far beyond what Moses could define. "I Am Who I Am," was the answer. The God revealed in Scripture history and the person of Jesus Christ stands in judgement over all tribes and attempts to fashion him to conform to our own images. A god made captive is no God at all! The God worth worshipping is the God of all ages, all time, all creation: The God free to act and to move, who challenges, disturbs, moves… In such action we are moved along to be what we could never be in our wildest imagination. This is the God who took a handful of common people and with them changed the world. This is the God who takes a Cross and thereby draws all humankind unto Himself. This is the God who calls us to discipleship today.

Some churches are always building bigger and more beautiful cans into which they seek to squeeze their gods. With the passage of time, such cans turn into mausoleums… silent witnesses to passing fads and elaborate fancies. What about Christ Presbyterian Church? What kind of "God" do we serve?

No. 7 • November 1986

ONE HUNDRED AND TEN PERCENT

What does it mean to give "one hundred and ten percent?" It really does not make sense, for one hundred percent is all, it is a total life. Can one give more of oneself than that for any cause? Well, obviously one can, for I have heard of the great extra effort that athletes, for example, put into their contribution called just that. Evidently, to win, it is expected of players to do the impossible. And they do it!

Last week we all were thrilled to read about a mother paralyzed and confined to her wheelchair getting into the swimming pool and rescuing her little girl who had fallen in. "I don't know how I did it," she said when interviewed. "I didn't know I had it in me…"

Presbyterians across the United States don't give one hundred percent. They don't even give ten percent. They give, on an average, two percent! Asking us to raise that to five percent of our gross income is the request and the challenge. Cries of protest and amazement are heard all over because we think it is asking too much.

Are we going to win the contest of life? Is our witness in the world going to gain credibility? When people seek for God's touch of love, are we going to be there to demonstrate what that can mean by the caring that we share? Can we do all that with two percent? I don't think so!

On November 16th, we are going to be asked to make our annual commitment to Christ's church and mission via our financial pledge. With what kind of spirit are we going to make our decision? Jesus said, "Where your treasure is, there will your heart be also!" If football players can do it, if mothers with babies can do it, if soldiers on the front line, if runners on the track can do it, I think, and I know we can do it also for Christ and the church!

No. 8 • January 1987

ALL THINGS NEW

With the coming of the New Year, our minds and hearts turn to the future. We look back with nostalgia on the past, of course, but we look ahead with keen anticipation, wondering what the New Year will bring. New experiences, new people, new places, new relationships. That which we have not yet experienced maintains a sense of wonder and excitement for us.

We all hope and pray all of these new things waiting for us will be positive and will help bring us to a fuller and more love–filled life. We say "Goodbye" to the old and "ring in the new." We want to leave behind us the tears and the pain of yesterdays' traumas. We reach forward with faith, believing that much better things are ahead for us.

It is good and right that we feel this way about the future. No, it is not just wishful thinking. We are not dreaming when we believe our tomorrows will be filled with more love, joy and peace. Our belief is based in the God who also anticipates bright tomorrows. In the book of Revelation, it talks of God of the new. "A new heaven and a new earth" where there will be no longer pain and sorrow and death. The author climaxes his statement with a quotation from God, "BEHOLD, I MAKE ALL THINGS NEW!" (Revelations 21)

How strange it is that people who claim deep faith in God often seem to point to the past where God's greatest deeds are held in the concrete of history. The Bible always points to the future as the arena of God's mighty and coming action in the climactic acts of all history. Traditions centered in the past, without an open heart and mind for what God will yet do, act as balls and chains restricting faith and action. Faith, which anticipates new things which we have not even begun to dream of, helps us sprout wings, and we soar into the thrilling and wonderful future. Revelation, says, "Write this, these words are trustworthy and true!"

CHAPTER VIII

FIRST PRESBYTERIAN CHURCH
GARDEN GROVE, CA, 1996-1998

No. 1 • December 1995

A MODERN JOURNEY TO BETHLEHEM

Samira and I had the rare privilege and joy of journeying to Bethlehem last summer. It was not an easy trip. We were warned not to go because we were driving a rental car with Israeli license plates and were likely to be stoned if we attempted the journey.

After weighing the pros and cons, we decided to go anyway with some alteration of plans. We contacted an acquaintance who was the principal of Bethlehem Bible Institute, and he recommended that we go to the school, park our car there and then go by taxi to the Church of the Nativity. Thus we would not run the risk of having our car stoned or burned while parked in Manger Square.

Upon arrival at the Institute, we were most pleasantly surprised by two events there. First, three Muslim young men came in for their weekly Bible study in their quest to understand the Gospel of Christ. And then a group of American Jewish Christians arrived to visit the school. Principal Bishara Awad, a Palestinian Christian, welcomed them all and after a time of sharing thoughts about our faith, we all settled down for a delicious Middle Eastern lunch. I marveled as I pondered the miracle of Moslem, Christian and Jew sitting down together brought there by the Christ of Bethlehem!

We were then driven to Manger Square across from the Church of the Nativity and dropped off for our visit. The church was empty and we were the only visitors there. That was most strange for usually it is crowded with tourists. We soon found out why. Being Friday noon, the mosque situated next to the church was full of men for their noon prayers. Within minutes they came pouring out, agitated and ready for a confrontation with the Israeli soldiers patrolling the area. After shouting their slogans and demanding their rights, bottles began to fly toward the soldiers who retaliated with gun fire. We ducked into a souvenir shop and waited for the demonstrations to end. After an hour, the square emptied and quieted down, with crowds and soldiers withdrawing to their respective places, and business returned to normal. Tourist buses began to arrive and, most amazing of all, so did a black limousine. A couple soon to be married stepped out — the bride in her beautiful wedding gown and the groom in his tuxedo. They went into the church to be married, followed by a retinue of family and friends. As we gasped in amazement at the turn of events, I said to Samira, "Welcome to the Middle East!"

I then remembered that this is how it was two thousand years ago when travelers called Magi looking for Bethlehem were warned of the dangers awaiting them. I remembered Mary and her baby and the massacre of the innocents that followed His birth. Despite all of that, Bethlehem became the center of God's action in the birth of the Son and the revelation of God's love incarnate. So it is that Bethlehem continues today to be a place of divine action in the midst of continuing human tragedy. So it is also in our own inner Bethlehems where Christ continues to seek a place to be born while sin and sorrow, pain and conflict rage within our souls!

Be of good cheer, Christ is born in Bethlehem, be it in Palestine or Garden Grove! Don't' ever hesitate to journey to Bethlehem! You'll have to duck a bottle or two, or you'll have to take a few detours, but ultimately you will stand awe-struck in reverential silence as you contemplate and pray at the holy spot where Mary laid her baby.

No. 2 • March 1996

LENT: A TIME FOR REFLECTION

In recent years Protestant churches have begun to focus on Lent as being very significant times for us to reflect on who we are and the meaning of Christ's suffering, death and resurrection for us. It did not used to be that way, for Lent used to be emphasized by Catholic, Orthodox and Anglican churches only.

When I was a boy, we actually took pride in not observing Lent, and would even make fun of those of the Orthodox faith who did!

"And what are you giving up for Lent?" we would ask teasing.

"We don't have to give up anything, you know," we would quickly add, "Because we are Protestants!"

I am glad that false spiritual pride is giving way to more humility these days. We too need to reflect on our life in the light of Christ's death for us, and in times of prayer to renew our commitments. Lent is an excellent time for doing that.

The danger is to think that by doing something, like giving up a cherished dessert, we gain favor with God. Maybe it was because of that kind of mechanical way of keeping Lent that Protestantism reacted negatively. We are not trying to pile up good credit with God by our "good works." We have been redeemed by God's grace (undeserved love). However, we are called to pray and reflect upon our life and to seek the guidance of the Holy Spirit in our daily lives. What better time that Lent to do that.

Lent is forty weekdays before Easter. What can we do that would be helpful to us in strengthening our spiritual lives, and preparing us for the grand celebration announcing again that "Christ is risen from dead! He is risen indeed!" For the apostle Paul it was the desire "to know Him (Christ) and the power of His resurrection and to share his sufferings, becoming like Him in His death, that if possible I may attain the resurrection from the dead." (Philippians 3:10,11)

Suffering with Christ means taking on the pain and burden of reaching out in love and touching the lives of those in need. In the process, we give up our cherished comforts and make ourselves vulnerable to feeling in our hearts the pain of others. This is what Jesus meant when he said, "Take up your cross and follow me."

Here are some suggestions: Join one of our Koinonia study groups and seek to grow in your experiencing of the work of the Holy Spirit in your life; go to our Library and check out a devotional book, such as book on prayers and read it during Lent; read and pray at least one full Psalm every day, with special time spent on the 22nd and 51st Psalms; talk to a Deacon or Mission Commission member and offer your help in some kind of human help and support ministry; spend 15 minutes in prayer daily or more if you think that is too short. Above all, do it with Joy!

No. 3 • April 1996

"HE RESTORES MY SOUL"

This statement made by the Psalmist in the 23rd Psalm is one of an amazing affirmation of faith in God and celebration of the impact God's loving care has had in his life. He has faced time of want, wilderness places, raging waters, inner conflicts, lost paths, deadly perils, and vengeful enemies. All these negatives have turned to positives in the soul-restoring presence and guidance of the Shepherd Lord. The God who restores our souls leads us into a new year and soon into a new millennium. Are we going to go through these new times with old grudges, old wounds, old attitudes, prejudices, old perspectives on our life together? I have not seen it myself, but I am told that there is a message on a wall in the psychiatric wing at St. Joseph's Hospital in Orange. It asks: "DO YOU WANT TO GET WELL, OR DO YOU WANT TO GET EVEN?" For the souls that have been restored, deserts begin to look like green pastures and enemies become guests at our table!

Recently, we all gathered around the communion table at the conclusion of our worship service and participated in what I considered a spiritually soul-restoring act of commitment to our Shepherd-Lord. I shared with you a prayer that has come to me during my daily walks around Peter's Reservoir and Park. These series of affirmations came to me in a time when I was going through soul struggles and needed restoration. Thinking that you may wish to have a copy of it, since we all prayed it together, I share it with you:

PRAYERS FOR MY DAILY WALK

KYRIE ELEYSON
    Lord have mercy

Thank you Lord for your mercy
Thank you Lord for your love

Thank you Lord for your presence
Thank you Lord for your grace

Thank you Lord for your person
Thank you Lord for yourself

Thank you Lord for the journey
Thank you Lord for the paths

Thank you Lord for the struggles
Thank you Lord for the sighs

Thank you Lord for the laughter
Thank you Lord for the smiles

Thank you Lord for the mornings
Thank you Lord for the light

Thank you Lord for the evenings
Thank you Lord for the night

Thank you Lord for the vision
Thank you Lord for my sight

Thank you Lord for the silence
Thank you Lord for the calm

Thank you Lord for the beauty
Thank you Lord for your balm

Thank you Lord for your guidance
Lead me on through all my days

No. 4 • Easter 1996

CELEBRATE EASTER

I greet you, in anticipation of the celebration of our Lord's resurrection, with the ancient Eastern greeting, which is a responsive one between pastor and people:

"The Lord is risen" — Pastor
"He is risen indeed!" — People

I ask, why is He risen indeed? What prompts me or you to make such a forceful statement, or declaration of faith? For me, the answer is found in the statement Paul makes about <u>his</u> faith in Corinthians 15 where he mentions 500 people who experienced personally the risen Lord, and then he says in verse 8: "Last of all, as to one untimely born, He appeared also to me."

The genius of the Gospel of Christ is that the presence and influence of Christ is personally communicated to every believer, going far beyond an intellectual assent to the declaration of faith. It results from one's own commitment to Christ and invitation to Christ to "come into my heart, Lord Jesus" as we were taught when little. Through the power of the Spirit who responds to our prayer, Christ does indeed come to us and appears to us. Sometimes Christ meets us or confronts us unexpectedly. This may happen in crisis situations or times of quiet reflection. The mode or the form that appearance takes is not important, but the fact of His indwelling within and among us is. Anything short of this is, as Paul says, "holding to the outward form of godliness but denying its power." (2 Timothy 3:5)

Let us all this Easter time celebrate the true meaning of Easter. Let's go far beyond bunnies and butterflies and proclaim: "Death is swallowed up in victory... thanks be unto God who gives us the victory through our Lord Jesus Christ."

VARTKES M. KASSOUNI

No. 5 • May 1996

PENTECOST FOR PRESBYTERIANS

Pentecost is for Presbyterians as well as for Pentecostals, Baptists, Catholics or Methodists. It is an event just as central to the celebration of our faith as the faith of any other church. We claim Pentecost and celebrate it on May 26th. This may sound somewhat strange because Presbyterians are not known for their exuberance, or experience centered worships and actually have the reputation of being quite the opposite. That stereotype is hopefully changing, and we in Garden Grove First Presbyterian Church should welcome such change as well. God's people in Scripture times, both in the Old Testament and in the New, were openly and totally dependent on God's Spirit for their experience and their expression of the faith. They celebrated with joy and participated with gladness. They were not mere observers but were involved with body, mind, spirit and heart.

"The promise is to you and to your children," Peter declared on the Day of Pentecost as recorded in Acts 2. They were experiencing what the prophet Joel has said, "I will pour out my Spirit upon all flesh and your sons and your daughters shall prophesy, and your young men shall see visions, and your old men shall dream dreams." A church on fire for God is a vision and is a dream that we must all seek. And when God gives the vision, pray that we will not draw back in fear or timidity but let God accomplish among us God's new and great purposes.

308

No. 6 • June 1996

CLAIM THE FUTURE

Times of uncertainty test our faith. We are again coming into a period in our church life when the future is uncertain, but our hopes run high. Times like this can unsettle us, make us nervous and edgy, or they can be invitations to "test and see that the Lord is good!" We are again like the children of Israel anticipating our entry into the promised land but somehow feeling we are stuck in the desert. The desert can be a great place for self-discovery and adventure, or it can be a place where we feel trapped and die! What makes the difference? It is FAITH!

God has so ordered our life that our trust is the basic element of life that we must sustain to make it through times of joy and times of sorrow. The future is never revealed ahead of time, only the promise that God will sustain and guide us. Recently, I came across a quotation from Frederick Buechner, a highly respected Presbyterian minister and author, on this subject which I'd like to share with you:

"Faith is different from theology because theology is reasoned, systematic, orderly, whereas faith is disorderly, intermittent, and full of surprises. Faith is different from mysticism because mystics in their ecstasy become one with what faith can at most see only from afar. Faith is different from ethics because ethics is primarily concerned not, like faith, with our relationship to God but with our relationship to each other. Faith is homesickness. Faith is a lump in the throat. Faith is less a position on than a movement toward, less a sure thing than a hunch. Faith is waiting. Faith is journeying through space and through time."

Sam Keen (In Apology for Wonder) said it in a different and dramatic way: "Faith is a wild dove and not a tame pigeon!" may the "wild" flights of the Dove, the Holy Spirit, carry us into our great tomorrows!

No. 7 • July 1996

FAITH, FREEDOM AND FANFARE

On July 4th we will celebrate Independence Day. For us in America that is the most significant and precious day in our national calendar. Our Presbyterian forefathers had a big hand in the struggle for freedom in the War of Independence. Even clergy took part, some by providing the churches' hymn books to provide scarce paper as wadding for the guns. Others took up arms and joined the rag-tag army opposing the colonial rulers. Nine of the signers of the Declaration of Independence were Presbyterians and John Witherspoon was the only clergy who signed it. He was Presbyterian also. In the British Parliament some named the war "That Presbyterian rebellion!"

The struggle for freedom is never-ending. We stand firm in our resolve to maintain a society that seeks "liberty and justice for all." Why do Presbyterians get involved in social issues? People ask. The answer lies in our understanding of how faith in God translates to concern for our fellow human beings. John Calvin was deeply involved in the civil affairs of Geneva, even to the point of being thrown out of town because people got really mad at him!

Today, we have the Montana Freemen and all other kinds of forces and voices declaring their suspicion of our government and seeking to replace it with their version or model of authority. And what may that be? Paul cautioned his readers. "Do not submit again to a yoke of bondage." (Galatians 1:1) David Koresh (in Waco Texas) in the name of freedom, had his colony enslaved in his compound! Religion often acts with equal tyranny as civil forces in the very name of liberty and freedom they proclaim.

Let us look beyond fanfare, sloganeering, beer and brass bands this year, and with careful contemplation, prayers and commitment seek God's guidance in doing our humble part for the maintaining and growing of a free America.

No. 8 • August 1996

GOD'S CREATIONS

Summer is here! Children are home from school and clamoring to go to the beach or running through the house chasing each other, and you wish it were September already.

Summertime for the church means low attendance, drop in financial support and the absence of many leaders who are off to their cabins, vacations or visiting family members. We too wish it were September and church activities could go into high gear again. Or, maybe we wish it would be summertime all the time and keep thinks in low gear and low stress for all of us.

Summertime is recreation time. That spells v-a-c-a-t-i-o-n-s. However, with God's grace it could be and should be re-creation time, a time to get renewed in body and spirit. A time to be revitalized, for is that not the reason we have the cycles in nature?

In the song, "Morning Has Broken" there is a line I like very much. It's in the third stanza: "Mine is the sunlight! Mine is the morning born of the one light Eden saw play! Praise with elation, praise every morning, God's re-creation of the new day!"

Every morning introduces God's new creation for us. We are in Eden again, and the Light of God is breaking on us. The blazing summer sun is for us the symbol of the power and life-giving source of divine love. May we be re-recreated by God and God's Son to continue lives of praise to live the words, "Praise for the singing! Praise for the morning! Praise for them, springing fresh from the Word!"

No. 9 • November 1996

A TIME TO GIVE THANKS

Thanksgiving is a national holiday. However, for us, this is not a tradition, or a holiday, but a way of life centered in our commitment to God as sovereign, redeemer and sustainer of our life, individually and collectively as a church. The call, "O Give Thanks to the Lord!" is repeatedly made in Scripture history. It is the dominant theme in the Psalms. The Old Testament contains the history of God's people whose response to God's acts of salvation was thanksgiving.

In Jesus Christ, God's continuing actions on behalf of universal humanity have expanded the implications of the Old Testament to include the whole world. "He holds the whole world in His hands!" as the much-loved African-American spiritual declares. The essential response of faith to God's saving and sustaining love is thankfulness. It is not ability to articulate doctrinal concepts concerning our relationship with God in Christ, but a simple yet profound attitude of being thankful and saying so to God in prayer.

Our worship experiences are founded in thanksgiving and praise as the foundational element on which everything else we do is based. That is why, when we come together, we begin by singing hymns of praise and lifting up to God prayers of praise. To do otherwise is to fail to acknowledge God's saving and sovereign grace and love, and to replace God with our own selves as central to the meaning of our life together.

It is good, however, to take special times and focus on thanksgiving in concert with all peoples, Christian or not, and share our thankfulness. I am puzzled, however, who is to be thanked if it is not God as the ultimate source of all life and creation? "Be thankful" is fine but not fine enough! Be thankful to God and, because of God, to each other for reflecting to us God's goodness. We reach out with caring concern to others because we have first received it from God. Scripture says, "We love because God first loved us." That's it!

No. 10 • Christmas 1996

"WHERE IS HE WHO HAS BEEN BORN?"

The question was asked by the Wise Men (Magi) who came from the East seeking the Christ child. We must ask it again if we are to be saved from the arrogance of tradition which assumes we know where to locate Christ, and go right to the spot without any hesitation. It is by divine design not that easy, made so to prevent us from lapsing into the idolatry of locating Christ in our own self-made shrines and placed in the middle of a world in which we are usually in control. There is in us a need similar to that of King Herod who felt that his position was threatened by the news of Jesus' birth. When Jesus comes into our lives, He displaces the old, moves aside thrones set to preserve ourselves and forces us into situations and relationships that we would ordinarily reject.

God's self-revelation comes on God's terms and in places determined by God's will. It is the challenge placed on our faith to seek Him again and to locate the manger. Having found it, do we have the depth of love to accept Him and serve Him on his terms? That's the challenge of Christmas 1996.

No. 11 • January 1996

HERE COMES THE NEW YEAR

The word "new" is not a stranger to the Bible. For me, this has always been a fact that I have noted with joy. This observation has been a source of inspiration for my ministry: God-driven events recorded in Scripture history have been the means whereby God has allowed and even directed the passing away of the old and the introduction of the new. Our God is not static but dynamic!

From Genesis (creation of the heavens and the earth), to Revelation (creation of a new heaven and a new earth), we have event after event recorded in which God's renewing and liberating hand is at work. So, taking the past as prologue for what is yet to be, we anticipate the future to be the arena of God's continuing creative and re-creative work in us, among us and beyond us. This is the affirmation of faith!

Let us then welcome the New Year with joy and with keen anticipation. For our church the New Year is certainly going to usher in a new era through the leadership of a new pastor. Let us remember, however, that people are merely the instruments of God, and our anticipation should be centered in God's actions primarily. Don't' fall into the trap of thinking a pastor will do it all for us. We must present ourselves as people who have captured a new vision and with new enthusiasm make ourselves available to the new pastor to lead this church onto new things, which God only can reveal and make possible.

Claim Philippians 4:13 for 1997: "I can do all things in Him who strengthens me." If a boxer named Holyfield can beat a champion called Tyson and claim that verse as his motto, as he did, we surely can do it too!

No. 12 • Easter 1997

CHRIST IS RISEN!
HE IS RISEN INDEED!

There is a famous church in Jerusalem. It is called by Eastern Christians. "Church of the Resurrection." In the West it is known as "Church of the Holy Sepulcher." I think the Easterners' version says it as it should be for it is the location of the empty tomb of Jesus. The angel said it to Mary on that glorious day, "He is not here, He is risen!" The name "Holy Sepulcher" does not contain an affirmation that there is nobody in the tomb. It is empty. Hence, "The Church of the Resurrection!"

Scholars and others argue about that empty tomb. What happened? Was the body moved secretly? Was it stolen? Was the body not really dead and was it revived in the coolness of the tomb? Was this resurrection story a fraud or creative imagination on the part of the disciples? We could go on and on trying to explain the phenomenon and, in doing so, explain it away.

Christianity without the risen Christ is no Christianity at all but a weak and powerless reflection thereof. In 1 Corinthians 15, the apostle Paul says that over 500 people experienced the risen Lord, including many who were still living at the time of the writing of his letter. It is the cornerstone of our faith to affirm that Christ rose again from the dead. He says in 15:20 "In fact Christ has been raised from the dead, the first fruits of those who have fallen asleep, for as by man (Adam) came death, by man (Christ) has come also the resurrection of the dead."

We, like Mary, come to the garden tomb seeking to anoint His memory with devotion, but instead of finding a closed and sealed sepulcher, we find it empty. An empty tomb, in and of itself, is no proof of the resurrection of

316

Christ. It is only when we also have a voice address us, as it did Mary, we turn and encounter the living Lord, that we find ourselves in His presence! Ultimately, it is that experience which is the proof. Christ meets us, Christ calls us, Christ names us, Christ regenerates us! For, "As in Adam all die, even so in Christ shall all be made alive." Allelujah!

No. 13 • April 1997

CHURCH OR RESTAURANT?

The year was 1959. I was thrilled to receive my first call to be the pastor of a church in New York City. I was sharing the good news with all sorts of people among whom was a highly successful businessman. He was a rich philanthropist but unfortunately a weak churchman.

"Let me give you some advice," he said. "The church is like a restaurant and you are the chef. Cook well and have it served attractively and people will come to your church. Otherwise your church will suffer and fail!"

His philosophy reflected concepts which were very popular then and are still most popular today! Nevertheless, I did not agree with it then, and I don't agree with it today! This approach to church development encourages pastors to be prima donnas and congregations to be consumers who come, pay their fee (called offering) and sit back to be entertained, which was this businessman's extent of church involvement. This approach fills the church one day and empties it the next when the "customers" discover a new restaurant with enticing new menus.

The church that is faithful to its Lord is made up of people who claim ownership and invest their lives in it. The pastor may be the chef, but the members are involved in the cooking, serving, dish washing, cleaning and running of the establishment. It is more like a home with mom and dad and everyone accepting their role as members of the family and accepting whatever they are able to put on the table for food, according to the best of their abilities.

I grew up in a home like that. I often wished I could eat at our rich neighbors' table because they had such delicious food, but my mom would say, "Son, you eat what we can provide. It is simple but good and nourishing food. You are our son and this is your home. You take what we can afford to serve!" I learned that lesson early in life, and it has served me well all my life. My mon's food was healthy food and you know what else? It was a home filled with love which attracted other kids, including those of our neighbors. A church should be like that!

CHAPTER IX

GENEVA PRESBYTERIAN CHURCH
LAGUNA HILLS, CA, 2000-2002

No. 1 • January 2000

STEPPING INTO THE UNKNOWN

My brother tells the story of sponsoring a new immigrant family to this country which included a mother and several children. The father had been executed some months before by the authorities in their country of origin. The family included a little girl scared, confused, lonely and afraid. She kept clinging to her mother, asking over and over again, "Mommy, what's going to happen to us?" Stepping into the unknown was a terrifying experience for her.

I remember standing on the deck of the ocean liner bringing me to America when the skyline of New Your City began to come into view. Along with hundreds of other immigrants I strained my neck to catch that first exciting glimpse of the Statue of Liberty. The cheer that went up when we did see it cannot be matched by the roar at a football game following a touchdown! Stepping into the unknown was an exhilarating experience for me.

We are stepping into the unknown: A new millennium? Y2K? A new pastor, and for me a new congregation? Our jobs? Our health? Our relationships? The list could go on and on. It's how we face the unknown that makes the difference between panic or peace. When the unknown is faced with faith, the result is joy and peace. When the unknown is faced with fear, the result is panic.

Which will it be for us in the year 2000? Fear or Faith? May our trust in God, centered in the person of Jesus Christ, make the difference, for "perfect love casts out fear."

No. 2 • March 2000

LIVING STONES

When Jesus responded to Simon Peter's confession that Jesus was "the Messiah, the Son of the living God," Jesus called him "a rock" and said, "On this rock I will build my church" (Matthew 16). It is quite fascinating to me that years later, writing to believers throughout Asia Minor, Peter calls them to be "living stones," allowing themselves to be built into "a spiritual house," the living Temple of God (1 Peter 2)

What makes the difference between a dead stone and a living stone? Stones are lifeless in and of themselves but are made useful at the hands of the mason. They are completely passive. This is not what God requires of us!

Spirit-activated stones are people whose wills have come under the captivating love and vision of God, who joyfully commit themselves to join other "living stones," and together allow the Divine Architect to build that most exciting of structures called the living Temple of God. That is what we are again being reminded that Geneva Church is all about! God does not want lifeless rock with which to work.

We are people made alive in Christ, having our own minds, or own wills, our own personalities very much in place. Peter, "a rock," is calling on us, "living rocks," to come together, to allow the Master to shape us, to form us and to place us within God's grand scheme. I can think of no other enterprise worthy of such devotion and commitment on our part. Can you?

No. 3 • April 2000

CELEBRATING THE RISEN LORD

On Christmas Day, I shared with you how the churches of the Middle East proclaim the birth of our Lord with the greeting: "Christ is born and revealed. Great news to us all!"

On Easter Day the greeting is: "Christ is risen from the dead, Blessed is the resurrection of our Lord!" I greet you with this ancient proclamation and share with you the joy of celebrating our Lord's resurrection. The central tenet of our faith is belief in the risen Lord. Paul says in First Corinthians 15:17 "If Christ has not been raised, your faith is futile…" the corollary to this is our own life after death, for our hope flows from our belief in and experience of the living Lord. " (1 Corinthians 15:19)

Skeptics and unbelievers have always ridiculed this tenet of our faith, Paul himself encountered the skeptics on Mars Hill, next to the Parthenon in Athens, who were very happy to hear him talk about "the unknown god," but as soon as he mentioned the resurrection of Christ , they mocked him and left. Scholars tell us that since ancient Athens was the center of all kinds of philosophy and of "scientific inquiry" Paul failed in establishing a church there. Hence we have no "Letter of Paul to the Athenians!"

It is not logic that proves Christ's resurrection but faith responding with joy to the evidence of history. Christ still has a way of coming to the doubting Thomases of our day and saying, "Put your finger here and see my hands, and place it in my side, do not be faithless, but believing" (John 20:27, 28) I pray that our response will be the same as that of Thomas: "My Lord, and my God!"

No. 4 • July 2000

BUILDING THE INVISIBLE CHURCH

Yesterday I was privileged to place a stone in the <u>invisible</u> Church of Jesus Christ! It exists in an office building I have passed by hundreds of times on the way to my home in Orange without knowing its existence. Yesterday, I also was privileged to place a stone in the <u>visible</u> Church of Jesus Christ when I met with our Building Construction Team and discussed the progress of Geneva's plans in that regard. Both churches are absolutely necessary, and the mission of the visible church is to build hundreds of invisible churches all over the map. Without that mission, its God-given purpose for its existence is denied, compromised or rejected.

Let me give you some insight into what I mean. Yesterday I was invited by a young man, who has attended our Saturday night service, to meet with a group of men at his place of work where once a week they meet for prayer and Biblical reflection. I had never met them before, but after I left that room I knew I had been in church with Christ where "two or three had gathered in His name." We shared our common experiences and insights from the Word, and then prayed for each other. In the course of this experience I was greatly edified and encouraged to carry on my ministry, and I know they were also. It then occurred to me that there are scores of these small gatherings taking place within the context of our congregation also, whether they be organized "Christ Care" groups or spontaneously gathered ones. This is Christ's invisible church! The visible church exists to nurture God's people in the invisible churches whose existence is in homes, offices, restaurants, hotels, living rooms and basements and a thousand other locations known only to God!

Get active in the invisible Church! Be a part of this dynamic force unleashed by God's Spirit to bring life to us and to the world we live in.

No. 5 • October 2000

HYPHENATED CHRISTIANS

Most of us are familiar with the term "Hyphenated American." The practice of attaching the name of one's country of origin to the term "American" used to be looked down upon as being quite "Un-American" (which is itself a hyphenated term!). Today, however, it is accepted and people are proud to share their national roots while they affirm their being American. i.e. African-American, Italian-American, Irish-American, etc.

Perhaps you've heard me say, "There should be no hyphenated Christians (such as Presbyterian-Christians, Baptist-Christians, Independent-Christians, etc.), only Christians," Well, I've been doing some thinking about this and hereby share some thoughts on the subject. It seems to me that this kind of emphasis continues the issue faced by the Apostle Paul in Corinthians, where he encountered believers who said, "I belong to Peter, or I belong to Apollos, or I belong to Paul." Some said, with apparent pride, "I belong to Christ!" Were they more Christ-centered than the others? I don't think so.

I still say there should be no hyphenated Christians, but I do also say that all Christians, or believers, have come to a point of faith within the context of a tradition, heritage, or school of interpretation of Christianity, be it Presbyterian, Baptist, Catholic or Independent. For example, churches that say, "We are non-denominational," are denominational anyway! An "independent" church is a denomination of one, just like a dollar bill is a denomination of one and a hundred dollar bill is a denomination of one hundred. Within that denomination of one, there exists a system of government and a heritage of belief, just like in all others.

We do not encounter Christ in solitary confinement. We do so in some community of faith, or ministry established by some community of faith located somewhere. Study and acknowledge the identity of the source from where you are getting your teaching about Christian faith. In our church it is clear: The Reformed tradition with a time-tested and proven belief system centered solidly in the person of Christ. With all kinds of churches and para-churches cropping up which claim "We are just Christian," there is a tendency to consider them more authentic and more Christ-centered. Beware!

Whether intentionally or naively so, somebody's approach or tradition is being propagated, whether acknowledged to be so or not. Stand firm in your faith and within the community of Geneva. As the saying goes, "Grow where you are planted."

No. 6 • November 2000

AND THE WORD BECAME FLESH

While it is still fresh in my mind and heart, let me share with you what I shared with the CBS (Community Bible Study) women's group this morning: **"The Word became flesh and dwelt among us full of grace and truth."** John 1:14

The objective of Bible study is not Bible knowledge but the Word becoming so internalized and connected to our own lives that we become bearers of the body, the person of Christ. Anything short of that, the word turns into words, words, words!

We have too much of "words" among us throughout our church communities, and not enough of the Word incarnated in and through us. The early church got caught in that trap of arguing theology, doctrine, practices, observance, beliefs, convictions and thinking that by so doing they were demonstrating faithfulness to God. Paul warns his readers not to become enmeshed in worthless arguments about philosophy, beliefs and practices, which are used as litmus tests for true piety.

Someone has said that the church is a "community of touching." Talking is not touching, touching with hand and heart is! God spoke, but the Bible is merely the record of that while Jesus Christ is the person of God, the Word alive, touching us by taking on our humanity and loving us to the point of death. Christ continues to be "enfleshed" in and through His disciples today, otherwise He is inaccessible and unknowable. The Holy Spirit acts through people, filled with the Spirit, who transmit the presence and the person of Christ. Have you touched someone lately?

No. 7 • February 2001

WALKING FORWARD, LOOKING BACKWARD

There were many fascinating scenes in the Rose Parade this year, as in every year. One scene that meant something special to us at Geneva was to see our own Jean Brokaw riding with her son Tom, the Grand Marshall, and family in the vintage car leading the parade! Jean, you looked great!

One scene that fascinated me was seeing a drum majorette leading her band walking straight ahead but doing so walking backwards, with her gaze fixed on her band. "Now, that's quite interesting," I thought to myself. "Why does she do it, and how does she do it without losing her balance and walking crooked? In thinking about it, I began to reflect on my ministry at Geneva and to see similarities between what she was doing and what I often do as a pastor. Looking backward is necessary to make sure we have not lost sight of the congregation in our desire to move forward with vision!

We look back to make sure we are "face to face," understand and know each other. We look back to know our history, appreciate our heritage and then move forward together. Looking back does not mean moving backward, for that would spell disaster and death.

In Geneva, we are at the opening of the New Year. Doors of new opportunity and challenge are opening before us. Revelation 3:8 says it: "Behold, I have set before you an open door." The door is in front of us, not behind us! I call on you, the congregation, to follow our leadership. Be fully assured that I am focused on you, your needs, your performance as the people of God. You are the band and I do not wish to lose sight of you! You make the music, you excite the crowds! However, you cannot do it without the discipline, the dedication, the love it takes to be in this band.

No. 8 • April 2001

TO LIVE AGAIN
(EASTER)

Job asked, "If a man die, shall he live again?" He asked this out of the pain and suffering he was enduring waiting for the end to come. Feeling utterly alone and abandoned by God and man he sat on the ash-heap of his days searching for some sign of meaning, purpose, and support from his God.

Paul said, "I die daily…" referring to the struggles of soul and body he encountered in the midst of his passion to carry on for Christ. God said to Adam and Eve, "The day you eat of it (the forbidden tree) you will die."

So, there are a variety of kinds of death which we experience: Death of conscience, death of relationships, death from persecution and tribulations and ultimately and finally death of the body.

However, the celebration of Easter is the declaration of triumph of life over death! "As in Adam all die, even so in Christ shall all be made alive!" (1 Corinthians 15:22) This is our message and our faith. Christ, the second Adam brings us back to Eden, back to Paradise, back to a life of relationship and joyful reconciliation with our God. "Today you shall be with me in paradise" is the word he speaks to each one of us who prays, "Remember me Lord…"

What kind of death are you facing? What are the demons that are attacking you? Are you in the darkness of your soul entering a tomb of aloneness and despair? Take heart! The risen Lord stands by you calling your name as he called out to Mary on resurrection morning. Turn and grasp your Lord with the cry, "My Lord and my God!" Christ is risen! He is risen indeed!

No. 9 • July 2001

MOVING INTO THE FUTURE

All of us who comprise the Geneva church family have been involved for several months in an extremely important task of analyzing our present and discerning our future. We have prayed for God's guidance and now are at the threshold of moving into our future with a God-given plan and vision. Paul said, "I press on toward the goal for the prize of the mark of the upward call of God in Christ Jesus." (Philippians 3:14) We do no less as a body of people called into being as the church of Jesus Christ.

Frances Bryson, our Church Historian, has written for us an excellent article of thoughts and comments about our 35 years of history (we are actually in our 36th year of life together), on the occasion of our Chapel Dedication and Celebration. In it, she comments about the vision of the founders (who were all from Leisure World) and yet they were determined to have a Sunday school to bring in young families and children. Geneva was the first church in this area to have a Sunday school! The founders' vision was "to build a church for the Present and the Future." This vision of our founders should fire us up again to claim the future, which is going to be different from that of the last 35 years of our life together. We believe, we have held together, given generously, built imaginatively and prayed vigorously. We can do it because God is with us.

Changes called for and necessary to realize our vision demand from us continuing unity and sacrifice. Do it for the sake of many who are not here yet, but will come if we remain faithful to the call. Let God give us the spirit of our pioneers again!

No. 10 • August 2001

WHAT IF?

Yesterday, five darling children were laid to rest in a cemetery in Houston, Texas. A disturbed mother had drowned them all in the family bathtub! I am sure you know the story and have gasped, along with everybody else, over this ghastly and utterly terrible tragedy.

Everybody has been asking, "Why did it happen? What went wrong in the life of this family? Could it have been averted?" Many reasons have been advanced, including that of post-partum stress, overwork with no time for herself, total devotion to parents and family (father had Alzheimer's and she spent much time devoted to him), total exhaustion and a sense of being trapped, etc.

They were a religious family, with prayers at home, and even at T-Ball games that her husband coached. He was a member of Fellowship of Christian Athletes, an Evangelical organization well known throughout the United States. Something very significant caught my attention, however, when I read that the pastor of the church where the funeral service was held said, "You have never seen the children in church. I really don't know this family." In other words it seems they had a very private kind of faith, with no connection whatsoever to a community of faith. Now that, too, is tragic indeed!

What if they had been active in the church and involved with a support group? Could this tragedy have been averted? I think very much so! Her stress, her pain, her anguish over the situation would have been shared by brothers and sisters surrounding her with the love of Christ. That's the difference between a private faith and one experienced and celebrated in community. Next time you hear someone say, "Oh, I can pray at home; I don't need the Church," please remember this tragic story.

No. 11 • March 2002

RESURRECTION POWER

"That I may know Him and the power of His resurrection."
(Philippians 3:11)

During Lent we have been studying what it means to grow together into Christ, centering our gatherings in the study of Ephesians 4: "speaking the truth in love, we are to grow up in every way into Him who is the head, into Christ." Why Christ? What is there so special about him? Why not say the same thing about other great people on whose teachings great religions have been built?

Our answer is found in our Easter celebration of the resurrected Lord! Herein is found the one unique and overwhelming difference between Christ and others: RESURRECTION POWER! Peter declared on the day of Pentecost that the pangs of death could not hold Christ. "He arose! Alleluia, Christ arose!"

Resurrection power is now available to all who enter their faith in the person of Christ. This is Paul's aspiration: "That I may know Him and the power of His resurrection!" This goal can be, must be, ours also. We are not talking here about theology or philosophy of religion, but of a life force, which makes the difference between hopelessness and joy-filled living.

Resurrection power is ultimate power. All other powers eventually die, but in Christ life in its eternal dimensions is assured, beyond the limits of our ability to comprehend it. In a world surrounded by death of all sorts, what a glorious truth we have to affirm and proclaim again this season: "Christ is risen!" He is risen indeed!"

No. 12 • August 2002

A NEW DAY DAWNING

Having been among you as your Interim Pastor for close to three years, my time has come to bring this ministry to a close and to move on to another assignment. With the coming of the Rev. Dr. Jeff McCrory, Geneva begins a new chapter in its great history. A new day is dawning! What an exciting time this is for you! I am most thankful to God and to all of you for having given me the opportunity to serve you and to prepare you for this great moment.

First, I welcome Dr. McCrory and wish him and his family a ministry at Geneva which is blessed of God and filled with the joys and the blessings of a happy and fruitful pastor-people union. He brings to Geneva precious skills and gifts for ministry, which will be used to inspire and to enable this congregation to grow and to prosper in its life and mission. Let each of you be a bearer of support and love, as instruments of God's grace, to encourage him and to stand with him in full solidarity. I too will continue in prayer for him and for all of you in that regard.

Let me also share with you how much Samira and I have enjoyed and appreciated our time among you. We have had nothing but positive experiences and your support has been exemplary. I began my work as your Supply Pastor, in response to a crisis. Those were difficult days but God enabled us all to close ranks and to pull together. And that we have done beautifully! You received and accepted us as your own and your love has shone through. In her own and unique way, Samira added her contribution also (mostly by way of baklava and sesame cookies!) and she joins her voice to mine in expressing to you all a profound "Thank you!"

As the Apostle Peter put it in his letter, each of you is a "living stone," connected to each other in the building of the "spiritual house," the church of Jesus Christ. You successfully completed our Light on the Hill building program, which is made of concrete, wood and stone. The saga of the "spiritual house" is never completed, however. I call on each of you to continue bringing to her your daily presence, prayers, participation and support. Keep on growing yourselves, and as you do so, you grow the church. Only God knows to what heights and dimensions the church can and will grow.

My parting word to you is the admonition given by Paul to the Philippians: "Complete my joy by being of the same mind, having the same love, being in full accord and of one mind. Do nothing from selfishness or conceit, but in humility count others better than yourselves. Let each of you look not only to his own interests, but also to the interests of others."

CHAPTER X

YORBA LINDA PRESBYTERIAN CHURCH,
YORBA LINDA, CA, 2003-2005

No.1 • May 2002

WHAT'S IN OUR NAME?

I've been doing some thinking about the word "Grapevine." It is the name of our monthly newsletter, of course. But since no one has enlightened me yet on the reason why we have chosen it, let me share with you some of my thoughts in that regard. I do not think it was chosen for the popular use of the term meaning, "the gossip line." Although, I suspect gossip in the church often is the source of our information for our life together! I would rather guess that it is in reference to Jesus' words in John 15:5, "I am the vine, you are the branches." So, it is a reminder that we are to be connected constantly to the source of our life, together, Christ "the true vine." The objective is for us to become His productive disciples. Following up on the metaphor of the vine, we are to be branches "bearing fruit." How do we do that? Jesus has the answer for us. They are found in a series of directives:

First, Jesus says, "Abide in me" (v4). Then he says, "Abide in my love" (v9). He then says, "If you keep my commandments, you abide in my love" (v10). He then proceeds to give us his commandment in verse 12: "This is my commandment, that you love one another." He repeats the statement in verse 17. How is it then that we can "abide" in Christ? By loving one another in the body of Christ, the community of faith! No idealized, imaginary of "Jesus" here, but a clear, down-to-earth, achievable directive "Love one another."

The essence of true spirituality is practiced in our relationships with one another. The preacher prayed: "Lord, I love humanity, but I can't stand people!" Idealized love with no connection to people, especially those in the body of Christ, who to us are not worthy of our love, may sound spiritual but in actuality is meaningless. Picking and choosing our friends in the congregation but ignoring others is not how it's done. It is a matter of Christ's command and not our choice! Learning to love, as Christ calls on us to do, is the core focus of our life together. Hence the name of our newsletter and it is a good one.

No. 2 • April 2004

IT'S A CROSS, NOT A CRUCIFIX

The fact and message of Easter is that Christ is risen. He is risen indeed! Easter faith focuses on this reality and our mental and emotional image of the Christ is the living Lord, and not a dead man on a cross! I've been thinking more and more about this fact since I saw "The Passion of the Christ." The abiding image in this film is that of Jesus the Christ suffering and dying on the cross. This image is in keeping with the Roman Catholic Church's fixation on this image, made evident by the prominent place crucifixes hold in their churches and other places of spiritual gatherings, such as retreat centers. This is in keeping with Mel Gibson's strong attachment to traditional Catholic faith and practices.

I cannot forget the impression I had when I was at a Catholic Retreat center in the hills of Pasadena some years ago. I was walking down a corridor, when I suddenly and unexpectedly was confronted with a huge crucifix with a bloodied Jesus on the cross! From then on, I purposely evaded going that way again!

What concerns me about "The Passion of the Christ" Film is that the crucifix will again become for us Protestants the focal point of our faith when it should be the empty tomb!

Peter declares in Acts 2:24: "God raised Him up, having freed Him from death, because it was impossible for Him to be held in its power."

Emotions may be stirred by crucifixes, still or animated, as in a film, but faith is stirred and made alive by the presence and power of the living Christ. Emotions are like the mists of the morning, but faith is grounded in fact and in the bedrock of Christ's teachings, life, death and resurrection.

The cross is empty, not because Christ is absent, but because He is no longer there. **"Death has been swallowed up in victory. Where, O death, is your victory? Where, O death is your sting? Thanks be to God, who gives us victory through our Lord Jesus Christ."** (1 Corinthians 15:54, 55)

No. 3 • June 2004

WHY WE NEED THE CHURCH

Coming to America as an 18-yeard-old young man, I was stranded in the city of Naples, Italy, with no knowledge of a word of Italian or any acquaintance whatsoever. What could I do? Knowing that I just had to find some support or else I'd be in very deep trouble very quickly, I decided to look for a Protestant church. I began by knocking on doors of every church I encountered. One can imagine how hard it was to find a Protestant church in a city that was totally Roman Catholic! After a long search, a kind priest directed me to a church he called "some kind of religious monument." I looked it up and finally found it. It turned out to be a Methodist church. The kind people there took me in and included me in their fellowship as if I were a long lost brother. During the two months I stayed in Naples trying to untangle my mixed up immigration papers, these kind people were invaluable for my health and sanity. It was there that I learned the absolute importance of a Church family. Their love and warmth towards me was truly inspiring.

Our faith must lead us to a connection with a family of faith (the church) or else it remains abstract and mostly wishful thinking. Connectional faith leads us to people and new relationships in the church that help us to grow and expand our boundaries in wonderful ways. I thank God that I learned that early in life, and it has served me well ever since.

We make a big mistake when we say to people: "Please come. The church needs you!" we should say instead, "Please come. You need the church!" You need the church family just like you need your physical family. Living alone is a miserable existence. It is also dangerous to our health.

Help us to develop and maintain YLPC in such a way that we too can be an inviting and warmly embracing family of God's people. There are a lot of lonely people out there.

No. 4 • September 2004

PULPIT, PEWS AND POLITICS

What is the proper role for the church in the midst of political struggles for control of our nation and our destiny? How do we define "proper?" Should the pastor ever speak of related issues from the pulpit? If so, what are the parameters within which he should speak out?

In my own approach to this very important question I do the following:

Consider how the faith communities in the Bible (Old and New Testaments), dealt with this issue. In the Old Testament, there were three branches that dealt with issues of public life and welfare. The political branch (kings), the religious branch (priesthood, usually under the control of the kings), and the prophetic community (often in conflict with the first two). In the New Testament, we have Jesus and His approach. He clearly stayed clear of national struggles to overthrow the Romans, but was prophetic in espousing the rights of the people otherwise ignored and abandoned by the powers (religious and political). The apostles drew a line between being obedient to God and following orders from the courts to keep them quiet (civil disobedience?). While living under the authority of Imperial Rome, they did not espouse revolt. On the contrary, they encouraged the churches to be loyal subjects, to pray for the Emperor, while working for the welfare of the people within their circles. The book of Revelation, however, makes it clear that the destruction of Rome (Babylon) is in God's plan and imminent.

Remember that there is a clear line of demarcation in America defining how far churches can go in political action. No advocacy of candidates is allowed (if we wish to maintain our tax exemption). This extends to using the church or its apparatus on behalf of promoting party-endorsed political action. The "wall of separation" between church and state clearly exists, even though there are increasingly loud voices being heard these days (interestingly from conservative Christian spokespeople) that there is no such restriction in our Constitution. Taking this fact into consideration, there can be no restriction placed on the conscience, however, when it comes to addressing issues affecting our life and well-being.

What then is "proper" for us? A conscience schooled by Biblical principles of justice, peace and mercy, centered in the life and teachings of Jesus, must continue to speak and act with courage. This is a far cry from partisan politics and has nothing to do with who should or should not be our elected officials. Such ministry addresses the needs of the audience (the church) who may be caught in the dilemmas of the day (such as the church in the Roman Empire). It also helps raise the consciousness level of the people, to see beyond their own immediate perspectives and needs, and addresses the just cause of neglected or oppressed people.

VARTKES M. KASSOUNI

No. 5 • October 2004

DISCERNING TRUE NEED

Last week I got taken in again! I pulled up to the gas pump, and as I began to put money in the machine a woman came up to me from the pickup up in the next stall. "I forgot my wallet at home," she said. "Could you give me two dollars to pump some gas? I have no money at all on me." Well, I felt somewhat cheap when I said, "Sorry, I can't do that." She kept on until I relented and gave her the money, "How about the man at the wheel?" I inquired. She gave me another slick answer as she took the money. However, instead of pumping gas, they turned the pickup around and drove off. I noticed they went across the street to another station with a grocery store in it. I almost took off after them to ask what brand of beer they were going to buy!

How do we discern true need versus con artists who pick on us all the time? We get them at the church. They know when to come and for whom to ask. Usually it is just before or just after church service, and they want to talk to the pastor. Yesterday I had a phone call from a man who claimed he had AIDS, was "messed up," and was looking for a caring Presbyterian church. After I inquired where he was, I began to give him the phone numbers of churches much nearer to him than ours, but he hung up on me!

My policy here at our church (which I have ignored a number of times), is to say. "We do not have aid funds to disburse to people outside our own congregation and the needs of people referred to us by them. Unless you are willing to be interviewed by a Deacon to establish legitimacy of your need, we cannot help you. This means that you may have to wait a day or two." That usually does it. "We can't wait that long" is the usual response. By the way, yes, we have given support from the Deacons Fund to people referred to us by our own members.

346

Jesus said, "Be wise as serpents but harmless as doves." I think this saying applies to our strategies for helping the needy. Discerning true need versus giving in to sharp operators is a necessary and sometimes gut-wrenching procedure we need to follow.

VARTKES M. KASSOUNI

No. 6 • November 2004

"THANKSGIVING," A TIME TO ACT

This year, by design, we have planned to coincide our Thanksgiving Service with our Stewardship Dedication Service on November 21. The theme, as stated above, is intentionally focused on the word Giving. Our belief is that the basic reason we are thankful is that God has blessed us, and that we in turn express our gratitude by giving. Eva Stimson, writing in "Presbyterians Today," in an article titled "Generous Givers, what motivates people to contribute to the church?" Identifies five common themes after interviewing Presbyterians throughout our country on this issue:

1. CHALLENGED TO STRETCH
Years ago, when he and his wife had decided to give $50 a month to a special building fund, Bill Saul was taken aback and challenged to give $50 a week! He and his wife agreed to make that commitment, "and we never missed a payment," he says. Bill is a leading layman in our Presbytery. The challenge stretch is a tithe, or 10% of our income to be dedicated to God's service.

2. IDENTIFYING WITH NEED
In an area of Alaska identified as being economically depressed, 72-year-old Adeline DeCastro has been known to write a personal check to cover needs in her church, a tiny congregation where they understand what need is. She is a simple woman with modest income. She loves her church and is intent on serving need through it, in the church and around in the community.

348

3. BECAUSE WE HAVE RECEIVED

Lucimariam Roberts says the first check she writes every month is to the church. "I can't help but give," she declares. "So many have given to me!" And so much has God given to us! Gratitude for God's saving grace, God's mercy of forgiveness and freedom to grow in Christ, for relationships of love in the family of God, the church. These are but a few of the more directly "spiritual gifts," God has given, apart from the physical blessings we so much enjoy.

4. A HEART FOR MISSION

We give because the church believes and serves the world in Christ's mission of love, mercy and redemption. From feeding the hungry, providing shelter, education, medical missions to evangelistic outreach, this is our local and global challenge. This is how "we can be part of the bigger picture," says Ginny Iacone, of Paoli, Pa.

5. FROM SCARCITY TO ABUNDANCE

La Mesa, New Mexico Presbyterian Church used to function formerly in what the pastor calls "a theology of scarcity." Pinching pennies was so prevalent that they even had their own "grungiest stationery" (hand-stamped with the church logo!) things changed when they began to function within a "theology of abundance." It began when they took seriously his message, "money is always available if we take the gospel seriously." And things have changed indeed. It can for us also if we also take the gospel seriously.

No. 7 • December 2004

JOURNEY TO BETHLEHEM AGAIN

We journey to our beloved places again and again. That special place where you used to go swimming as a kid, or that special resort where you and your family spent your summers, or the houses where you grew up, or the restaurant where you proposed to marry your sweetheart. For us Christians, Bethlehem holds a very special place in our hearts. It is where Jesus was born. Our journeys to Bethlehem, spiritual, or physical are special experiences. I've made that pilgrimage physically at least six times, and each time I was filled with a deep sense of awe and wonder. It is time to go there again.

There are many obstacles on the way to Bethlehem. This year there is an ugly twenty-foot high wall there, near where the angels sang "Peace on earth, good will to men!" there is neither peace nor goodwill. Hatreds separate people and fears isolate them from each other. Why bother with Bethlehem anymore?

When I think of Bethlehem today I remember a painting by George Frederic Watts that hung on our living room wall when I was a child. It was titled, "Hope." It depicted a woman seated atop our planet, her head sadly bowed, plucking on a single unbroken harp string, with all the other strings broken and dangling from the instrument. Every time I am ready to give up hope, I remember that painting and I take heart.

The Church of the Nativity in Bethlehem has a main entry though which all pilgrims must pass to enter the holy site of Jesus' birth. It is about four-feet high only, and one must bow low to go through. We are told that it was built so because invading soldiers on their horses could not gain entry unless they dismounted first. Others say it was built so as to force all to enter with humility. I like the second version. The whole story of Jesus' birth is one of humility. He was born in a stable, but we build our palaces (cathedrals) for him! He lived to love and to give of himself to the whole world. We live to hoard our wealth, power and privilege, and we reject in hatred those who are not like us. GOD, TAKE US TO BETHLEHEM AGAIN!

No. 8 • January 2005

NEW BEGINNINGS

God is a God of beginnings and new beginnings. Not only nature demonstrates this to be true but so does Scripture history. Autumn and winter are times of falling leaves and hibernation. Spring is a time of renewal and awakening. There is no death in nature, only changes and the continuation of life in new forms. So is it also with the God of the Bible.

God began with the creation of heaven and earth. Humanity had its beginnings in the Garden, but soon this went wrong and a downward spiral ensued. God began again with the flood and gave us a rainbow as a sign of God's continuing love for all humanity. The patriarchs, such as Noah and then Abraham, experienced new beginnings. The Israelites flight from Egypt and entry into the Promised Land were new beginnings. When things went wrong, again the promise was for judgment, exile, and then new beginnings. Jeremiah said that God would make a new covenant with them, and "write the law on their hearts."

God began again and recreated Adam in Jesus Christ, who is called the first of a new creation, and his followers the new humanity. Jesus talked of new beginnings when he said a "new birth" or "birth from above" generated by the Holy Spirit is what humanity needed. He himself talked of His death and resurrection, which took place after His crucifixion. The apostles carried on this message, making the fact of resurrection central to the reality and power of the Gospel. Peter said. "You have been born anew of imperishable seed... the word of the Lord. That word is the good news that was announced to you." (1 Peter 1:23)

As we begin the New Year, are we energized by this imperishable seed, or are we still feeding on the perishable and the old? Is it merely new resolutions, or is it new life with Christ that is leading us into the unknown? We believe in the future, we claim our tomorrows in Christian hope, and we walk forward with confidence, not because all things are going to be rosy and nice, but because Christ in us is the hope of glory. I invite you to walk hand in hand with the One who holds the future.

No. 9 • February 2005

WHAT A MORNING!

From our bedroom window, which faces east, we are often filled with wonder and awe as we witness beautiful sunrises. I usually rise before dawn and with a cup of coffee settle down to read the morning paper. On some mornings, brilliant streaks of gold and red begin to illumine the skies as the sun begins to come up. Overwhelmed by the sight, I call up to Samira, "Open the drapes and see the beautiful sunrise!"

Easter is that one morning when we also call to each other. "Open the drapes and see the beautiful sunrise!" It is the rising of the Sun of Righteousness, the resurrection of the Lord! My, what a morning it must have been when Mary and the other apostles came upon that fantastic scene of the empty tomb. Even more fantastic was the message declared to them, "He is not here. He is risen!" And even more fantastic was the experience they had of the risen Lord appearing to them and saying "Peace be with you!" The Shalom of God was personally appearing to them.

There are drapes of unbelief which prevent people from seeing the sunrise of the resurrected Christ. There are also drapes of doubt, indifference and fear which prevent us from experiencing the wonder of it all. So, our call goes out again this Easter: "Come celebrate the rising of the Son!" Actually, our celebration is every Sunday and not just on Easter Day, Sunday is known as "The Lord's Day" and our worship is always a celebration of His resurrection.

The resurrection of Christ makes it possible for us to have the kind of living and victorious faith which enables us to transcend obstacles of all sorts, chief of which is the specter and fear of death. We too can declare with Paul: "Death is swallowed up in victory. Where, O death, is your victory? Where, O death is your sting? Thanks be to God who gives us the victory through Jesus Christ." (1 Corinthians 15:54-56)

No. 10 • May 2005

THE CHRISTIAN FAMILY

Mother's Day is May 8, and that whole week is designated as being "Christian Family Week" in our church calendar. There is much being written these days about family life, and much debate going on as to what constitutes a family. I don't mean to get into the debate now raging about "traditional family values" and what those are from my perspective, except to say that God's love brings us all into a family life together, and that is the church! The church as family is an encouraging concept, but can also be a threatening one because many people who "go to church" these days don't want to be incorporated into a family. They wish to attend, observe, enjoy, and then go away to live their life as they please, without the responsibility that entering into a family would entail.

All people, nuclear families including parents and children, as well as single people are invited into church to participate in our family life together. Worship services should include us all in a way that no one feels left out or alone, even though no other family members may be present. We have intergenerational fellowship here and we value the contribution of love, attention and support that each one brings. Seeing families sitting together in church is a heart-warming scene, which should be repeated every week!

Jesus pointed to His disciples and said "these are my family" when He was told His mother and siblings were outside the house waiting for Him. These may sound like harsh words, but in the love and grace of God, all people are brought together into a family relationship which transcends even our earthly family ties. Now, that's powerful stuff! In other words, the spiritual glue which helps us bind ourselves to each other is discovered and experienced in our spiritual life together as a church.

No. 11 • June 2005

JUNE GLOOM OR JUNE BLOOM?

This time of the year, just about every morning and sometimes all day, we have a weather condition called, "June gloom." The overcast hangs around and at best turns into haze. The first time I traveled from New York to Los Angeles, it was in June. Not knowing about this condition, I was very disappointed that the sun, for which California was legendary, was not breaking through.

This time of the year, it is a time for the roses and our gardens to bloom with color and beauty. The splendor of spring is in full view all over the region. Being somewhat of a gardener myself, I wait for this time of the year to place my "green thumb" into service. The rewards are many and varied indeed.

I see a correlation between these phenomena and our lives as Christians, and our life as a church community. Will it be a time for "gloom" or for "bloom" for us? In many ways, it is a time for us to bloom. June weddings, June graduations, June excursions and travels are signs of life and exuberance. That's wonderful, of course! We have a number of our young people who are graduating from High School and College. We rejoice with them and their families. Our church life has several special events that herald our "bloom." We have a special Men's Breakfast on June 11, recognition of graduates, confirmation of over a dozen of our youth on June 12, and our Praise and Celebration Service that afternoon. Recognition of the Accomplishment of Women will take place on June 26. Here are signs of life and growth among us. Celebrate it!

June is also the gateway to summer and usually the beginning of decline in attendance and giving. Let it be different this year! Let us keep blooming as a church community right through the summer with no letup. As we continue to come, give, pray and serve, we will have a "blooming" good summer.

No. 12 • June 2005

THE CHURCH IN BODIE

Returning from vacation last week on Route 395, Samira and I decided to go off the main road and explore the ghost town of Bodie, situated a few miles north of Lake Mono. I've always wanted to do that, but knowing it was out of the way, and would take at least an hour, we'd never done it before. This time we did and were richly rewarded for the effort.

In this authentic and non-commercialized ghost town, which some time ago had as many as 75,000 people living there, there is a little church still standing. It is the old Methodist Church. Being a pastor, I am always attracted to church buildings whenever I travel, and this time was no exception. Standing at the entrance of this little building with a mesh screen that prevented us from going inside, I peered through and in the few minutes spent there made some observation I would share with you.

The pulpit was there, massive and central to the chancel which had a message, or a prayer quoting a Psalm and praising God. Off to the left is an old pump organ with pipes on it, whether real or not I could not say. The pews were still there. In the middle of which was the old heating stove. I stood there in respectful silence and tried to recapture the scenes that had transpired there as long as the city was alive.

My thoughts were those of wonder and admiration for a church that dared to address the needs and challenges of a bawdy and crime-ridden city filled with people seeking gold and riches. One little girl's diary said on the occasion of her family's move to Bodie, "Goodbye God, we're going to Bodie!" It must have taken a courageous pastor and church leaders to maintain a ministry in such circumstances.

And then I thought of Yorba Linda! What a piece of cake in comparison! However, on second thought, I believe it takes just as much courage, vision, dedication and faith to grow a church here as in Bodie. The pioneering spirit that empowers people to build a church in the wilderness is what it takes to grow a church in affluent Yorba Linda!

Will Yorba Linda, including our church buildings, be a ghost town some day? I doubt it. However, imagining that it might, I wonder what a visitor peering through our glass doors would say about us. What kind of ministry, of church life and mission did we have? Were we a vibrant and active church? I pray that their impressions will say, "Those Presbyterians! They must have been some kind of dedicated people of God!"

No. 13 • August 2005

IDENTITY THEFT

IDENTITY THEFT is the fastest growing crime in America today. Hardly a day goes by without some new revelation of stolen or lost computer disks and files reported by banks, credit card companies and businesses. They tell us that our identity is at risk and that we should take steps to prevent us from suffering grievous losses. It is of utmost importance that we heed such advice and take steps to protect our identity. However, our identity is lodged not only in our credit reports and cards but in our character. Who we really are is not revealed by our bank accounts but by our inner person shaped by unseen forces of all kinds. Who am I? This question can be answered in many ways.

I am a child of my heritage. My parents and their community, or their "village" raised me up to be who I am. The same is true for you and your identity as well. If your "village" had a vibrant and active church, as mine did, then you have been fortunate to have had at the center of your identity development, spiritual forces drawing from the person of Christ, meaning and values more precious than any bank account.

We have developed our own "village," which is our church community. Our identity continues to be shaped thereby, at the center of which is Christ Himself. It is of utmost importance that we maintain the kind of heritage within our own ranks which will continue to shape the identity of our children. What a thrill it is, for example, to see so many children walk up every Sunday morning and with rapt attention listen to Kim Wisnia share our spiritual values with them in the Children's Message!

How do we rob ourselves and our children of their spiritual identity? We do so by not taking seriously our spiritual education; hit and miss attendance at church, hardly any serious Bible study, and by giving more attention to secular pursuits. These are only some ways we allow precious inner identity of Christian character to be stolen from us. And we do the stealing ourselves! The loss of that treasure is irreplaceable! Jesus said. **"What shall it profit a man if he were to gain the whole world but lose his soul?"** (Matthew 16:26 KJV) Have you checked your spiritual credit report lately?

No. 14 • October 2005

PARTNERS IN MISERY AND OPPORTUNITY

When the earthquakes and tsunamis hit Indonesia last Christmas time, we were all filled with astonishment and horror at the ensuing havoc in surrounding countries viewing it from our positions of relative comfort and safety. When Hurricane Katrina struck with devastating force in our own southern gulf states last month, we were shaken much more deeply. This time the horror of it all struck us much more where we could feel it in our own hearts and minds. The ensuing response of concern, support and aid has been fantastic to observe. In our own church we gave over $8,000, and what really touched my heart was that our own children stood at the corner of our church, at Palm, and raised over $300 offering shaved ice and popcorn, and then went to Eastlake Village and raised another $200 there for disaster relief! Obviously we have been touched as seldom before, and that is a gift from God to us.

On October 2, we celebrate World Communion Day. What better demonstration can God give us than these disasters to remind us that we all belong to one world community? We are no different from Indonesians, or Chinese or Africans… we are all God's creatures mutually dependent on each other to sustain our fragile life. There is no partiality with God! Americans are just as vulnerable to tidal waves of destruction as people anywhere else. Peter said to the Roman centurion Cornelius: **"I truly understand that God shows no partiality, but in every nation anyone who fears Him and does what is right is acceptable to Him."** (Acts 10:34)

Offers of aid and support came to the gulf states and New Orleans not only from around the United States but many nations overseas as well. Included among them were nations we ordinarily would consider our adversaries. It was a humbling thing for our nation's President to accept these offers, but I am most happy he did. We have become aware that we are interdependent with people across the globe, and that is a good thing! God has reminded us that we cannot continue to think we have it all and need no others to come to our aid. So we are partners in misery and opportunity as well. My prayer is that God will enable us to celebrate our unity as human beings no matter what color, race or nationality to which we may belong across this wonderful world of ours.

No. 15 • December 2005

HERE COMES CHRISTMAS!

Pray with me this prayer: "Lord God, as Christmas approaches, help me to look beyond all the lights and the decorations and the commercials, so that I may be able to think of the Christ-child and His humble birth in a stable. Help me to think past all the jingles and the sound of carols played over and over again in stores and streets and malls, so that I may be able to hear the angels whisper in my heart the awesome news of Christ's birth. Help me to rediscover the joy of giving of myself in love to those in need, and not to worry so much about giving the right gifts to people who already have so much.

May the spirit of Christ reawaken in me sensitivity to the peace that He brings, and may the peace we all wish for so much these days begin with me. Help me to celebrate His birth with a simple and sincere faith in the company of my brothers and sisters in Christ at home and at church. Thank you, dear God, for your indescribable gift of your Son. May that gift be received with humble joy throughout this sad and war-weary world! Amen."

We all share with some sense of panic that Christmas will be upon us so soon! We are not ready yet... the cards have not been sent, the gifts have not been bought, the decorations have not gone up yet.. and on and on. Don't' get caught up in the frenzy of it all. Don't get swept away by this tidal wave of voices and commercials to buy, buy and buy.

Take a few moments in the beginning of each day to pray the prayer I suggest above, or pray a prayer that expresses your own personal thoughts. Then, renewed in God's grace, go out to address the challenges facing you. Remember, Christmas brings good tidings of joy.

CHAPTER XI

MORNINGSIDE
PRESBYTERIAN CHURCH
FULLERTON, CA, 2005-2007

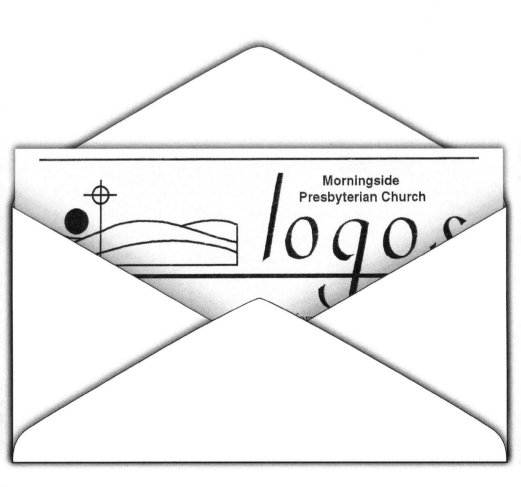

No. 1 • August 9, 2006

GETTING TO KNOW YOU

As we begin our journey together as pastor and people, it is very important for me that I get to know you. Along the way in my training as a pastor, I have received counsel which has been very good. Among these are two: One is that "A shepherd has to know his sheep. Get to know your people!" The other is, "Don't get stuck in your office. Get out among your people!" I have followed that advice, and I have found it to be very helpful indeed. I intend to do no less at Morningside.

I have a threefold strategy to accomplish my objectives:

First, is to visit just about everyone on our list, and continue to do so, including hospital and home visits.

Second, is to visit all our Elders, Deacons and church Leaders in their homes if at all possible, or in special meetings like lunches or office visits. I want to know who our leaders are and to listen to them concerning their work, needs, challenges and to make myself available to them.

Third, I want to visit our members at large in their homes. I have found it extremely helpful to do so, because seeing people only in church is not enough. Who people are, and their full identity is revealed and communicated in person to person meetings. I also welcome small group gatherings. I would welcome your calling some friends into your home and then calling on me and Samira to join you for an informal evening together.

There are other strategies to be used in my ministry. I will share more of these as we go along. For now, it is "Getting to know you." If you agree, give me a call. Don't wait for mine, please.

VARTKES M. KASSOUNI

No. 2 • August 23, 2006

FOCUS ON THE WORD

In my previous LOGOS articles, I shared with you my initial strategy for pastoral ministry. It centers in getting to know our people and in addressing their personal and spiritual needs. I have begun to meet with our leaders to hear them, to get to know them and to respond to their concerns. Our office administrator, Lynda, has begun to make calls for me in this regard, and I have already met with a number of our people.

Another key strategy on my part is to preach sermons that are Biblical in content and relevant to our lives. I call my sermons, "messages" because they are the Word of God communicated to the listeners. You may have noted that in the worship bulleting the Scripture reading is followed by the statement. "The Word of God Written." And the Message is followed by the statement "The Word of God Proclaimed." No, I do not go to the "old barrel" to use old sermons. Each one is fresh and new.

The kind of preaching I do is called "Expository." The points I make are already made in the Word. I merely have to "mine" them and pass them onto the hearers. Most sermons these days that we hear are "topical" wherein a certain topic is chosen and then the Scriptures are used to support the position taken by the preacher on the subject. In expository preaching, the preacher is limited to and by the written Word. Personal biases are left out, or are supposed to be left out. We don't always succeed in doing so, however!

Christ, who offered Himself to us as "The bread of life," is the living Word of God. Hence, the spiritual nourishment you will receive in every worship service ultimately is the sharing of Christ our Lord.

No. 3 • September 13, 2006

WORLD COMMUNION AND OUR PEACE OFFERINGS

October 1, the first Sunday in October, is the day for World Communion celebration within our churches throughout the world. It is also the day we receive our Peacemaking Offering. The body of Jesus Christ, the church, is formed by peoples from every nation, race and tongue. It is an international reality which is exciting to think about and a cause for real celebration.

In 1969, I had the rare privilege of going around the world on a preaching mission. In early November, while in Moscow, I had the pleasure of worshipping in a packed out Protestant church. There was no seat available for me. Noting that I was a visitor, the usher asked a church member to get up and give me his seat, which he did gladly. Then communion was served. Ushers had no room to walk down the aisles, so the elements were passed on hand to hand. As the holy cup was passed onto me by a Russian believer, I was overcome with emotion and had a flashback to July 20 of that summer. That's the day that American Neil Armstrong stepped on the moon, bringing America's mission to the moon to a successful conclusion. All of us were gathered in our family room, watching the TV screen with great intensity. When he took that historic first step, we all shouted. "We beat the Russians, we beat the Russians!" Included in the group was my six-year-old son. After a while, when things were quiet again, he came and whispered in my ear, "Dad, what's a Russian?" Yes, at that point in the communion service in Moscow, at the height of the Cold War, a Russian and an American became one because of Christ!

"In Christ there is no east or west, in Him no south or north, but one great fellowship of love, throughout the whole wide earth." We sing that song, and on October 1, it becomes a reality in our thinking. However, there is an added dimension to our celebration, when we say "World Communion." We celebrate the fact that all humanity is one, created by God, linking us to each other, whether we like it or not! Benjamin Franklin once prayed, saying, "God grant that not only the love of liberty but a thorough knowledge of the rights of man may pervade all the nations of the earth, so that anybody may set his foot anywhere on its surface and say: This is my country." Happy World Communion Day!

No. 4 • October 11, 2006

LOOK AT US

On Sunday, October 22, our message will be based on the incident recorded in Acts 3:1-10, where Peter and John encounter a lame man begging for alms at the temple gate. Their response to his quest is not money but something far more precious: healing. Peter said to him, "Look at us… silver and gold I do not possess, but what I do have is what I give you in the name of Jesus Christ the Nazarene, walk!"

What a wonderful story this is. It holds for me the essential core of our Gospel ministry, to which we are dedicated as a church. It is not the accumulation of money, but a ministry of bringing life to people in the name and power of Jesus Christ. During stewardship campaigns, such as the one we are entering here at MPC, the focus becomes money, finances, budgets, deficits and surpluses. In other words, "silver and gold." We need to be reminded that "the bottom line" in our life together is not financial reports, but lives changed, challenged, healed and renewed in the Spirit. That is what we are here for!

Inviting attention to us is usually considered an egotistical thing to do. However, if we have something to offer others, the invitation is a valid one. Peter did not want to be recognized as a famous apostle, he wanted to heal this poor man. I dare say that when church folks are filled with this Spirit, then lives around them are changed. And you know what? Silver and gold comes pouring in because people want to support such a church and give through the church to spread the love of Christ near and far. How about us? Dare we say, "Look at us?" I certainly hope so.

No. 5 • October 25, 2006

WHO WILL WIN?

Election Day is almost here. On Tuesday, November 7, we will go to the polls and cast our ballots. Who will win? What a question to ask! Winning and losing is so relative, is it not? As the old saying goes, "One person's food is another person's poison!" Your candidate of choice may not be mine, and vice versa. You may vote "Yes" on an initiative, and I may vote "No" on the same issue. Thank God for America where we can agree to disagree and cast votes without fear of retaliation from the opposing camp. What we must all agree on is that freedom of choice is a God-given gift to us, and we must preserve and protect it at all costs. God does not coerce faith from us. Religion that forces beliefs on its adherents is not a gift from God! In Galatians 5:1 Paul says, "For Freedom Christ has set us free; stand fast therefore, and do not submit again to a yoke of bondage."

Ah, freedom! How precious, and yet how elusive! Cast your ballots in faith that what you do will preserve our freedoms in America.

First century Christians lived under the yoke of imperial Rome. Their freedoms were severely restricted, and many died as martyrs under its oppression. How amazing, then that Paul says in Roman 13:1 "Let every person be subject to the governing authorities. For there is no authority except from God, and those that exist have been instituted by God." Yes, there is a seeming contradiction there, but people of faith must always live knowing that the ultimate authority belongs to God, and even the Roman Empire eventually learned that fact. So, we take seriously the reminder that "Vengeance is mine, I will repay," says the Lord." In the light of that fact, we vote our conscience, and live our faith. We accept the teaching of Scripture. "Do not be overcome by evil, but overcome evil with good." (Romans 12:21)

No. 6 • November 8, 2006

THANKS-GIVING

"Get to the point!" We often say this to people who are beating around the bush about some topic or other. They either cannot or will not come to a clear concluding point and frustrate their hearers in the process. The Apostle Paul is different when it comes to giving in the name of Christ's mission. "The point is this: The one who sows sparingly will also reap sparingly and the one who sows bountifully will also reap bountifully. Each of you must do as you have made up your mind, not reluctantly or under compulsion." (2 Corinthians 9:6,7)

Our Thanksgiving Service this year is also our Stewardship Dedication Service. The point is this: Our Thanksgiving is tied to our Thanks-GIVING. The expression of our gratitude to God for all that we have so lavishly enjoyed during the year culminates in an expression of our own giving in return. My mother never received a gift from anybody without returning a gift in turn. We used to tease her about it at times. However, the lesson stuck! We learned to give and to give with love and generosity. At the top of our list of those who receive our expression of thanks have always been God and the church. Hence, we cannot have thanksgiving without Thanks-GIVING.

Our Stewardship emphasis calls on us also to act on what we have decided to do in this regard. "Not reluctantly or under compulsion." I can hear us say, "But we have to hold on to what we have because our needs are so great." So, we sow sparingly! Then we grumble because our harvests are so spare also!

The promise that motivates and encourages us follows the call to generosity made by Paul: "God is able to provide you with every blessing in abundance, so that you may always have enough of everything and may provide with abundance for every good work." (2 Corinthians 9:8) Yes, "Always have… and always provide." Inflow and outflow. That's how the abundant life works.

No. 7 • November 22, 2006

ADVENT IS PREPARATION, CHRISTMAS IS CELEBRATION

Anticipation precedes celebration. Celebration without anticipation robs the event of its true value and meaning. If a child were given the gifts he wished for (his birthday for example), without waiting for the actual day, the meaning of the gifts would be lost, and the day itself would be anti-climactic. There is great value in waiting. By waiting in patience, the people of Israel were taught what faith was all about. Habakkuk was told by God: "There is a vision for the appointed time, wait for it; it will surely come... the righteous live by their faith." (Hebrews 2:3)

Advent is a time for waiting, preparing and contemplating the meaning of the coming of Christ at Christmas. It is not Christmas yet! Isaiah talks of "A people waiting in darkness." Yes, we too wait in darkness today. Times are bad and headlines scream the statistics of death and destruction daily! This one month of Advent, starting on December 3rd, is our time waiting in prayer, meditation and contemplation. We need to do this in the midst of our frenzy in planning Christmas.

We all have been given an Advent Booklet of meditations and prayers to help us in this season of preparation. Use them personally and with those in your household. Make your dinnertime a time of doing this together and read the prayers included or pray your thoughts seeking the guidance of the Holy Spirit. Meditate on the promises of God concerning our life and times. Write down a thought or two each day starting with, "My prayer is that with the coming of Christ God will..."

May the silence of anticipation be followed by the exclamation of the angels, "Christ is born in Bethlehem!" On that day, the people sitting in darkness will see a great light! However, until that day comes, let us learn how darkness can be our friend in waiting.

No. 8 • December 27, 2006

HERE COME THE MAGI

On January 7, we will be celebrating Epiphany Sunday. In the West, this day celebrates the coming of the Magi to worship the newborn King and to give him significant gifts of gold, frankincense and myrrh. In the East, Epiphany celebrates the baptism of Jesus at age 30! Why such a significant difference? It is because the birthday of Jesus was not celebrated for several centuries. The revelation of Christ to the world (Epiphany) did not happen at his birth but at his baptism, when Jesus went to the Jordan River, to John the Baptizer, to be baptized, and a voice declared. "This is my beloved Son with whom I am well pleased."

The Magi, also called "wise men," were actually astrologers who read the stars to find meaning and follow their message. So it is that the "star in the East," declared to them of a momentous event, and they came to Jerusalem inquiring about the birth of a King. Herod, who was already "King" obviously took this news as an alarming development! He was to be replaced, and this was untenable, hence the subterfuge and intrigue to locate the Child. Unable to locate him, since Joseph had taken Mary and Jesus and fled to Egypt. Herod ordered the massacre of all male children, two years and under. This is known as "the massacre of the innocents."

The wise men were from a foreign country, probably modern Iraq or Iran, signifying that the birth of Jesus was a momentous event with international implications. Jesus made this clear when during his ministry he opened the doors of God's house to include people from other nations. Eventually, the universal church of Christ grew to include people "from every tribe and nation," and the wall separating Jew from Gentile was removed forever. All this is foreshadowed in the worship of the Magi, and all of us are blessed because of it. And so the 12 days of Christmas come to a conclusion!

No. 9 • January 24, 2007

50 YEARS AGO

On January 20, 1957, I was ordained to the Christian ministry by the Congregational Association of Churches of New York City. The ceremony took place in a little church in that city to which I was called as pastor in 1959. In 1958, I moved my ministerial standing to the United Presbyterian Church (USA), which joined with the Southern Presbyterian Church in 1982 to form our present denomination, PC (USA).

Fifty years is a long time, and I thought I would share some thoughts with you about it.

First, I give profound thanks to God for giving me the health and fitness it has taken to survive fifty years of ministry! I also thank God for the grace I have received, affirming me, and my calling, through all the trials and changes I have experienced these years. Second, it has been a distinct joy for me to serve as pastor to a number of churches from New York to California! I have served small and large churches as solo Pastor as well as head of multiple-staff churches. In all of them, I have come alongside people who faced challenges and issues of life, and shared the love and the presence of Christ as best I could. That is the heart and soul of ministry! Third, I have discovered that leaders who lead because they seek recognition and power are disappointed sooner or later. Congregations respond to love in actions, leaving the Pastor often in vulnerable positions. That's where the risk of ministry comes in. If pastors are not willing to take that risk, they should not even think of ministry as their vocation.

Beyond pastoring churches, I worked as a church developer for our presbytery for nine years. It has been a great source of joy for me to be used by God as the person starting new fellowships, which grew to become full-fledged churches. For example, last Saturday our Presbytery met at Laguna Niguel Presbyterian Church, which was my first assignment back in 1986.

My ministry at Morningside is another dimension of the variety of pastorates I have had. This very unique and challenging model of church (Korean and Anglo together as one congregation) is daunting indeed. I gladly join a number in our congregation who have the vision and the energy to carry on to see their vision realized. Toward that end, we are now in a review process. It is a privilege to be among you at this time and stage in my pastoral ministry. What's next for me after Morningside? I'd be reluctant to speculate.

No. 10 • February 21, 2007

TERRORIZED BY TERROR?

Verse 5 of Psalm 91 says. "You will not fear the terror of the night, or the arrow that flies by day, or the pestilence that stalks in darkness, or the destruction that wastes at noonday."

The word "terror" has been used so many times since 9/11 that everything we do and say anymore seems to be controlled and overshadowed by it. We are literally being terrorized by our own fears and reaction to terror. Which is worse, the original source of terror or our own over-reaction to it?

It is not the first time that such obsessive fears have taken charge of our lives. Back in the time of the Psalmist, the forces surrounding the people of God seemed overwhelming. However, the word spoken by God's messenger was sent to calm the people and assure them that God's presence and guidance in their lives would overcome the fears that haunted them. "You will not fear the terror of the night." Whether the fears that haunt us are from human terrorists, wartime casualties, economic disaster or disease borne pestilence, we are assured that we can maintain our calm and inner peace through it all.

I am afraid we have turned into a nation "terrorized by terror." Or even worse, we have become a nation that is capitalizing on the theme of terror to advance partisan interest. Think of the drug industry, for example. "Ask your doctor" is constantly made by all-pervasive ads urged on us to make, pushing all kinds of drugs for treatment of diseases, real and imagined. One could spend all day pursuing these ads, turning us into hypochondriacs!

The way to prevent terror from terrorizing us is to place absolute trust in the love and mercy of God. When the Psalmist prayed, "The Lord is my Shepherd, I shall not want…" this is what he was talking about. In Psalm 91 he says, "You who live in the shelter of the Most High, who abide in the shadow of the Almighty, will say to the Lord. "My refuge and my fortress; my God, in whom I trust." There you have it: a choice between terror and trust. Which will it be with us?

POINTED **REFLECTIONS**

No. 11 • March 28, 2007

HOLY WEEK AHEAD

We are heading into Holy Week! This Sunday is Palm Sunday, which gets us started on the grand preparation for and celebration of the resurrection of Christ, on Easter morning, April 8. This is the most important week in our calendar, bringing us to the mountain top of our faith. Come, let us go to Jerusalem and join in the procession welcoming Jesus to the Holy City.

There is destiny in the air. It is mandated by God that Jesus is to come and meet the climax of His ministry here. When the crowds shouted, "Hosanna in the highest, blessed is He who comes in the name of the Lord," He was requested to quiet the crowd lest the Roman soldiers think an insurrection was in the offing. Jesus reply was, "The very stones will cry out if the people do not!"

There have been times in history when the very stones have cried out, calling on God to act with justice and redeem God's people. This occasion is the most important one in that regard for all humanity. On Calvary, time stood still as the whole universe heard the cry of victory. "It is finished!" Echoes of the cry ring in our ears today, as we climb the hill again to stand at the foot of the cross. As the old spiritual says it in haunting melody: "Were you there when they crucified my Lord?…sometimes it causes me to tremble, tremble, tremble. Were you there when they crucified my Lord?"

More thrilling is the verse that says, "Were you there when He rose up from the tomb?" Yes, like Mary, while waiting in the Garden, we suddenly hear our name! The risen Lord meets us there! Our faith has brought us there and our faith is rewarded with the experience of Christ's spiritual presence. "Do you believe because you see me?" Jesus said to doubting Thomas, "Blessed are those who have not seen and yet have come to believe." May the impact of the risen Christ be real and life-changing for us this Holy Week.

381

No. 12 • April 25, 2007

TRAGEDY STRIKES AGAIN

The massacre of students and faculty at Virginia Tech has left us all in shock and deep sorrow. Even though this event took place thousands of miles away, it still has touched us as if it were happening here in Fullerton! Owen and Sylvia Dean's grandson is an ROTC cadet attending there, so it hit some of us much more closely than others. Thank God he is safe and not included in the list of casualties there.

I write to call on us all to be in prayer for the grieving and hurting families of those who died. No one recovers easily from this kind of a tragedy. I write to call on us all to remain also in total and caring support of our Korean-American friends and members of our church. Being from the Middle East, I know how we are made very self-conscious when people from our background are involved in acts of terror! So it is with all of us, whether Korean or German, Irish, etc. we pray for you, dear Korean friends, that you will sense the love and support we have for you at this difficult time in your community's life in the U. S.

May God sustain us all in God's grace and enable us to reach out and surround everybody with the love which flows from God's heart for all people.

As we did after 9/11, Columbine school shootings and other similar events, we ask again the question "Why?" I dare not try answering a question that has no logical answer. The question to ask is "What now?" What are we to do and how are we to cope? In times like these we dig deep into our souls and draw from wells of peace which God has poured into our hearts. We then pass on that "peace which passes understanding" to those around us and beyond. May we do so again in response to this gigantic tragedy.

No. 13 • May 9, 2007

PENTECOST AND PRESBYTERIANS

May 27 is Pentecost Sunday, Presbyterians are not known for their emphasis on this subject. We are known for emphasis on "decency and order" as we are constantly reminded at presbytery meetings! One does not find tongues of fire, speaking in strange tongues and uncontrolled enthusiasm and excitement in worship services in our churches. That is what Pentecostalism stands for, does it not? The Pentecostal movement throughout the world is growing by leaps and bounds, but not Presbyterians. We are declining everywhere. Is there a link between our lack of "Pentecostal fire," and our decline? I think so.

The Day of Pentecost is traditionally considered to be the birthday of the Church and is celebrated as such. However, we need to consider Pentecost to be more than a historical marker, but our focus for the continuing work on the Holy Spirit. Jesus emphasized the role of the Holy Spirit when he addressed His disciples during his Maundy Thursday discourse. "The Holy Spirit, whom the Father will send in my name, will teach you everything, and remind you of all that I have said to you." (John 14:26) In other words, the continuing presence and power of Christ among us and through us is to be experienced in the ministry of the Holy Spirit. When he said, "Without me, you can do nothing," we can confidently assert that to hold true for us today as well.

Appropriating the work of the Holy Spirit to our worship life today, we need not be afraid of what God can do for us. More dependence on the moving of the Spirit and less on the predictable dictates of our traditions? Yes indeed, if it is done in prayerful devotion to our God! Do not quench the

Spirit is an admonition we need to listen to as we go about maintaining not only our worship but our community life together.

At Morningside, we're going through some significant changes as we look to the future and pray that God will shape it in accordance with God's direction. Planning is necessary, but planning without the guidance and power of the Holy Spirit is nothing more than human machination and manipulation! The church of Jesus Christ was not only born on the Day of Pentecost, but it has been maintained, nourished and grown by the Holy Spirit ever since. Let us pray that it continues to be so at Morningside Presbyterian Church.

No. 14 • August 22, 2007

WHAT DO YOU SAY?

In September we are going to focus on the theme of sharing our faith as we emphasize evangelism. We are going to have a workshop on this subject on September 23rd, and then we are going to celebrate "Evangelism Sunday" on September 30. What do we say when we share our faith? This is the question people ask me when we talk about it.

"Will you go to heaven when you die?" or some similar question is used by many churches to train their evangelism callers. We do not do that. Actually, it was never used by Jesus or others in sharing the faith. Even the well-known dialog between Nicodemus and Jesus did not include that question. When Jesus said, "Unless a man be born again (or born from above) he cannot see the kingdom of God," He did not use the term "heaven." His focus was God's reign in our lives and the ultimate establishment of the reign of God on earth. His focus was here and now.

The Good News we share (the "evangel") is the difference Christ has made in our lives now, and the impact of God's love in our lives as we experience it daily, in our church, and in our community of faith. Or, how left alone, we are in spiritual poverty and unhappy, alienated from God's love. Putting that in our own personal words is what evangelism is all about. In other words, "If you've got it, share it!"

Promotion of the church is not evangelism. Sharing our faith is. The church is the community where we hear and respond to the Good News, so talking about our church is certainly important and necessary. Saying something personal is very important. When salespeople sell their product, they always focus on what a difference using their product has made in the lives of people. Sharing our faith is no different. Follow through with an invitation to meet with a Bible study group, visit with others who are believers or to attend church as your guest. You'll be happy you did.

No. 15 • September 26, 2007

WORLD COMMUNION

Sunday, October 7, is World Communion Day. It is also the day we receive our Peacemaking Offering. The two go together in a beautiful way because what the world needs now is peace. As little as we can do, it is important that the church of Jesus Christ promotes peace throughout the world. There is so much war going on in the name of God that it is about time we spoke up for peace in the name of God!

Flying to Cleveland recently, I heard what I've heard before. A voice thanked us for flying with their airline and then added, "We are members of One World Alliance." I've wondered what that means, but have never asked. One of these days I will. What does it mean to celebrate "World Communion"? We should be aware of its meaning and with conscious effort do our part in its support. When it first began, the day was called "Worldwide Communion," meaning the conscious effort to remember our sister churches throughout the whole world and celebrate with them Holy Communion as a visible expression of our unity in Christ. That has changed to now read "World Communion," the meaning has been diluted to mean positive peace-building relationships with all peoples, Christian and others as well. For many years I resented this change and thought it a watering down of our witness to the world, but now I think it is good that we do so.

Christian churches throughout the world can take this opportunity to build and maintain visible bridges of understanding and support with their neighbors, for after all, we are one world! One tangible way to do this is with our participation in the Peacemaking Offering. A significant portion of this offering is held in our own church's possession and used for projects in our own community to promote peace and support. One such project this year is our newly adopted Power4Youth program of tutoring young people in our own community.

Benjamin Franklin once prayed this prayer, which I commend to us all. "God grant that not only the love of liberty but a thorough knowledge of the rights of man may pervade all the nations of the earth, so that anybody may set his foot anywhere on its surface and say: This is my country!"

No. 16 • November 28, 2007

WAITING IN HOPE

The season of Advent begins on December 2. As you look over the scripture readings I have for us for this season, you will note that they are all from the prophet Isaiah. Why so? Because they languished in despair in the Babylonian exile. He looks ahead and assures the people that times of despair, war and death will be followed by days of new light, new growth, new life, in the fulfillment of God's word. He is the prophet who talks of swords being shaped into plowshares, and the lambs lying down with the lions in the peaceable kingdom. All this was prophesied hundreds of years before the coming of Christ. Hence, waiting in hope is the key to one's faith. It does not give up!

We need to experience Advent also. Please, don't' rush Christmas in too soon. We need to understand what it means to wait in hope. Hold off on the Christmas carols and the decorations, and all the festivities. Jesus is not born yet! The season of waiting in hope is necessary for us to deal with unfulfilled promises, and with looking into the future knowing that today things are still not right. Death and destruction are still dominant in relations among peoples. Learning to live with and to deal with such realities is most necessary if our faith is not going to end up into being mere wishful thinking and evasion of what's going on now.

I pray for the day when swords will be reshaped into plowshares, but I know that it won't happen soon. Therefore, I read the prophets and seek to understand their mentality and their spiritual frame of heart and soul as they carried on and never gave up hope. I know Christmas is coming, but not quite here yet. We know Christ will come again, but not quite yet. However, we live and we labor with that conviction so strong that it shapes our thoughts and actions today. That is what it means to be participants in the season of the Advent of Christ.

No. 17 • December 5, 2007

WOULD YOU GO TO BETHLEHEM?

"Come ye, O come ye to Bethlehem…" Would you go to Bethlehem today? Unfortunately it is no longer the little town we sing about, sleepy and quiet while the stars go by. It is an embattled town surrounded by an ugly twenty-foot high wall, holding the citizens in and preventing them from having easy access to their fields and properties outside the wall. Christians, who used to comprise 75% of its population, have dwindled down to around 25% only. Crowds that used to come to Manger Square and visit the Church of the Nativity, no longer come. There is a spirit of gloom that has settled on the people and their calls for support go mostly unheard. Literally, "the people sit in darkness waiting for a great light."

Samira and I were there several years ago, and experienced first-hand the growing storm over Bethlehem. We fled to a little shop off of Manger Square and witnessed the fury of a mob that gathered following Friday prayers in the mosque nearby and filled the square, shouting and throwing bottles and stones at the Israel occupation forces watching them. How sad to see this blessed town, the birthplace of Jesus, reduced to such a level of hostility and violence!

If I were to go to Bethlehem today, I would no longer go as a tourist. Tourists look at buildings and stones but are usually blind to the people living there and do not hear their stories, hopes and aspirations. I would go to support the remaining faithful who are staying there to keep the light of Christ burning. I think of the good folks at the Bethlehem Bible College, for example, who are there and keep the witness alive. They are living in Advent hope! A new day shall come! In the meantime they need our prayers and assurances that they are not forgotten. So let us go again to Bethlehem this advent season. But may our journey be a spiritual one looking for Jesus again, past the noise, the violence and the confusion surrounding this birthplace. Come to think of it, it really was no different the day He was born, was it?

No. 18 • December 19, 2007

POSSIBLE IMPOSSIBILITIES

The story of the birth of Jesus is quite fascinating. What is also most fascinating to me is the story of the angel who appeared to Mary and announced to her that she was to be the mother of the Savior. What the angel said caught my eye in the reading of this story again (Luke 1:26-38). "Nothing will be impossible with God" (vs 37). Then Mary said, "Here I am, the servant of the Lord; let it be with me according to your word."

When I was on the staff of our Presbytery, I would sometimes say to our Executive, as we discussed developing situations that taxed our energy and intelligence in some of our churches. "It just does not make sense!" To this he would reply, "Kass, that's your problem! You expect things to make sense all the time. Sometimes they just don't, but we accept them anyway!" The Virgin Mary conceiving by the power of the Holy Spirit and giving birth to a child is "impossible" enough, but it goes further than that. This child is to be the Savior of the world! He will be great and will be called the Son of the Most High, and the Lord God will give Him the throne of David forever, and of His kingdom there will be no end" (vs. 33) Wow!

Mary learned to accept the "impossible" and lived to experience in person the power of God at work in and with her. Today, she is admired and revered even to the point of being called "God bearer." ("Theotokos" in Greek), which was the title given to her by the church fathers at the council of Chalcedon in 453 A.D. As Protestants, we do not go that far, but we do maintain a high place of honor and regard for being the mother of our Lord. Can you imagine the amount of derision she faced for giving birth to a child that was assumed to be illegitimate? Can you imagine what she went through raising Him up and helping Him overcome the same derision directed at her? She often wondered about the turn of events, but never doubted the power of God at work in her. She lived with so many "impossibilities" in her life that she must have come to expect them as being normal.

"To you is born this day in the city of David a Savior, who is Christ, the Lord." (Luke 2:11) This message given to the Shepherds is our message. To us also, He is born today! The promise of Advent has turned into the fulfillment of Christmas Day. We need to wait no longer. The "impossible" birth has taken place and soon the "impossible" life will follow. Let us respond as Mary did, and say, "Let it be to us according to your word." Let us be people of faith again who step out boldly and claim "possible impossibilities" in the miracle of Bethlehem.

VARTKES M. KASSOUNI

ADDENDUM

VARTKES M. KASSOUNI

REFLECTION ON AN ASSASSINATION

Recently, Samira came across in her papers this long lost article, dated back to 1982. I had misplaced mine or else I would have included it in my first book, POINTS OF LIFE. I am delighted that it has been found and included in herein as an ADDENDUM.

The following statement was read in the United Armenian Congregational Church of Los Angeles on Sunday morning, January 31, 1982 by Senior Pastor Vartkes M. Kassouni, preliminary to the Pastoral Prayer during the regular worship service:

On Thursday the Turkish consul in Los Angeles was assassinated. Armenians calling themselves "Justice Commandos" claimed responsibility. An Armenian young man has been apprehended as a suspect. This event is now the subject of talk and discussion all over metropolitan Los Angeles. We are all disturbed and shaken. Feelings run the gamut of total revulsion and condemnation of the act on the one hand to outright glee and rejoicing on the other. Where do we fit in? What is our reaction and response? Let me give you mine.

Political assassinations, including this one, are deplorable. I can see no justifiable basis for resorting to such measures in order to publicize our case against Turkey. Yes, we are children of martyred people. Yes, our ancestral lands have been seized and our people have been forced by death and by exile to abandon their cherished soil. We have not forgotten, and we cannot remain silent. Unresolved grief fills our souls and justice denied haunts our spirits. We grieve alone for the world is too preoccupied to remember a forgotten genocide. However, we will not use violence against innocent people. To do so is to sink to the level of the Turks themselves who have for centuries used violence as their tools in their dealings with our people. If in my seeking of justice I must abandon all that has made me and my people noble and great, then I humbly ask, "What price revenge?"

Such assassinations do not succeed to place our history in Turkey in a positive light. They convince no one, especially the Turks themselves to acknowledge their guilt. The massacres are still considered "alleged" by the news media and the public. What is tragic, however, is that Armenians are now placed in the category of "terrorists" and the Turks in the category of innocent victims.

Since we are Christian people, let us use the tools of our faith to make our point. Martin Luther King, used non-violence successfully in his people's struggle against injustice, why not we? "Beloved, never avenge yourselves, but leave it to the wrath of God… If you enemy is hungry, feed him… for by so doing you will heap burning coals upon his head… overcome evil with good (Romans 12)." These words from the Holy Bible are still true and effective, as idealistic and unworkable as they may sound. Those who have tried it know how true they are. I suggest that we try them also.

Let us pray that the perpetrators of the crime will experience the hand of God's grace in judgment and forgiving grace, and that the family of the victim of this crime will find consolation, and that all of us no longer will foster feelings of hate and revenge. Let us pray that by lives lived in spiritual nobility and honor we will demonstrate, first to our own children and also to the world that Armenians have ample resources enabling them to rise above injustices done to them, to survive genocide and holocaust, and to live on as responsible members of the family of man. Let his be our prayer today. It is going to be mine.

REFLECTION ON 9/11

9/11/01 was a black day in the history of our country. Early that morning I was driving to the gym when I heard the news on the car radio. The horrible story soon unfolded, that Muslim suicide bombers had taken charge of four airliners in flight and crashed them, with hundreds of passengers, into the Twin Towers in New York City, the Pentagon in Washington DC, and a field in Pennsylvania. The whole country was engulfed in shock and horror, as we watched the unbelievable sights of the Towers crashing and thousands dying!

At Geneva Church, where I was the pastor, we gathered the staff for prayer and mutual counsel as to what we should do. We decided to get the word out to our people and call them to the church that evening for prayers on behalf of the victims, their families, for our country in crisis, and for ourselves in need of support because we were all in shock. This we did. There was no sermon, no liturgy, no attempt at talking but total silence for quite some time. After that people began to whisper their thoughts, their questions, their comments seeking some consolation and enlightenment.

How could this happen? Why did it happen? Was more to come by way of terrorist strikes? What could we do? Who had answers? I joined them all in asking these questions, for I was dumbfounded along with the rest of us there!

The words of the Lord's prayer kept coming up: "Deliver us from evil." So it was that we were witnessing, experiencing, suffering from the powers of pure, unadulterated evil! That prayer became our prayer over and over as we sought solace in and through our faith. Analyses, explanations, attempts at understanding and then responding to forces attacking our nation followed for days and months, and continue to this day. But that one day was one of utter darkness and horror!

Those events altered the course of our country drastically. We were shaken loose from our sense of national safety and smug comfort that we were immune from what was going on in the countries abroad but "could not happen here." We now know better and think we are prepared to prevent it from happening again. Are we?

POINTED CONCLUSIONS

Having come to the end of this book, I would take a nostalgic look backwards, and a probing look into the future. In my collective memories there are certain themes, as well as people, places and events, that are worth noting:

My ministry in Armenian churches (3 out of the 11) always celebrated their history and honored the work of their past leaders. We also celebrated the history and note-worthy accomplishments of the Armenian people throughout history. As a nation, they adopted Christianity as their religion early on (301 AD) and have suffered the consequences ever since! Whether Roman, Persian, Arabic, or Turkish, they were always surrounded with overpowering force, but they never surrendered their will, which was centered in their religious faith as Christians.

Our presence in America has always presented us with a dilemma: Choose, speak, worship and propagate Armenian only, and consider this to be our central mission. Or celebrate our presence in America as a gift, and flourish with English for worship and relations with our youth. My choice has always been the latter, I began with faltering and poor Armenian (New York City), following a pastor, (Rev. A. A. Bedigian), who was recognized as the premier communicator and teacher of Armenian life and history. However, I did not give up on Armenian, and continued a bilingual ministry to the very end. My reward is that my children and grandchildren are all proud of our heritage, and have very open desires to visit Armenia, with one already having served a year there as a volunteer teacher.

Crossing over into English speaking churches (via the United Presbyterian Church U.S.A), since 1984, has been the most fantastic, and rewarding experience for me. That move opened doors of opportunity and ministry that have challenged, stretched, and rewarded me in ways I would have never dreamt before. My understanding and experience of spirituality grew to mean much, much more than personal piety and fixation with subjective religiosity. It expanded to include social issues affecting the lives of people and segments of society far beyond my immediate self and circles. This social consciousness led me to national General Assemblies where issues now embroiling our country were addressed. On this level, I was involved with action on behalf of Armenians, leading the Presbyterian denomination to adopt the historic resolution recognizing the Genocide on its 100th Anniversary, in June of 2015.

What of the future? I've been retired from active ministry since 2015. I refuse to believe there is no longer a need for my witness and work for Jesus Christ. I remain keenly aware of what's going on in our churches, and in our world. I serve as called upon, speak and act up as circumstances demand it. I continue to write and to pass on my thoughts to whoever is willing to listen. Their number is diminishing, however, not because of my age, but because of changing times. Young pastors, both in Armenian and American circles, now march to the tune of different drummers. They are being wooed and mesmerized by "pied pipers" who are marching to the cliffs of history, and will go over the edges singing "Onward Christian soldiers ..."

In contrast, the faith that I urge my readers to adopt and follow is this:

• Centered in a personal faith in Jesus Christ, as Lord and Savior.

• Connected to a faith community, a church, vibrant in life and worship.

• Committed to the positive use of the Bible, not to deny science but to affirm it as the arena for God's continuing creative, sustaining, and loving action today. God bless you all!